PETER AND THE STARCATCHERS

PETER AND THE STARCATCHERS

By DAVE BARRY
and RIDLEY PEARSON

Illustrations by GREG CALL

DISNEP
EDITIONS

Hyperion Books for Children/New York

To Storey, Rob, and Sophie; Marcelle and Michelle;
and of course, Paige, whose idea this was

Acknowledgments

We thank whoever invented e-mail, because without it
we don't know how a guy in St. Louis could write a book
with a guy in Miami.

We thank Wendy Lefkon, who read the first few chapters
and decided she wanted to publish the book, even though at the
time she had no idea where it was going, and neither did we.

We thank Ridley's agent, Al Zuckerman, and Dave's agent,
Al Hart, because when you have two Als representing you,
you KNOW you're in good hands.

We thank Judi Smith, Nancy Litzinger, and Louise Marsh,
who keep us sane and organized, or at least organized.

And above all we thank Paige Pearson, for asking her daddy
one night, after her bedtime story, exactly how a flying boy
met a certain pirate.

—*Dave Barry and Ridley Pearson*

TABLE OF CONTENTS

CHAPTER 1

THE Never Land

THE TIRED OLD CARRIAGE, pulled by two tired old horses, rumbled onto the wharf, its creaky wheels *bumpety-bump*ing on the uneven planks, waking Peter from his restless slumber. The carriage interior, hot and stuffy, smelled of five smallish boys and one largish man, none of whom was keen on bathing.

Peter was the leader of the boys, because he was the oldest. Or maybe he wasn't. Peter had no idea how old he really was, so he gave himself whatever age suited him, and it suited him to always be one year older than the oldest of his mates. If Peter was nine, and a new boy came to St. Norbert's Home for Wayward Boys who said he was ten, why, then, Peter would declare himself to be eleven. Also, he could spit the farthest. That made him the undisputed leader.

As leader, he made it his business to keep his eye on things in general. And he was not happy with the way things were shaping up today. The boys had been told only that they were going away on a ship. As much as Peter didn't like where he'd been living for the past seven years, the longer this carriage ride lasted, the scarier "away" sounded in his mind.

They'd set out from St. Norbert's in the dark, but now Peter could see grayish daylight through the small, round coach window on his side. He looked out, squinting, and saw a dark shape looming by the wharf. It looked to Peter like a monster, with tall spines coming out of its back. Peter did not like the idea of walking into the belly of that monster.

"Is that it?" he asked. "The ship we're going on?"

He ducked then, avoiding the hamlike right fist of Edward Grempkin. He was always keenly aware of where this fist was; he'd been dodging it for seven years now. Grempkin, second in command at St. Norbert's Home for Wayward Boys, was a man of numerous rules—many of them invented right on the spot, all of them enforced by means of a swift cuff to the ear. He paid little attention to *whose* ear his fist actually landed on; all the boys were rule-breakers, as far as Grempkin was concerned.

This time the fist clipped an ear belonging to a boy named Thomas, who had been slumped, half asleep, in the carriage next to the ducking Peter.

"*OW!*" said Thomas.

"Do *not* end a sentence with a preposition," said Mr. Grempkin. He was also the grammar teacher at St. Norbert's.

"But I didn't . . . *OW!*" said Thomas, upon being cuffed a second time by Grempkin, who had a strict rule against back talk.

For a moment, the carriage was silent, except for the *bumpety-bump*. Then Peter tried again.

"Sir," he said, "is that our ship?" He kept an eye on the fist, in case *ship* turned out to be a preposition.

Peter was thinking about trying to run away, but he didn't know if that was possible—to run away from "away." In any event, he didn't see much opportunity for escape; there were sailors and dockhands everywhere. Carts and carriages. Near the back of the ship, fancily dressed people boarded via a ramp with a rope handrail. Toward the bow, some pigs and a cow were being led up a steep plank, followed by commoners dressed more like Peter and his friends.

Grempkin glanced out the round window and grinned, but not in a pleasant way. There wasn't a pleasant bone in his body.

"Yes, that's your ship," he said. "The *Never Land*."

"What's Never Land?" said a boy named Prentiss, who was fairly new to the orphanage and thus did not see the fist until it hit his ear.

"*OW!*" he said.

"Don't you be asking stupid questions!" said Grempkin, who defined "stupid questions" as questions he could not answer. "All you need to know is this ship will be your home for the next five weeks."

"Five weeks, sir?" asked Peter.

"If you're lucky," said Grempkin leaning out of the carriage now to study the sky. "If a storm doesn't blow you halfway to hell." He smiled again. "Or worse."

"Worse than hell, sir?" inquired James.

"He means if the ship sinks," said Tubby Ted, who had a gift for looking on the dark side, "and we wind up in the sea, swimming for our lives."

"But I can't swim," said James. "None of us can swim."

"I can swim," Tubby Ted declared proudly.

"You can *float*," corrected Peter. Even Grempkin cracked a smile at that, yellow tooth stumps showing through chapped lips.

Peter looked down the wharf and saw a much nicer-looking and bigger ship, painted a shiny black. Its crew wore uniforms, unlike that of the *Never Land*. It, too, was being loaded and seemed ready to set sail. If it came down to choosing between the two ships . . .

"It don't matter," said Grempkin, brightly, his mood improving. "Swim, sink, float—the sharks will take care of all you boys before you get a chance to drown."

"Sharks?" said James.

"Big fish with lots of teeth," said Tubby Ted. "They eat people."

"What if there's no people in the sea?" said Thomas. "What do the sharks eat then?"

"Whales," said Tubby Ted. "But they like people better, and there's plenty of people in the sea. Ships is always going down. I heard about one . . . *OW!*"

"That's enough of your jabber," said Grempkin, who had a rule against too much jabber.

The carriage pulled to a stop beside the ship. As Grempkin and the boys climbed out, a thick, bald man in a grimy officer's uniform thumped down the gangplank and approached the carriage.

"You Grempkin?" he said.

"I am," said Grempkin. "And you are . . . ?"

"Slank. William Slank. First officer, second in command of the *Never Land*." The man made a face as if he'd just bitten into a rancid prune. It occurred to Peter that Slank didn't like being second in anything. "These are the orphans, then?"

"They are," said Grempkin. "And you're welcome to them."

"I don't care for boys," observed Slank.

"Then you'll definitely not care for these," said Grempkin.

"We've had boys on board before," said Slank. "They was always stirring up the rats."

The boys glanced at one another. *Rats?*

5

"The thing to do," said Grempkin, "is keep them disciplined." To illustrate, he shot his fist sideways, not looking where it was going. It struck Prentiss, who, being fairly new, had not yet learned that it was unwise to stand immediately to Grempkin's right.

"*OW!*" said Prentiss.

"Sir," said James, to Slank, "there's rats on the ship?"

"Don't you be playing with the rats!" said Slank, cuffing James on the ear. "They make a tasty treat when the food runs out."

"The food runs out?" asked Tubby Ted, suddenly reluctant to take another step. "When?"

Slank slapped him across the ear and said, "After we eat *you.*"

Grempkin nodded approvingly, confident now that he was leaving the boys in good hands.

Peter scanned the area for a place to run and hide. He saw a supply store offering pulleys and hemp rope, some taverns—the Salty Dog, the Mermaid's Song. *Mermaids?* Peter wondered. But everywhere he looked, there were sailors and dockworkers, rough men with rough hands. He wouldn't get ten paces before one of them would collar him, if Slank didn't collar him first.

"I'll be getting back to St. Norbert's," Grempkin said. He turned toward the coach, paused for a moment, then turned back and said, "You boys better watch out for yourselves."

In seven years, that was the nicest thing Peter had ever heard Grempkin say.

"All right," said Slank, as Grempkin turned back to the coach. "You boys get on board. We're waiting for one more piece of cargo, and then we cast off."

Peter eyed the nicer ship down the wharf. Some soldiers were approaching it, carrying rifles with bayonets. The soldiers wore crisp blue uniforms and black, shiny boots. They walked on either side of a horse-drawn cart that carried a single trunk, black, done all around with chains and padlocks.

The boys hesitated, taking their first good look at the *Never Land*. It wasn't as big as they'd expected, and it looked old and poorly kept—frayed ropes, peeling paint, barnacles and green slime climbing the hull from the waterline.

"Get a move on!" said Slank.

"I can't swim," whispered James.

"We'll be all right," said Peter. "It can't be worse than St. Norbert's."

"Yes it can," said Tubby Ted. "The food runs out."

"Sharks," Thomas reminded them. "Rats."

"We'll be all right," repeated Peter, and he started up the gangplank, being the leader, but still thinking about finding a way to escape before the ship set sail.

THE SECOND TRUNK

Not far down the wharf from the Salty Dog and the Mermaid's Song, two men toiled in a dark, dismal warehouse, its enormous doors open to the harbor and the ships that were preparing for departure.

"Are we done, then?" asked Alf, the bigger of the two. He had a nose wart the size and shape of a small mushroom. "Because I could use some grog."

Alf, being a sailor, could always use some grog.

"Not yet," said Mack. "Slank says we got one more to get aboard, this one over here." Mack, a thin man, but as strong as any hand on the *Never Land*, had a tattoo of a snake's head on his neck, the snake's body disappearing into his sour clothes.

Mack pointed to a corner of the warehouse where a filthy canvas was draped over a bulky object. The two men trudged over. Mack grabbed a corner of the canvas and pulled it off, revealing a common-looking trunk made of rough wood but held shut by thick chain and secured by two—no, *three*—padlocks.

Alf studied the trunk, frowning. "Ain't this the trunk them soldiers brought in here this morning?" he asked

"It looks like it," said Mack. "But it ain't. There was *two* trunks come in together. The black one got loaded onto the *Wasp* by them soldiers. Heavy as lead, it was. Then Slank pulls me aside and says he wants us, real careful-like, to put this one aboard the *Never Land*. He says, tie the canvas tight 'round it and walk it up the main gangway like it belong to one of the travelers. He says if we do this right there's two bob more in our pay."

"Apiece?" said Alf.

"Apiece," said Mack.

"All right, then," said Alf, who was not one to ask questions when two bob was involved.

"Let's tie her up, then," said Mack. "You lift the end there, and I'll tuck this canvas underneath, and slip the rope 'round it."

"Why don't *you* lift the end?" said Alf.

"It's me back, Alf," complained Mack. "You know how it troubles me."

"No more than mine troubles me," said Alf.

"But I said it first," said Mack.

Alf sighed. The longer they argued—and Alf knew, from

9

experience, that Mack would argue this point a good long time—the less chance he'd have at some grog before they set sail.

"All right, then," Alf said, and he squatted to grab hold of the end of the trunk.

Alf was a simple man, of simple wants. What he hoped to get from life was food that was soft enough to chew, a place to sleep out of the rain, and some grog now and again. Alf had never known true happiness, and he didn't expect to.

And so he was not ready, not ready at all, for what happened when his rough, callused hands touched the trunk.

First, he felt it: a warmth, starting in his hands but quickly moving up his arms and down his back and into his legs, and everywhere the warmth went it was . . . *wonderful.* Like stepping into a bath. In an instant the pain in his bent old spine, the throbbing pain that he'd lived with since almost his first day on the docks, was gone. So was the aching weariness in his legs. Gone!

But there was more: there was a . . . *smell.* It was flowers. New grass in a meadow right after a spring rain. A fresh orange being peeled. It was cinnamon and honey, and bread just baked and pulled from the oven. And another smell even more wonderful than all the others, though Alf couldn't place it. *Like nighttime,* he thought.

Alf could see light now, swirling around his head, colors

and sparkles, moving to music, dancing to the sound of . . . *bells*, yes, it was bells, tiny ones, by the sound of them, and it was a sweet and joyful sound, though Alf could hear something else in it, something that seemed to be trying to tell Alf something. He strained to hear it, he wanted to hear it. . . .

"ALF!" said Mack, shaking Alf's shoulder harder now, hard enough so that Alf let go of the trunk. And when he did, the wonderful smells were gone, and so were the lights, and the bells, and Alf could feel the weight come back into his body, his back and his arms and his legs, along with all the old aches and pains, and he felt himself settling, as though he'd been—but that was impossible—floating above the warehouse floor, just a little bit of an inch, but *floating*. He brushed off his hands, thinking someone had put rat poison on the outside of the trunk. He'd seen sailors go into a crazy dance from messing with rat poison.

"ALF!" said Mack again. "What's wrong with you?"

Alf looked at Mack, then down at the trunk, then back at Mack. He put his fingers in both ears, looking silly.

"I . . . when I touched it . . ." Alf said. "Didn't you hear them?"

"Hear what?" said Mack.

"The bells," said Alf.

"What *bells?*" said Mack. "There weren't no bells."

"Bells," said Alf. "And lights, and . . ." He stopped, seeing the way Mack was looking at him. "Rat poison!" he said, slapping his hands against his pants, trying to get them clean.

"You already been to the tavern today?" asked Mack suspiciously.

"Rat poison!" said Alf, now rubbing his hands on a dirty old towel. Mack was looking at him all funny. "Got to gets it off me hands."

"Bells?" Mack teased him, shaking his head. He turned back to the trunk. Alf saw that Mack had slipped the canvas more tightly around the trunk, and the rope around the canvas. A tiny bit of the trunk still showed.

"Mack," said Alf. "I dares ya to touch it."

"What?" said Mack. "Me?"

"Just touch the trunk," said Alf. "On the wood there."

"I'm not messing with no rat poison! You remember what happened to Hungry Bob?" Mack considered himself a cautious man, and the truth was, he was afraid to touch the trunk now. He knew that something had happened when Alf touched it; somehow, he'd *felt* it. No, Mack had decided there was something strange about this trunk. Why else would Slank be giving special orders and offering two bob? Mack was not going to touch it, thank you very much.

"It's not our job to fool with it," Mack said, pulling the rope tight. The canvas now covered the trunk entirely. "Slank said put it aboard the *Never Land*, and that's that."

"But, Mack," said Alf. "I'm telling you, God's truth, rat poison or not, it felt good. "

"Let's just finish the job," said Mack, pulling the knot tight, "and take our two bob to the tavern, get our grog quick-like, and forget about this trunk."

"All right, then," said Alf, though he didn't think he would soon forget that feeling he'd just had. Maybe once the *Never Land* was under way he could sneak in and visit this trunk again.

Grunting, the two men lifted the canvas-wrapped trunk onto a handcart, and trundled it out of the warehouse, onto the wharf. A minute later they passed the *Wasp*, whose crew was preparing to cast off.

"She's a pretty ship, ain't she?" said Mack.

"What?" said Alf, who'd been thinking about the trunk.

"I say, the *Wasp* is a beauty," said Mack. "I'd love to sail on her someday. They say she's the only ship afloat that might outrun the *Sea Devil*."

The mention of the pirate ship won Alf's full attention. The *Sea Devil* was the ship of the most feared pirate on the Seven Seas. Sailors said that if you caught sight of the *Sea Devil*, it was time to make your peace with your maker, because you'd be with Him within the hour.

"No ship can outrun the *Sea Devil*," said Alf. "Nobody ever has."

"Till now," said Mack. "The *Wasp* was built for just that,

and Captain Scott is as able a seaman as ever sailed these waters. Unlike the idjit in charge of *our* bilge bucket."

Sneering, Mack nodded toward the *Never Land*, now just ahead.

"Aye," said Alf. "Pembridge could capsize a dinghy on dry land."

Cyrus Pembridge, the *Never Land*'s captain, was widely regarded as the most incompetent man to command a ship since the formation of water.

"Who in the name of common sense would put to sea on that ship with that man in charge?" wondered Mack.

"Well," Alf answered, "*we* are."

"True," Mack said. "But nobody else'd hire the likes of us."

They were alongside the *Never Land* now. The ship had been loaded and provisioned; the crew was preparing to cast off. Most of the passengers were on deck. Some were looking around anxiously at the decrepit ship, and the scruffy crew in whose hands they were placing their lives. Others were leaning on the dockside rail, watching the cast-off preparations. Among these, Alf noticed, was a group of five boys near the bow. They looked plainly scared, except for one, a wiry boy with bright orange hair—not the largest of the lot, but the one who seemed to be in charge. He had an air about him, Alf thought, the look of a boy who doesn't miss much.

"It's about time," said Slank, tromping down the gangplank, trailed by two more seamen. "You're late. Tide's begun to run." To the men behind him, he said, "Get this cargo trunk aboard."

As the men bent to heft the load, Alf—not thinking; not knowing why he did it—slipped his hand under the canvas flap, thrusting it forward until his fingers felt the smooth wood.

"Here now!" said Slank. "What the dickens are you doing?"

"Alf," said Mack. "What *are* you doing?"

But Alf didn't hear them. Instantly he was lost in it all again—the warmth, and the smells, the music and the floating—and it was so good, especially the sweet song. There was something else in there, too, something the bells were saying, trying to tell him. . . . *What was it?*

"HANDS OFF THAT CARGO!" Slank yelled. Alf felt himself yanked away from the trunk, and then the music was gone, and all the other good feelings with it. Alf was wobbly, but with Mack's help he managed to keep his feet. Alf watched two men carry the trunk onto the ship, and he felt a sadness come over him, because he knew might not hear the music again. He almost wept, except that a man like Alf didn't cry.

Then—he didn't know why—Alf looked toward the bow, and found himself looking right into the startlingly blue eyes of the orange-haired boy.

"Come on, Alf," said Mack, gently tugging at Alf's coat, concerned about his old friend's strange behavior.

But for a moment Alf held still, his gaze still locked with that of the orange-haired boy.

"Come *on*," repeated Mack. "We're casting off!"

Alf turned and followed his friend toward the lines that held the ship to the wharf. After a few steps, he looked back, but the boy was gone. *Boys gets into all sorts of trouble*, he thought, his ears still ringing from the music of those bells.

CHAPTER 3

MOLLY

PETER TROTTED AFT on the *Never Land*'s bustling deck, dodging the sailors making final preparations for casting off and getting under way. The forward gangway had been detached, hauled aboard, and stowed; now sailors were working on the aft gangway. When they were done, there would be no way off the ship.

Peter's plan was to dart down the gangway just before they finished the job and disappear into the bustle on the wharf. He figured the ship's departure wouldn't be held up just for him, a mere one boy out of five.

He had no plan for what he'd do once he got off the ship; all he knew was, he didn't want to stay on it. He'd seen enough of the *Never Land* to decide that it was an unpleasant, dirty place, run by unpleasant, dirty men. They were around him now, stinking of sweat, struggling with lines and sails as an officer shouted orders that consisted mostly of curses. *They don't seem like a happy group*, thought Peter.

He neared the aft gangway and stopped, looking for his chance to flee. Directly ahead, blocking his path, stood the first officer, Slank, supervising the gangway crew. Just beyond, two sailors were carrying the canvas-draped cargo that had been brought onto the ship at the last minute. Peter had watched the cargo's arrival and the little drama that had played out on the wharf. He'd seen the sailor, the one with the big nose wart, reach under the canvas and touch something; he'd seen the look that had come over the man's face. *He looked so happy*, Peter thought. *Why did he look so happy?*

Peter studied the mysterious cargo now being maneuvered into the aft hold. It didn't look heavy; the sailors handled it fairly easily. Peter wondered what was inside.

He was distracted by a giggle, and turned to see a rare sight: a girl. He'd not seen many girls over the past few years; St. Norbert's had had only one, the headmaster's daughter, an unpleasant, sallow-faced child who amused herself by dropping spiders onto the heads of boys passing beneath her third-floor window.

This girl he saw now in no way resembled the headmaster's daughter. She had large, wide-set green eyes, and long brown hair that curled slightly and turned to gold at the tips. She wore a long, straight blue dress that accentuated the slimness of her frame. She was perhaps an inch taller than Peter, and by the look of her she took baths. At

St. Norbert's, Peter took one bath a month, unless he could get out of it.

He straightened his posture and tried to look older.

The girl stood next to a stout woman, wearing a wide-ranging and complicated skirt and wielding a formidable black umbrella. The woman's hair was an unnatural shade of red, and she wore a great deal of powder on her face, caked and cracked at the edges of her mouth and nose. She was surveying the ship and crew, and it was clear she did not approve of either.

The canvas-wrapped cargo was lowered into the hold, and disappeared. The brown-haired girl watched it go, then glanced around quickly. Her eyes fell on Peter. He half expected her to look away, as strangers do when their gazes lock by accident, but she didn't; she kept her eyes on him, studying him openly, until finally it was he who broke the contact. Peter turned toward the wharf.

"Ready, sir!" shouted a seaman.

"Get aboard, then," shouted Slank. "We're wasting time!"

Peter's attention returned to the gangway, which he saw was about to be hauled aboard. This was it, his chance to escape. He tensed his legs as he prepared for the dash to the wharf. *Ready, set . . .*

"Peter!" He felt a hand grab his shirt from behind. "Peter!"

It was James. *"Not now,"* whispered Peter. *"Go away."*

"But I lost you—and—and—and I couldn't find you, and—and . . ."

"Go *away!*" hissed Peter, pushing James from him. He looked around quickly and saw the girl staring at him. He looked back to where several sailors were preparing to haul up the gangway. Again Peter stiffened, ready to run for it.

"*Please,*" James pleaded, weeping, his voice desperate. "I'm scared."

Peter looked—he didn't know why—back up at the girl. She was watching him intently. For an instant he thought her expression meant that she disapproved of his shoving James, and it bothered him. *Why do I care what she thinks?*

But then the girl shook her head side to side, barely moving it.

It's not disapproval, Peter thought. *She's warning me.*

The girl nodded her head toward the gangway. Peter looked that way and saw a huge man—more a horse than a man—who hadn't been there a minute before. His enormous black-booted feet were braced on the deck. His right hand held a long, coiled whip.

I wonder what he . . .

It happened in a second, at most two. A sailor bolted for the gangplank, his bare feet slapping wood. He had taken perhaps three long strides when the whip cracked—it moved much too fast for Peter to see it—and wrapped itself around this man's ankle like a snake. The sailor crashed to the deck as the giant jerked the whip back, dragging the man effortlessly, as if he were no more than a dead cat, to the feet of the scowling Slank.

Slank spat on the sailor.

"Having second thoughts, were you, now?" he said. "Somebody always does, come cast-off time. That's why we have Little Richard, here." Slank nodded back at the huge man, then drew back his leg and kicked the would-be escapee hard in the ribs. The man moaned and squirmed on the deck.

"You'll be starting out this voyage with a week in the brig," said Slank. "Hardtack and water for a week. You can sleep with the rats for a while, and if that don't improve your attitude, we'll give you another taste of Little Richard's lash—only this time he won't be so gentle."

Slank glared around the deck. "Anybody else having thoughts of leaving?" he said. The sailors, avoiding Slank's stare, busied themselves with their work.

"I thought not," said Slank. "Now, get this bag of lice out my sight."

As the sailor was lifted, still moaning, and hauled below, Slank resumed his supervision of the gangway crew. "READY!" he shouted. "HEAVE TO!"

The sailors grunted, and the gangway was raised up off the wharf and slid back onto the deck. Slank gave the order to cast off the lines. The bow, pushed by the tide, began to slowly swing away from the wharf. No getting off the ship now.

Peter glanced up again at the girl. She was still watching him. If not for her warning, it would have been his ankle snared by the whip, and his bruised body being hauled off the brig. He nodded to the girl, just a bit. It was the closest he could come to thanking her.

The girl nodded back, her face serious, but her eyes betraying a hint of amusement. And then, to Peter's surprise, she walked over to the short set of ladderlike stairs that led from the aft deck cabins to the main deck, collected her skirts into a fistful of fabric, and descended.

The stout woman leaned over the rail and called after her. "Miss Molly! Miss Molly!" But the girl paid no mind. She walked up to Peter, who made himself as tall has he could. They were just eye to eye.

"Thinking of leaving us, were you?" she asked.

"I don't know what you're talking about," Peter said.

"Don't you?" she said, smiling now.

"No, I don't."

"Good," she said. "Because it would be a shame to miss a voyage aboard such a lovely ship as the *Never Land*."

The stout woman leaning over the upper rail snorted, making a noise like an irate duck.

"Lovely ship, indeed," she said. "It's a floating stinkhouse, is what it is, pardon my French. And barely floating at that."

"That's Mrs. Bumbrake," said the girl, still looking straight at Peter. "She's my . . . governess."

"Your father buys us passage on a garbage scow," said Mrs. Bumbrake, "but does *he* sail with us? Oh no. Not him. *He* sails on the *Wasp*, the finest ship in all of England."

"I'm sure Father has his reasons," said the girl.

Mrs. Bumbrake made the duck sound again.

"My name is Molly Aster," the girl said to Peter. "What's your name?"

"Peter," he said.

"What's your last name?

"I don't know," he said. It was true. Back at St. Norbert's, he'd once asked Mr. Grempkin what his last name was, and Grempkin had boxed his ear and told him it was a stupid question. Peter never asked again.

"Well, Mr. Peter Nobody," said Molly, "do you know how old you are?"

"How old are *you?*" said Peter.

"I'm twelve," said Molly.

"I'm thirteen," said Peter.

"Wait," said Molly. "I just remembered. "Today is my birthday. I'm fourteen."

Peter frowned. "Wait," he said. "If you were twelve, and today's your birthday, you'd be thirteen."

"Not in my family," said Molly. "In my family, we only celebrate even-numbered birthdays."

Peter was impressed. He'd never thought of that.

"I just remembered something myself," he said. "Today is

also my birthday, and I am now"—he paused dramatically—"sixteen."

"No," said Molly. "Too much. I'll accept fourteen. We'll both be fourteen."

Peter thought about it.

"All right, then," he said. "Fourteen."

"So, Mr. fourteen-year-old Peter Nobody," said Molly, "why are you going to Rundoon?"

"What's Rundoon?" asked Peter.

Molly laughed. "You really don't know?" she said.

"No," said Peter.

"Well," said Molly, "you'll know soon enough, because that's where this ship is sailing. My father is to be the new ambassador there, in the court of His Royal Highness, King Zarboff"—she held up the three middle fingers of her right hand—"the Third."

"The daughter of an ambassador!" said Mrs. Bumbrake. "And he puts *us* on this seagoing dirtbucket, pardon my French."

"What kind of a place is Rundoon?" asked Peter.

Mrs. Bumbrake made the duck sound.

"Not a terribly pleasant one, I'm afraid," said Molly. "The people are nice enough, but the king is not nice at all."

"The king?" said Peter.

"His Royal Highness, King Zarboff the Third," said Molly, and again she held up three fingers. "He's a bad man."

"What do you mean, he's bad?" said Peter. "And why do you hold up your fingers when you say his name?"

"I'm practicing," said Molly. "If you don't salute with these three fingers when you say his name, and he finds out, he has these very fingers cut off."

"He *does?*" said Peter.

"He does," said Molly. "There's a shop in Rundoon that sells nothing but two-fingered gloves. Does a brisk business, too."

"Oh," said Peter.

"But that's not the worst part," said Molly.

"It's not?"

"No. The king's late father, His Royal Highness, King Zarboff the Second, was eaten by a snake."

"So?" said Peter.

"It wasn't just any snake," said Molly. "It was the pet snake of His Royal Highness, King Zarboff the Third." Both Molly and Peter held up three fingers this time.

"His *snake* ate his *father?*" Peter said.

"Yes, said Molly. "Somehow"—she arched her eyebrows knowingly—"the snake got loose in the father's bedroom while he was sleeping. They say the son wasn't a bit upset—didn't even seem surprised—when it ate his father. And now, as king, he keeps the snake by his throne, and feeds it by hand."

"What does he feed the snake?" asked little James, speaking up for the first time.

"And who's this young gentleman?" asked Molly.

"He's James," said Peter. "And don't ask him his last name, because he doesn't know it either."

"What does he feed the snake?" repeated James. "I mean, now that his father is gone."

"Pigs, mostly," said Molly. "But Father says that sometimes, if one of his servants has disappointed him, the king . . ."

"Molly!" interrupted Mrs. Bumbrake. "That's enough!"

James was crying again. "Peter," he sniffled, "I don't want to go to where there's a mean king and hungry snakes!"

"Here, now!" boomed an angry voice behind Peter. Recognizing the tone, Peter was already ducking before the "now" ended, and thus he received only a glancing blow from First Officer Slank.

"You runts ain't supposed to be here!" shouted Slank at Peter and James. "This here is for first-class passengers. These here ladies . . ."

He glanced up toward Mrs. Bumbrake, whose skirts swirled in the wind, revealing a plump ankle, a pink flash of shin. Slank's mouth went slack for a moment, then he smacked his lips. Mrs. Bumbrake blushed and tilted her head down, raising her eyes so she could bat them at the smitten Slank.

". . . these here *lovely* ladies," he said, turning back to Peter and James, "do not want to be bothered by riffraff like you."

Molly said, "But they aren't bothering us!"

"Forward with you right now!" said Slank, ignoring Molly and giving Peter and James a rough shove, so that Peter had to grab James to keep him from falling.

"There's no need for that!" said Molly.

"All due respect, miss," said Slank, "but I knows how to handle this here riffraff. We've had these orphan boys aboard before, and if you let 'em . . . ."

"Orphans?" said Molly, her eyes widening. "These are the orphans?"

"Yes, miss," said Slank. "We got five of 'em this voyage."

Molly, somber now, stared at Peter.

"What?" said Peter.

"Oh, my," said Mrs. Bumbrake.

"*What?*" repeated Peter. But Molly said nothing.

"Get moving," said Slank, shoving Peter and James again. "And if you don't want to feel Little Richard's lash, you'll stay forward until we reach Rundoon. After that, your sorry hides belong to Zarboff."

Peter froze. "King Zarboff?" he said, slowly raising three fingers. "The Third?"

Slank laughed, pleased by the fear on Peter's face. "Why, yes!" he said. "You didn't know? You'll be spending your days as a servant in the court of His Royal Majesty! He goes through a *lot* of servants, does the king. Seems we got to bring him a new lot every trip we make. So my advice is, step lively, unless you want to see his snake from the inside."

Slank, roaring with laughter, gave Peter and James another shove. The two boys stumbled forward, James sobbing. When they reached the bow, Peter turned and saw that Molly was still watching him. The *Never Land*'s sails were almost all hoisted now; the ship was moving out of the harbor. Peter glanced over the side at the dark water, gauging the distance to land, but he'd never tried to swim, and knew this was not the time or the place to learn. Besides, the way James was clinging to his shirtsleeve, if he went over the side they'd both end up drowning.

No, there was no escaping it now. They were on their way to Rundoon.

CHAPTER 4

The Sea Devil

FAR FROM THE WHARF, well across the bay and almost to the open sea, was a tangle of rocks so treacherous that no captain familiar with these waters would sail his ship there. Over the years, many ships had struck these rocks and sunk; they lay in pieces scattered everywhere, masts, bows, keels. It was the perfect place to hide a ship. Angels' Graveyard, it was called, and it so frightened most sailors that they would not even look in that direction.

But there was a ship in there now, amid the huge rocks, long and low, black as coal, with three masts pointing toward the sky like skeleton fingers. On the foredeck stood two men, one squat and one tall.

"Can you see her?" said the squat man. He wore a striped shirt and blue wool pants that didn't quite reach his ankles; his blistered bare feet were dark as tar.

"Not yet," replied the tall man, squinting through a

spyglass. He was a strikingly unpleasant figure, with a pockmarked face and a large red nose, like a prize turnip, glued to his face. His long black hair, greasy from years without washing, stained the shoulders of the red uniform coat he'd stolen from a Navy sailor on the high seas, just before escorting that wretched soul over the side of the ship. He had dark, deepset, piercingly black eyes, overshadowed by eyebrows so bushy that he had to brush them away to see through the glass. But his most prominent feature was the thick growth of hair on his upper lip, long and black, lovingly maintained, measuring nearly a foot between its waxed and pointed tips. It was this feature that gave him his name, the most feared name on the sea: Black Stache.

"There's a hunk of worm food in the way, the *Never Land*," he said. "What kind of fool name is that for ship?"

"It's a fool name, all right," said the squat sailor.

"Shut up," said Black Stache.

"Aye, Cap'n."

Black Stache moved a few steps to his right, then squinted through the glass again.

"There she is!" he said. "The *Wasp*. Clear as day. Now, *that* there is a rival worthy of the *Sea Devil*. So she thinks she can sting us, does she? Outrun us?"

He laughed, and so did the squat man, and so did the dozen or so pirates within earshot, though they didn't know what they were laughing at. The crew of the *Sea Devil* understood: if Black Stache laughed, you laughed. If he snarled, you snarled. If he breathed in your direction, you ran for cover. "Ratbreath," his sailors called him behind his back. It was said that he liked to eat vermin raw, with a touch of sea salt.

When Black Stache had heard enough laughter, he raised his arm, and the crew quieted immediately. He turned to the squat man, who had been the *Sea Devil's* first mate for a year now, the longest anyone had ever gone in that position without being heaved overboard by the captain.

"We've got the Ladies ready, don't we?" asked Black Stache.

"Aye, Captain, we do at that."

"Then we'll just see who's the faster ship, won't we, Smee?"

"Aye, we will, sir," said Smee, "if the Ladies hold."

"The Ladies" were Black Stache's secret weapon—a special set of sails he'd had the ship's sailmakers make, using patterns that Black Stache had obtained from, of all places, a ladies' corset maker. Though they had not yet been tested at sea, Black Stache was convinced that his invention would revolutionize the pirate industry. He was saving the Ladies for just the right moment, when he was heading downwind, closing on his prey for the kill.

"They'll hold," he said. He spat on the deck, then turned to the sailors gathered near.

"We'll see who's the fastest ship afloat, eh men?" he said. "And when we do, the *Wasp* won't be floating anymore!"

The sun-bronzed pirates cheered, and not just because they had to. They knew there would be treasure on board soon, with a share for them. Black Stache saw the greed in their eyes.

"Treasure, lads!" he shouted. "The greatest treasure ever taken to sea!"

The pirates cheered again, louder this time.

"Or so some have said," said Black Stache, and he turned to stare at a cage on the main deck. There was a man inside the cage, a uniformed sailor. He huddled in a corner, shaking at the sound of Black Stache's voice.

"And if this scurvy dog is wrong," said Black Stache, his black eyes boring in on the terrified prisoner, "then he'll wish he'd never been born, that I vow."

"The treasure's on the *Wasp*. I promise," cried the prisoner. "I heard it with me own ears."

"It'd better be," Black Stache said. "Or I'll wear them ears on a necklace."

Ignoring the man's whimpers, Black Stache turned and raised the glass to his eye again.

"They're hoisting sail," he said. "Making to catch the tide. Tell the men to make ready to follow."

Smee relayed the order, and the pirates swung smoothly

into action. They didn't look pretty, but they were an efficient crew, well trained by the whip.

Black Stache ignored them, his gaze still aimed through the glass.

"You're mine, *Wasp*," he mumbled on foul breath, a rare smile on his thin lips. "You, and everything you hold. *Mine*."

CHAPTER 5

CAPTAIN PEMBRIDGE

THE BOYS WERE SHOWN TO THEIR QUARTERS in the *Never Land* by a gaunt, hollow-eyed sailor called Hungry Bob. He led them down a ladder and along a narrow passageway belowdecks, stopping in front of a low opening.

"Here you go, lads," he said. "Your home away from home."

Peter, followed by the others, ducked through the opening. What they found was depressing, even measured against the low standards of St. Norbert's: a tiny, gloomy, windowless space, lit only by a sputtering oil lamp. The air reeked of smoke and rotten fish. The floor was bare, except for a chipped crockery pot in the corner.

"We're all supposed to sleep *here?*" Peter said. "But there's not enough room!"

"Oh, you'll be glad you're close together," said Hungry Bob. "Keeps you warm."

"But it *smells*," said James.

"It does?" said Hungry Bob, sniffing. "Not so's I can tell." Hungry Bob was not exactly a fragrant flower himself. "Anyways, you get used to it." He pointed to the crockery pot. "I put your dinner in the corner, there. You eat once a day, and you want to eat it right quick when I brings it, or the rats'll get it first."

The boys, who hadn't eaten since the night before, brightened at the prospect of food. They gathered around the pot.

"Where's the plates?" said Prentiss. "And the spoons?"

Hungry Bob had to grab the wall to keep from falling over with laughter. "Plates!" he roared. "Spoons!"

"Then how do we eat?" said Prentiss.

"Like the rest of us," said Hungry Bob. "With your hands."

The boys peered doubtfully into the pot, which contained a darkish liquid. It looked far from appetizing, but they *were* hungry. Tubby Ted, always the first to take action where food was concerned, cupped his hands and scooped out a handful of the liquid with some small grayish lumps floating in it. He sniffed it, wrinkled his nose, then shrugged and took a lump into his mouth. Immediately he spat it onto the floor.

"IT'S ALIVE!" he screamed.

The boys looked at the lump on the floor, and sure enough, it was wriggling.

"It's a worm!" said Tubby Ted. "He fed us *worms!*"

Hungry Bob picked up the worm and looked at Tubby Ted.

"You ain't gonna eat this?" he asked.

Tubby Ted shook his head violently.

"Your loss," said Hungry Bob. Then, as the boys watched, slack-jawed, he popped the worm into his mouth, chewed thoughtfully, and swallowed.

"Moth maggot," he said. "I prefers fly, but moth is good, too."

Tubby Ted turned away, retching.

"You eat *worms?*" said Peter.

"I eats what I can, on this ship," said Hungry Bob. "Ate a piece of rope once. Two months at sea, we was. Mr. Slank had me lashed for that, but it was worth it. That was tasty rope. You boys'd be wise to eat whatever you get, because you won't get much."

"But," said Peter, "I mean . . . *worms?*"

"If you don't fancy worms," said Hungry Bob, nodding toward the communal bowl, "you don't want to know what else Cook puts in there. Let's just say worms is one of the choicer items."

Thomas, peering into the pot again, gasped.

"There's something *swimming* in there!" he said. "It's . . . it's a mouse!"

"Really?" said Hungry Bob, looking into the pot. "Why,

so it is! Cook must be in a generous mood. Usually he don't serve mouse 'cept on special occasions like Christmas."

Thomas moved away from the pot. "I'm not hungry," he said.

"Nor me," said James, and then Prentiss. Tubby Ted was still retching.

"Sir, we can't eat this," said Peter.

"As you like," said Hungry Bob, picking up the pot. "This'll make a fine dinner for me. But in a day or two you boys'll get hungry, and I'll be taking this pot out polished clean by your tongues."

"I don't think so," said Peter. "Look, sir, there must be better food on this ship."

"Oh, there is, there is," agreed Hungry Bob. "But not for me or you."

"But, sir," said Peter, "please, if you would . . ."

"Listen, boy," interrupted Hungry Bob. "You're wasting your time talking to me. I ain't the one who decides these things. I'm a deck rat, not the captain."

"Well," said Peter, "what if I ask the captain?"

That struck Hungry Bob as even funnier than the request for spoons.

"Ask the captain?" he roared, almost choking. "Ask the *captain?* Yes! You do that! You ask Captain Pembridge for a nice dinner!"

Chuckling, muttering "Ask the captain!" to himself,

Hungry Bob ducked back through the opening, carrying the dinner pot. The younger boys looked at Peter, who was not sure he liked being the one who was supposed to know what to do.

"All right, then," he said.

The boys kept watching him.

"All right, then," Peter repeated. "I'll be back."

"Where are you going, Peter?" asked James.

"I'm going to go see the captain," said Peter. He wasn't sure this was a good idea, especially after Slank's warning to stay away from the aft part of the ship. But he figured he had to do *something*.

"You wait here," he said to the boys, and ducked out into the passageway.

As Peter climbed the ladder, he heard a drunken voice bellowing. Reaching the deck, he looked around and saw that the voice was coming from amidships, where a red-faced and very round man in a comically elaborate, too-small uniform was shouting odd orders to an audience consisting of Slank and a half-dozen crewmen.

"AVAST THE MAIN MIZZEN!" the round man shouted.

"You heard Captain Pembridge!" shouted Slank. "Avast the main mizzen!" His voice was stern, but Peter saw he was smirking.

"Aye, aye, sir!" shouted the men, and, grinning, they began fussing busily with various lines, tying and untying knots. Peter didn't know anything about ships, but he could see immediately that they were merely pretending to do something nautical.

"KEELHAUL THE SCUPPERS!" shouted the captain.

"You heard Captain Pembridge!" shouted Slank, struggling to keep his tone serious. "Let's get them scuppers keelhauled!" The men were smiling openly now, making no effort to hide their contempt for the little round man.

They had good reason. Cyrus Pembridge was easily the worst captain in British nautical history. He had never bothered to learn even the basics of seamanship, choosing instead to occupy his time consuming vast quantities of rum. He held command of the *Never Land* solely because his wife's family owned a shipping line, and his wife detested him. She had insisted that he be given a ship, her thinking being that he would be away from home most of the time; ideally, he would manage to sink his ship, and thus be out of her life altogether.

The shipping company, following sound business practices, had given Pembridge its most worthless ship, staffed with the most incompetent and disposable crew. The crew had quickly recognized that it was suicide to try to follow Pembridge's commands, which never made sense anyway. It was Slank who ran the *Never Land*. But on those rare occasions when Pembridge staggered out on deck, Slank and the crew amused themselves by pretending to obey him.

"CAST OFF THE AFT BINNACLE," Pembridge was shouting.

"Cast off that binnacle!" repeated Slank to the grinning crew.

Pembridge turned and looked at Slank, as if seeing him for the first time.

"Who are you?" he said. "And why are you shouting?"

"I'm your first officer, sir," said Slank. "Mr. Slank. I'm just relaying your orders to the crew."

"Ah," said Pembridge.

"The aft binnacle has been cast off, sir," said Slank.

"The what?" said Pembridge.

"The aft binnacle," said Slank. "As you ordered."

"I did?" said Pembridge, squinting suspiciously. "When?"

"Just now, sir," said Slank.

Pembridge blinked at Slank.

"Who are you, again?" he said.

"Your first officer, sir," said Slank.

Pembridge blinked again.

"My head hurts," he said.

"Perhaps the captain would like to go to his cabin," said Slank.

"You don't tell me what to do," said Pembridge. "I'm the captain."

"Yes, sir," said Slank.

"I'm going to my cabin," said Pembridge.

"Yes, sir."

The round man took a step, then stopped, frowning, his round body teetering.

"Which way is my cabin?" he said.

"That way, Captain Pembridge," said Slank, pointing aft.

Pembridge teetered off. Behind him, the crewmen burst into laughter, only to be silenced by a scowl from Slank.

"That's enough," he shouted. "Back to work."

From behind a mast, Peter watched Pembridge stagger aft. Now seemed as good a time as any to try to talk to him. Peter stepped out from behind the mast and . . .

"YOU! RUNT!" bellowed Slank. The man saw *everything*. "WHERE DO YOU THINK YOU'RE GOING?"

"Nowhere, sir," said Peter.

"That's right," said Slank, striding toward Peter. "You're going nowhere. You're to stay below, and you're to come out when I say you can. We got work to do on this ship, and we don't need you in the way. You follow me, runt?"

"Yes, sir."

"Can you swim, runt?"

"I don't know, sir."

"Well, you'll find out quick enough if I see you on deck again without my permission."

"Yes, sir," said Peter. Feeling Slank's glare on his back, he turned and went back down the ladderway, back to the cramped and smelly little cabin. As he entered, the other boys all looked at him hopefully.

"What did the captain say?" said Tubby Ted. "Can we have some real food?"

"Yes, Peter," said James. "What did the captain say?"

"I . . . well," said Peter, ". . . I didn't talk to him just yet."

The boys' faces fell. James looked down, and sniffed.

"But I will!" said Peter. "I'll talk to him. Just not right now. But don't you worry," he said, putting his hand on James's shoulder. "We'll be fine. I have a plan."

"You do?" said James, looking up. "Really?"

"Of course I do," said Peter, patting his shoulder.

"Oh, good," said James. "Because I'm hungry."

"I'm starving," said Tubby Ted.

"We'll have real food soon enough," said Peter. "I promise."

And as he saw the hope return to the eyes of the other boys, Peter thought: *I need a plan*.

CHAPTER 6

BLACK STACHE IN PURSUIT

"SHE'S GETTING AWAY!" Black Stache bellowed. "Hurry up with Preston and Harbuckle! And ready those barrels!"

"Aye, Cap'n!" came a shout from below.

Through his glass, Black Stache saw the *Wasp*'s gleaming black hull race for the horizon, cutting a foaming white wake in the deep blue-green of the ocean. Black Stache had never seen a ship sail like that. He knew now that he no longer wanted only the *Wasp*'s treasure; he wanted the *Wasp* herself. He'd strip her flag and fly his own on her mast.

"What flag should we be flying, Cap'n?" First Mate Smee leaned his bulging belly over the open chest of flags captured from ships the *Sea Devil* had scuttled.

"Let's make it something colorful," said Black Stache. "The Union Jack would do just fine, eh? She'd like that wouldn't she? Kissing cousins?"

Black Stache liked the British flag—he had a dozen or

more in his collection—and felt especially proud when he sank a ship belonging to the Queen. Black Stache had no love for the Queen, no love for women of any sort, except for his ma. He had a real soft spot for his ma, and was truly sorry for the time he'd marooned her.

"What's the delay down there?" Black Stache thundered. On the main deck, several men were tying a fat crewman's ankles to his wrists behind his back, so he looked like a rocking horse. A gag covered the man's mouth, or he would have been heard screaming for his life.

The Union Jack was run up the *Sea Devil*'s mainmast and snapped loudly in the wind. Black Stache held the glass to his eye again, watching the retreating *Wasp*, getting farther away each minute.

"How do you plan to take her," said Smee, grinning. "Fire?"

One of Black Stache's many tricks was to sail close to another ship at night and, using a smoking barrel of tar, make it appear the *Sea Devil* had caught fire. His prey would turn and come to help, only to be rewarded for this act of mercy by being attacked. But Black Stache knew that even if he could get the *Sea Devil* close, the *Wasp*'s captain, Scott, was too experienced to fall for that ploy.

"We'll have to think of something better than that," Black Stache said.

"The broken mast trick?" Smee slapped his leg. "I love that broken mast trick, Cap'n."

Black Stache snorted. "She's carrying the richest treasure ever taken to sea," he said. "She won't fall for the broken mast."

Below, the crew had finished hog-tying the first man and had started on a second, also a portly fellow. He looked just as terrified, his cries muffled by a gag. Black Stache smiled. He loved other people's misery.

"Cap'n," said Smee, very timidly, "why're they tying up Preston and Harbuckle?" Preston and Harbuckle were both very good sailors, and Black Stache seemed to be preparing to toss them overboard for no good reason.

Black Stache spat a gob onto Smee's bare foot.

"Smee," he said, "I've decided we're going to take the *Wasp* the old-fashioned way."

"Sir?"

"I mean without cheating," said Black Stache.

"Without *cheating*, sir?" Smee said, shocked. Black Stache *always* cheated.

"Not this time," said Black Stache. "Captain Scott won't stop the *Wasp* for no trickery. We got to pure run her down, Smee."

"But how, Cap'n?" said Smee. "Are we going to use the Ladies?"

Black Stache shot Smee a look of contempt, which sent a chill down Smee's spine.

"You idjit," the captain sneered. "We can't use the Ladies

on this heading. We've got to get abeam of the *Wasp*, then turn downwind. *Then* we raise the Ladies and run her down."

"But, Cap'n," Smee said timidly, "how do we get abeam of her? She's fast as the wind, and pulling away."

"Yes," said Black Stache. "We need more speed, and that means we need to get rid of some weight. So I've ordered the crew to throw most of our water overboard."

He pointed toward the stern. Smee turned, and saw crewmen rolling heavy wooden barrels toward the rail, and heaving them over the side.

Smee gasped. Even for Black Stache, this was insane. At sea, there was nothing more precious than water. *Nothing.* Not even rum. Nobody *ever* threw water away.

"Cap'n," Smee sputtered, "sir, we can't, I mean . . ."

"Smee," said Black Stache, savoring his own malignant brilliance. "Water is heavy, right?"

"Yes, Cap'n, but . . ."

"And we'll run faster without the weight, right?"

"Yes, Cap'n, but . . ."

"And if we run faster, we'll have a better chance of catching the *Wasp*, right?"

"I s'pose so, Cap'n, but . . ."

"And when we catch the *Wasp*, we'll have the *Wasp's* water, won't we now?"

Smee fell silent now, finally grasping the lunatic plan.

"Don't you see?" said Black Stache. "It's a carrot for the

men. They know we're carrying just enough water for a few days. So they know we *have* to catch the *Wasp* in that time, or they die of thirst. Isn't it a *fine* plan, Mr. Smee?"

Insane, thought Smee. But what he said was "Aye, Cap'n. Brilliant."

"Of course it's brilliant," said Black Stache. "And to make it even more brilliant, I'm going to give the crew another carrot."

"Another one, Cap'n?" Smee did not like the sound of that at all.

"Yes," said Black Stache, admiring his own genius. "Smee, aside from water, cannon, and cargo, what're the two heaviest things on the *Sea Devil*?"

Smee thought for a moment, then said, "That would be Preston and Harb—"

He looked down at the deck, where the two fat pirates had been hefted into the dory, which was now being lowered alongside the ship.

"You see, Smee?" said Black Stache. "This'll teach the men that they got to work hard. They must be worth their weight to me, Smee, or it's over the side."

Smee looked down at his own belly. It was not a small belly. Black Stache caught the look and smiled broadly, showing his brown tooth stumps. He continued to smile as the dory, with its squirming and terrified passengers, was cut loose, and quickly fell behind the *Sea Devil*, growing smaller by the minute, until it was gone. Along with most of the *Sea Devil's* water.

"Good riddance," Black Stache growled, and he spat again, a major gob, this time hitting Smee's other foot. He turned to face the crew, now watching him warily.

"The deadweight is gone, men," he said. "We're picking up speed." He gestured toward the dot on the horizon that was the *Wasp*. "She's a fast ship, but we're going to be faster. We'd better be, because your water rations are gone in three days' time. So work hard, men. Work hard, if you don't want to join those two bales of lard drifting astern."

Black Stache glared at the crew, daring anyone to challenge him. His glare was met by a fearful silence.

"Good," said Black Stache. "Now, let's get more sail up."

The pirates scurried into action as if their lives depended on it, which they did. Black Stache turned to Smee.

"I'll be in my cabin," he said. "When I come back, I want that ship"—he pointed to the distant *Wasp*—"to be closer. If it's not, we'll have to toss some more weight over the side."

He looked pointedly at Smee's belly, then turned and stalked off.

Smee pushed the men hard all afternoon, and ate no dinner that night.

CHAPTER 7

ᏢETER ᏤENTURES ᎯFT

Bʏ ᴛʜᴇ ᴛʜɪʀᴅ ᴅᴀʏ the boys were so hungry that when
Hungry Bob brought their daily slop, they actually ate some
of it. They picked carefully through the lumps, still (to
Hungry Bob's delight) passing on the wriggling ones, and
choking down others as best they could. But it wasn't enough
food, not nearly enough. Hunger now clawed constantly at
their bellies.

Peter, still wondering if it was such a good thing to be the
leader, was feeling intense pressure to do something. He had
given up on pleading the boys' case to Captain Pembridge.
Several times now, the boys had heard the captain staggering
around on the main desk, shouting senseless commands
("HEAVE TO ON THE STIZZENS! FURL THE
YARDARM!") to the vast enjoyment of the crew.
Pembridge sounded even more confused than he'd been the
first day; the sailors mocked him openly now.

No, Pembridge would be no help. And Peter didn't dare approach Slank; to ask *him* for better food would be to ask for a lashing. And so, as the third day turned into the third night, and the boys prepared for another restless, hungry night in their dank little cabin, listening to James whimpering—and rats scuttling—Peter made up his mind: he would steal some food.

There had to be decent food on the ship. Slank surely wasn't eating the swill that the boys got, and he just as surely wasn't feeding it to the first-class passengers, like that girl Molly and her governess. No, they were eating decent food, and Peter meant to have some of it.

He figured it was stored in the aft part of the ship, where the important people slept, and the valuable items were stored. He'd done some poking around, and determined that there was no way he could go aft belowdecks without passing through the crew's quarters, where he would surely be seen. His plan, then, was to wait for dark, then sneak aft on the main deck.

He waited until an hour past sunset, then carefully detached himself from the clump of dozing boys huddled together on the floor for warmth, and protection from the rats. Tubby Ted continued to snore, but James sat up, rubbing his eyes, and said, "Peter, where are you going?"

"*Quiet*," Peter hissed. "I'm going to look for food."

"I'll go with you," said another voice. Prentiss.

"And I," said Thomas.

"Bring me a ham sandwich," said Tubby Ted, awakened by the talk of food.

"I'm going alone," said Peter, ducking out of the room. "And I'll bring back what I can."

"Be careful," said James, behind him.

"Also, some cheese," said Tubby Ted.

Peter climbed the ladderway to the deck, poked his head up and looked around. He saw a small knot of crewmen a few yards aft, looking off the ship's port rail, talking; otherwise, the deck appeared to be empty. He eased himself out of the ladderway and slid on his belly to the starboard side, away from the men. Then, on hands and knees, he crawled aft.

As he neared the stern of the ship he heard loud talk and laughter coming from a cabin window. He recognized Slank's booming voice, and the high-pitched giggle of Molly's governess, Mrs. Bumbrake.

"Oh, Mr. Slank!" she was saying. "You are a devil!"

"That I am, Mrs. Bumbrake!" boomed Slank. "And you know what they say!"

"What do they say, Mr. Slank?"

"They say," roared Slank, "the devil take the hindmost!"

Then Peter heard Mrs. Bumbrake emit a very un-governess-like squeal, followed by what sounded like a slap, followed by some thumping, then more squealing, then more thumping, and then much laughing. From the sound of it, Peter figured they wouldn't be breaking up the party any time soon.

That takes care of Slank, he thought. *Now all I have to worry about is the big man with the whip.*

He checked around to make sure nobody was watching, then got to his feet, tiptoed aft, and descended some steps to a dimly lit corridor, flanked by four cabin doors. *Molly is probably in one of these cabins*, he thought, moving silently, until he reached a narrow ladderway leading down. Heart pounding, he descended the ladder, and found himself in darkness. He felt his way along the floor with his feet, toes outstretched. He then stood still for perhaps a minute, waiting as his eyes began to pick up what little light filtered down the ladderway from above. He saw he was in a long, low space. At the end was a doorway, and . . .

Peter froze. On the floor by the doorway was a man's body. It lay slumped against the wall, head lagging sideways, and . . .

. . . *and it was snoring.* Peter relaxed a little. He peered at the sleeping man's face, and recognized him as a member of the crew. Next to the man, on the floor, was a lantern, which apparently had gone out. The man's right hand was loosely curled around a wooden club, about two feet long.

He's on watch, Peter thought. *He's guarding the door, and he let the lantern go out, or he put it out, and he fell asleep.*

Peter thought about it some more. *If he's on watch, whatever's in that room is important. Maybe they keep the good food in there.*

He hesitated, weighing the risk of waking the guard against the hope of finding food. Then his stomach growled, making the decision for him. Peter crept forward keeping an eye on the sleeping man. He reached the door and put his hand on the knob, worried that the door would be locked, only to find that not only was it unlocked, it was slightly ajar.

That's odd.

Peter gently pushed the door open and stepped inside. Again, he waited for his eyes to adjust, as this room was even darker. He heard a scuttling sound, but it was one he'd become all too familiar with: rats.

Please don't bite me, he thought. *I'm here for the same reason you are.*

In a few moments he began to make out a bulky shape perhaps five feet in front of him. Holding his hands before him, sliding his feet, he started toward it, and . . .

What was that?

It was a noise in the corner, something moving.

It sounds too big to be a rat.

Peter froze again, peering toward the source of the sound, and he saw something green—no, *two* green things—glowing, hovering. Peter stared at them and realized . . .

Those are eyes. But what has eyes that glow like that?

Peter was not interested in finding out. He turned and bolted for the doorway and . . .

WHUMP!

Peter bounced off a stout body and fell backward onto the floor. He'd run into the guard, who was now awake, and unhappy.

"OW!" said the guard, stumbling backward. He caught himself and lumbered forward into the room, shouting, "What do yer think yer *OW!*"

The guard, seeing poorly in the dark room, had tripped over Peter's legs. He stumbled and pitched forward headfirst, falling and striking something behind Peter. Seeing his chance to escape, Peter scrambled to his feet and darted through the doorway, determined to get out of there as quickly as possible, only to stop when he heard the sailor's astonished *"Wha . . . ?"*

Unable to control his curiosity, Peter risked a backward glance. The guard was on his hands and knees, next to the bulky shape on the floor. Peter, his eyes now fully adjusted to the darkness, recognized it as the canvas-wrapped cargo he'd seen being carried aboard the ship. The guard, his mouth agape, was staring at something above the shape.

A rat.

In midair.

A rat floating in midair.

Peter blinked his eyes, but there was no question: the rat was suspended in space, as if hanging from a string, but there was no string. As Peter and the guard stared at the rat, it

waved its legs slowly, almost languidly, as if swimming, and began to drift toward the doorway, toward Peter.

Peter knew he should run, but could not move his legs, could not take his eyes off the airborne rodent now coming through the doorway. When it was about two feet away it seemed to notice him and, moving its right feet in a paddling motion, altered its course to the left, so as to just miss Peter's head. Riveted to the spot, Peter watched it come, swiveling his head as it drew closer, closer, and . . .

Peter jumped as a hand gripped his arm.

"Peter," a voice whispered.

Peter jerked his head around and saw: Molly.

Where did she come from?

"Molly," he said, "what are . . ."

"You need to get out of here *now*," she said, pulling him away from the doorway.

Behind him, Peter heard the guard stumbling to his feet.

"Here, now!" the guard was shouting. "Stop, whoever you are!"

Peter felt Molly dragging him to the ladder.

"Come *on*," she said, reaching the ladder and swiftly ascending it. Peter followed, his mind swirling now, thinking about the flying rat, remembering the eyes he'd seen glowing in the dark.

Molly has green eyes.

They reached the next deck. Behind and below them,

the guard was still yelling for them to stop. Peter started toward the stairway leading up to the main deck, but Molly grabbed his arm, opened a door, pulled him inside, and closed the door behind them. It was a small cabin, but cozy—two bunks, one slung over the other; a tiny bureau. The cabin smelled of lavender and face powder. This was obviously where Molly and Mrs. Bumbrake stayed.

"Molly," said Peter, "what . . ."

He was silenced as Molly clapped her hand over his mouth. She nodded toward the door. Peter heard the sound of boots clomping down the stairway, then past the cabin door. Big boots.

The man with the whip, thought Peter. *Little Richard.*

Molly silently opened the door just as the top of the huge man's head disappeared down the ladderway.

"Go," said Molly, pushing Peter out the door. "Before Slank gets here."

"All right," said Peter, "but what was . . ."

"There's no time," said Molly. "Here, take this." She turned, snatched a brown-paper package from the bureau, and shoved it into his hand. "Now, *go.*"

Peter heard more bootsteps on the deck. Clutching the package, he raced up the stairway and, keeping low, scooted forward along the ship's starboard rail. Behind him, he heard more yelling; one of the voices was Slank's. But Peter's path was clear, and he reached the forward ladderway unnoticed.

He darted down it and, with great relief, ducked into the boys' cramped little space, which, at this moment, seemed almost pleasant.

James sat up. "Peter," he said. "You're back."

Peter slumped to the floor, breathing hard, his heart pounding.

"What happened?" said Prentiss.

"Are you all right?" said Thomas. "You look scared."

"I'm not scared," said Peter, too quickly.

"What happened?" repeated Prentiss.

"Well," said Peter, not sure how much he should tell, or how much the others would believe, "there was this room, and . . ."

"Did you get food?" interrupted Tubby Ted.

"Well, said Peter, "I was trying to . . ."

"You did!" said Tubby Ted, spying the package and grabbing it from Peter's hands. "You got food!"

"But that's—"

Peter was interrupted by the boys' shouts of delight as Tubby Ted ripped open the brown paper and triumphantly held up a loaf of bread.

"Peter!" said James. "You did it!"

"Yes," said Peter, quietly, looking at the bread. "Of course."

They managed to pry the loaf out of Tubby Ted's hands long enough to divide it five ways. Although they could have eaten several more loaves, the worst of their hunger pangs were satisfied, and after they finished the last crumbs, they all quickly drifted off to sleep.

All, that is, except Peter, who tossed restlessly, reviewing his strange experience in the aft hold, questions swarming in his brain.

How could a rat fly? What was going on in that hold? Why were they guarding it? Why was Molly down there? Had those been her eyes he'd seen in the dark? They had to have been! But what kind of person has eyes like that, eyes that glow in the dark? *How on earth could a rat fly?*

The more Peter pondered these questions, the more he became convinced that the answers, whatever they were, had something to do with the trunk, the same trunk that had made that sailor act so strange on the day the ship left port. Peter went over it again and again in his mind, trying to remember if he'd seen anything else in the hold; there was nothing, he decided. Only the trunk. That's what they were guarding.

I'm going to find out what's in there.

CHAPTER 8

$\mathcal{A}$DRIFT IN A $\mathcal{D}$ORY

$\mathcal{P}$RESTON AND HARBUCKLE, their hands tied to their feet behind their backs, lay on their fat bellies on the bottom of the dory, looking like a pair of pudgy rocking horses. Their situation—bound and gagged, abandoned at sea without food or water—had been bad enough to begin with, but it was getting worse.

They'd been drifting for a while now, each man struggling in vain to get free of his ropes. And now Preston, exhausted from the effort, could see that the water sloshing around the bottom with him was definitely higher.

The dory was leaking.

Figures, Preston thought. *Black Stache wouldn't waste a good boat just to kill us.*

Preston strained to look around. He could see that the dory was riding lower now. As the waves rolled it, water sometimes sloshed over the sides.

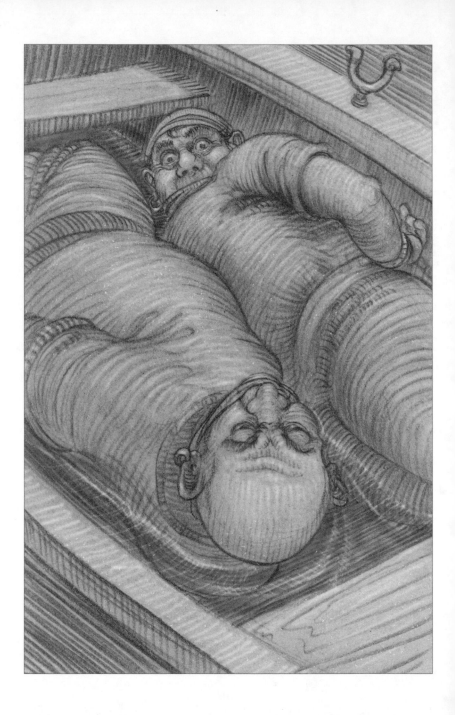

The little boat was going down.

I'm going to drown, thought Preston. He felt a momentary pang of regret that he had not spent more time with his beloved wife. But it passed when he remembered that the reason he'd gone to sea in the first place was that he had never really liked his beloved wife.

The water in the dory was definitely higher now. Preston, who was not the world's foremost thinker, was doing his best to formulate some kind of plan, when he heard Harbuckle, in the front of the dory, say something through his gag.

"Bmmmgh!" it sounded like.

Preston craned his neck to see his shipmate, who was looking back at him with a certain urgency in his eyes.

"Gmmmmph!" Harbuckle said, arching his eyebrows in a meaningful way.

Preston sensed that Harbuckle was trying to tell him something.

"Wmmmmbh?" he queried.

"Gmmmmph!" repeated Harbuckle, adding, "GMM-MMPH!"

Harbuckle rolled sideways, so his back was to Preston. He looked over his shoulder and made a violent, look-down-there nod with his head toward his bound hands, the fingers of which were wiggling.

"GMMMMMMMMMMPH!" he said, sounding very impatient now.

Ah! thought Preston. *He wants me to do something.* This seemed to Preston like a sound idea, doing something. But what? Preston made a frowny face at Harbuckle, to indicate, *What?*

Looking exasperated, Harbuckle rolled toward Preston, then rolled away again, again nodding violently toward his hands.

"GMMMMMPPPHH!!" he said, and suddenly Preston understood. *He wants me to roll over, so he can untie my hands. What a good idea!* He nodded his head violently, to indicate that he understood. Then, with a massive heave, he rolled his bulky body toward Harbuckle's.

The good news was, Preston's roll took him just the right distance; he and Harbuckle were now back to back, their hands just touching.

The bad news was, by shifting his massive weight forward to join Harbuckle's, he had overburdened the bow of the dory, and cold seawater was now sloshing into the tiny boat.

"GMMMMMMMPPPHH!!!!" shouted Harbuckle, and Preston felt his shipmate's hands clawing frantically at the knots on his own. He tried to hold still, but as the water rose, he had to squirm and struggle to keep his head above it—but the water was coming in fast, and Preston could no longer grab any gasps of air, and so he held his breath as long as he could, until his lungs screamed in agony and he grabbed at his aching chest and . . .

Wait a minute. He was grabbing his chest, which meant...
His hands were free!

Desperately thrusting himself up, Preston got to his knees, tore the gag from his mouth and gulped sweet sea air. He saw that the dory was now swamped, but he was still alive! He could barely believe it: a moment ago, he'd been at death's door, but now here he was, still breathing, and he owed it all to . . .

Harbuckle!

Preston plunged his head back underwater and found his shipmate's body, not moving. Frantic, Preston grabbed Harbuckle by the hair and yanked his head to the surface, where—*thank goodness*—it made a faint moaning sound. Preston yanked the gag from Harbuckle's mouth, which began to cough, and then spew seawater, and then, finally, to speak.

"You *idjit!*" it said. "You rock-headed, lobster-brained MORON!"

"I'm sorry, mate!" said Preston. "I forgot you was down there!"

"You *forgot I was down there?*" said Harbuckle. "I untie your hands and save your worthless life and YOU FORGOT I WAS DOWN THERE?"

"Only for a minute," said Preston.

"Untie my hands," said Harbuckle, "so I can wring your neck."

Harbuckle calmed down as Preston untied him, and both men began to understand that, although they had escaped immediate death, their long-term prospects were not good. They tried using their hands to bail out the dory, but it was hopeless: for every handful of water they scooped out, the waves brought more in. Eventually they stopped trying, as exhaustion, cold and despair settled in.

And then Preston saw it, on the horizon.

"Look," he shouted, pointing.

Harbuckle squinted, and he saw it, too.

A mast.

Harbuckle said, "You don't suppose . . . ?"

"They're coming *back* for us?"

"That couldn't be good," Harbuckle said.

"No," agreed Preston. Perilous as their situation was, it was probably better than whatever Black Stache would have in store.

"Wait a second," said Harbuckle, squinting hard. "That ain't the *Sea Devil*."

Preston took a long look.

"It ain't the *Wasp*, either," he said.

The two pirates looked at each other, then both rose up, nearly capsizing the swamped dory, and began waving their arms frantically.

"Over here!" they shouted. "We're over here!"

With agonizing slowness, the distant ship drew closer;

the two castaways, their voices growing hoarse, kept shouting and waving, desperate for a sign of recognition. Finally, Preston saw it.

"Someone's waving at us!" he shouted, jumping up so violently that the much abused dory finally did capsize, leaving the two pirates swimming, or trying to.

But there was no question; the ship was steering toward them now, and as it drew close, both men could see clearly see the person who'd been waving at them, the person who'd seen them first, and saved their sorry lives.

"Why," said Harbuckle, "it's a *boy*."

CHAPTER 9

The Rescue

Peter leaned over the port rail to watch as the two fat, wet men, clinging to knotted ropes, were hauled slowly aboard the *Never Land*. The seas swelled and shifted, the fat men crying out as they swung like pendulums.

Peter had seen the drowning men first; he'd pointed them out to a sailor, who'd run to tell Slank. Peter had kept waving as the *Never Land* drew closer, to let the men know they'd be rescued.

And now, as they were hauled aboard, Peter was as curious as everyone else to learn who they were, and how they got into their predicament. He joined the crowd forming a circle around the men as they sat on the deck, dripping, panting, looking apprehensively up at their rescuers. Peter noticed Molly on the other side of the circle. Their eyes met for a moment, then Peter looked away.

Why do I always look away?

"Move aside!" said Slank, shoving his way through the crowd. He stood over the two men and said: "Do you speak English?"

The fatter of the two (though not by much) nodded, coughed and said, "Yes, sir."

"What're your names?" asked Slank. "What ship are you from? And how did you end up in the sea?"

"My name is Harbuckle, sir," said the fatter one. "This here is Preston. We thank you, sir, for saving our lives. We was surely—"

Slank interrupted. "I asked you what ship you're from," he said. "And how you wound up in the sea."

"We're from . . . the . . . ah . . . the *Marcelle*," said Harbuckle.

The slightly slimmer fat man, Preston, look at his mate, puzzled. "No we're not," he said. "We're from the *UNH*—" His sentence was cut short by a sharp blow to the side of his head from Harbuckle.

"Hey!" said Preston, rubbing his head.

"Don't pay him no mind," said Harbuckle to Slank. "He's confused from swallowing seawater. He knows good and well we're from the *Marcelle*." Harbuckle was glaring at Preston now. "Got that, mate? The *Marcelle*."

"Is that so?" said Slank, quietly.

"Yes, sir," said Harbuckle. "It surely is. She went down in a storm, a bad one. We was lucky to get the dory launched, sir, and if you hadn't come along, we—"

"I know the *Marcelle*," interrupted Slank.

"You do?" said Harbuckle, looking surprised.

"I do," said Slank. "Tell me, did Captain Ferguson go down with the ship?"

Harbuckle hesitated, then said, "Aye, sir, that he did. He was a courageous man, Captain Ferguson."

"Yes," said Slank. "He was. Now, there's one more thing I need you to tell me . . ."

"What's that, sir?" said Harbuckle.

Slank drew his knife, the blade's honed edge glinting. "What part of you do I feed to the sharks first?"

The crowd gasped, some drawing back, some moving in for a better view.

"No!" said Harbuckle, his fear-widened eyes riveted on the knife. "Please, sir! *Why?*"

"Because you're a lying piece of kelp," said Slank. "The *Marcelle* is commanded by Captain Paige. Captain Ferguson died twenty years ago."

Slank took a step toward Harbuckle, who scrambled backward.

"Please, sir!" he screamed. "No! NO! I'll tell you the truth!"

"And what would that be?" snarled Slank.

"We was thrown off the *Sea Devil*," said Harbuckle.

Another gasp from the crowd.

Slank barked out a laugh. "D'you expect me to believe

that Black Stache would sail with a pair of fat slugs like you?"

"It's true, sir!" said Harbuckle. "I swear it!" He turned to Preston. "Tell him, Preston! Tell him what ship we're from!"

Preston frowned. "The *Marcelle*," he said.

"NO!" shouted Harbuckle.

"But you said . . ."

"TELL HIM THE TRUTH BEFORE HE KILLS US, YOU IDJIT!" screamed Harbuckle.

"Well, make up your mind!" said Preston. To Slank, he said: "I tried to tell you. We're from the *Sea Devil*."

Slank studied the two men. "All right, then," he said. "If you're from the *Sea Devil*, what were you doing in the sea? And before you answer, know this: if I think you're lying, you'll go right back into the sea." He flashed the blade. "In pieces."

Harbuckle gulped. "Sir," he said, "Black Stache put us adrift in a dory."

"And why would he do that?" said Slank.

"To lighten the *Sea Devil*," said Harbuckle. "To give her speed. He even threw most of the water barrels overboard."

Another crowd gasp.

"You're lying," said Slank, stepping forward again. "No captain throws water overboard."

"It's true!" said Harbuckle. "Black Stache is mad! He says now the crew will have to catch the *Wasp*. To get the water."

"The *Wasp*?" said Slank. "Black Stache is after the *Wasp*?"

Peter noticed that, across the circle, Molly had moved forward a step.

Her father is aboard the Wasp.

"Yes," said Harbuckle. "He says there's a treasure on the *Wasp*."

"And what would that be?" said Slank.

"He didn't specify," said Harbuckle. "He just said it was a great treasure. The greatest treasure ever taken to sea, he says."

Peter saw Molly frown.

"The greatest treasure ever taken to sea," repeated Slank, softly.

"That's what he says," said Harbuckle.

"Any clue to the *nature* of this treasure?" Slank asked.

"A trunk," Harbuckle said. "It's in a trunk. Black Stache has a prisoner, an officer of the Royal Guard. He's the one told Black Stache about the trunk. Says a fine trunk was brought aboard just before the *Wasp* set sail, escorted by a dozen armed men."

"What's in this trunk?" said Slank.

Molly was staring hard at the pirate now.

"I dunno," said Harbuckle. "The Guardsman prisoner don't know, neither. Just that it's to go from the Queen of England to the King of Rundoon by the fastest ship afloat, under the heaviest guard. Whatever it is in there, it's important enough to have two royals concerned about it."

Slank stared out to sea for a long moment, then looked back down at Preston and Harbuckle, who watched him fearfully, awaiting their fate. Another long moment passed. Finally, Slank spoke.

"You're pirate scum," he said.

"Yes, sir," said Harbuckle, "but we . . ."

"Shut up," said Slank. "You're pirate scum, and what I should do is throw you both over the side right now."

Harbuckle whimpered. Preston wet his pants, but nobody could tell, as his clothes were already soaked.

"But I'm going to let you live," said Slank.

"THANK YOU, sir!" said Harbuckle. "A thousand . . ."

"Shut up," said Slank. "I'm going to let you live *for now*, because you might be useful. *For now.* Little Richard!" The giant loomed behind Slank, his whip coiled on his fat leather belt. "Take this pirate scum below. The rest of you men get back to work."

The crowd dispersed, the sailors murmuring about the drama they'd just watched. Peter edged his way toward Molly, who was still staring at the spot where Harbuckle had lain.

"Molly?" he said.

She looked up at him, her face blank, her green eyes devoid of their usual sparkle.

"What?" she said.

"I, uh . . . I . . . I know your father is on the *Wasp*," he said.

"Yes."

"Well, I hope he'll be all right."

"Thank you."

Molly turned to go. Peter could see she didn't want to talk, but he burned with curiosity.

"Molly," he said.

She turned back.

"I wanted to thank you for last night," Peter said. "For helping me."

"You're welcome." She started to turn again, but Peter put his hand on her arm.

"Wait," he said. "How did . . . I mean, what were you doing in that room? What are they keeping in there? And did you see the rat? In the air? Did you *see* it?"

Molly was staring at him now.

"Peter," she said, "listen to me. This is very important. You mustn't . . ."

"MOLLY!" The two youngsters were suddenly separated by the massive form of Mrs. Bumbrake, her front side toward Molly, leaving Peter face-to-face with her formidable backside. "I've told you a thousand times, you are *not* to be on this deck without me, and you are to stay away from the riffraff."

"But . . ."

"No back talk, young lady! You come with me!" With Molly in tow, Mrs. Bumbrake barged away, leaving behind a cloud of lavender.

Peter watched them go.

I mustn't what?

He drifted forward, toward a knot of sailors who were pretending to work while they gossiped. There was much to gossip about. There were the two rescued pirates, of course, but also something else, something that had happened last night, news of which was circulating around the ship.

". . . guarding the door," one of the sailors was saying. "He says one minute he was wide awake, next minute he wakes up on the floor. Like there was a spell cast on him, he says."

Peter moved closer.

"Magic spell?" scoffed another sailor. "Not hardly. Too much rum, that's your magic spell."

"No," said the storyteller. "Not John. He don't drink, not a drop. That's why Slank give him the guard duty. No, he says something put him out, and when he woke up, there was people in the room, voices. So John goes running in there, and somebody runs right into him!"

"Who?"

"He didn't see. It happened sudden, he says. But whoever it was, he trips John, and down John goes, headfirst into that trunk."

"What's in that trunk, anyway?"

"Dunno," said the storyteller, "but whatever it is, Slank

guards it like gold. So anyway, John's trying to get up, and his head feels bust open, and he looks up, and then he sees it." The storyteller paused dramatically.

"What?" asked one of the listeners. "He sees what?"

"A rat," said the storyteller. "A *flying* rat."

"You mean it was jumping? 'Cause I've seen 'em jump as far as . . ."

"No," said the storyteller. "John says it was flying."

"That's the bump on his head talking," said one.

"I dunno. It ain't like John to imagine things."

"Well I don't believe it. I've sailed with rats for thirty years, and they don't fly."

"I think it's true," said a new voice, from a big man with a big wart on his nose—the sailor Peter had seen acting strange around the mysterious cargo on the first day. He looked around at the group.

"I believe John," he said.

"Why's that, Alf?"

"Because the rat was in the room with that trunk. I touched that trunk, the day we set sail. There's something strange about it."

"Strange is one thing, Alf. Flying rats is another."

"But I'm telling you, I *felt* it," said Alf. "I felt something, I dunno, *magic*. I felt like . . ." Alf looked around, hesitant.

"Like what, Alf?"

"Like . . . like *I* could fly," said Alf.

There was a pause, and then the crowd erupted in laughter.

"Sure, Alf, you could fly!"

"You're a regular bluebird, Alf!"

"Look out," said somebody. "Slank's coming."

The sailors, still chuckling, quickly dispersed, leaving Alf, red-faced, staring at his feet. Peter hesitated, then approached the big man and tugged at his sleeve. Alf looked down at him.

"What is it, boy?" he said.

"I believe it, too," said Peter. "About the rat."

Alf frowned. "Why?" he said.

Peter hesitated, then said, "Because I saw it."

Alf bent over, his face now close to Peter's.

"You saw it, boy? You was down there?"

Peter nodded.

"Did you see anything else?" said Alf. "Did you happen to see what's in the trunk?"

"No, sir," said Peter.

Alf studied him, then spoke softly. "But you want to," he said. "You want to know what's in there."

Peter nodded again.

"Me too, boy," said Alf. "Me too."

CHAPTER 10

BLACK STACHE CLOSES IN

BLACK STACHE HEARD THE SHARP WHISTLE pierce the night air—sounding like a gull's hungry cry—and lifted his head to see his lookout wave from the crow's nest.

We're in range.

Stache banged the butt end of his sword on deck twice—*thump, thump.* Instantly, the eight long oars sticking out from the cannon bays lifted from the sea in unison, dripping water, and withdrew into the ship's hull. The crew, desperate now for water as well as treasure, had been hard at it 'round the clock for almost two days straight, working both the sails and oars, reading the winds perfectly, closing the gap on the *Wasp.* Now they were ready for the final run.

She's mine.

Black Stache thumped his sword three more times to summon his officers, then retreated below to his cabin, taking a seat at a table covered with navigational charts. Also

on the table were also two small, delicate models of sailing ships, one painted a shiny black like the *Wasp,* the other a replica of the *Sea Devil.*

There was a tentative tap at the door.

"Come in," growled Black Stache. Smee entered and gagged; the cabin smelled like a dead cow. This was because there were, in fact, several pieces of dead cow on Black Stache's bunk, as well as the half-eaten carcass of a turkey. Gnawed remnants of other meals littered the floor. Flies buzzed everywhere. Smee held his hand over his nose, trying to be discreet about it.

"You called, Cap'n?" he said, his voice muffled.

"It's time," said Stache, staring at the model ships. "The moment is at hand."

"Yes, sir," said Smee, turning, desperate to escape the eye-watering stench. "I'll just go up and tell the—"

"*Wait,*" said Black Stache. "I want to go over the final plan with you and Storey."

As Smee reluctantly turned back, there was a second knock, and Storey, the *Sea Devil's* crew chief, entered. He fell back, momentarily staggered by the odor, then scrunched up his face and forced himself forward into the cabin, like a man walking against a gale.

"Aye, Cap'n?" he said, through gritted teeth.

"Sit down, men," said Stache.

Smee and Storey looked around. There was nowhere to

sit except the bunk, which was covered with rotting food, and a wooden stool, upon which sat a large fur-covered lump—an old cheese, perhaps, or a dead cat.

"If it's all the same, Cap'n," said Storey, "I'll stand."

"Me, too, Cap'n," said Smee.

Black Stache looked around his cabin, apparently noticing its condition for the first time.

"Smee," he said, "where the devil is my cabin boy? This place is a mess."

"You had him walk the plank, Cap'n," said Smee.

"I did?"

"You did, Cap'n," said Smee. "For touching your model ships." Smee chose not to add that the cabin boy had walked off the ship almost cheerfully, knowing he would no longer have to try to clean Black Stache's cabin.

"Ah, so I did," said Stache. "I'll want you to get me a new cabin boy when we take the *Wasp*."

"Aye, Cap'n," said Smee. This would be the sixth cabin boy in less than a year.

"Now, about the *Wasp*," said Black Stache, looking at Storey. "Are we ready?"

"We are, Cap'n," said Storey. He pointed toward the ship models, careful not to touch them. "We've been gaining steady, with the rowing. Now we're sitting just right for a downwind run. Your plan was right on the money, Cap'n. I don't care how fast the *Wasp* is; with this wind, and this heading, when we raise the Ladies, we'll close on her in no time."

"And the Ladies are ready?" said Black Stache.

"Aye, Cap'n."

"All right, then," said Black Stache, pausing dramatically, savoring the moment. "Raise the Ladies."

"Aye, aye, sir!" shouted Storey and Smee, lunging for the doorway, and fresh air.

After they left, Black Stache turned his eyes to his model ships. He put his hand gently, almost lovingly, on the model of the *Sea Devil*. Slowly, he moved it forward until it touched the *Wasp*. He kept pushing until the *Wasp* reached the edge of the table. Then, smiling, he gave it a vicious shove; the *Wasp* model fell, its delicate hull smashing into pieces on the floor. Black Stache laughed, his breath further befouling the rancid cabin air. Then he stood and, stepping on the remains of the *Wasp*, stalked out of the cabin.

Time for the kill.

CHAPTER 11

THE MESSENGERS

IT WAS JUST BEFORE MIDNIGHT, an overcast night, no moonlight or starlight reaching the dark deck of the *Never Land*. The wind was steady at about five knots; the fat ship plowed forward on a following sea.

Molly, wearing a blanket like a cloak over her nightgown, emerged from the ladderway and looked quickly around. Seeing no one, she walked swiftly to the stern rail, her feet bare on the scarred wood of the deck. She'd not dared to put on shoes when she'd left the cabin, for fear she'd wake the snoring Mrs. Bumbrake.

After glancing quickly around again, she leaned over the stern rail and peered out at the dark water. She saw only the ship's churning wake, ghostly pale by the light of the ship's lone stern lantern. Her eyes strained to see more.

Where were they?

She wondered if she was too early. Or, worse, too late.

Telling time on the ship was a problem, especially when overcast skies kept Molly from seeing the stars.

Five minutes went by. To Molly, it felt like an hour.

Where were they?

Molly heard a man's voice, and she tensed, ready to race back to the ladderway. But then she heard another voice, and realized it was two sailors, well forward, passing another long night watch with the endless gossip of a ship at sea.

Molly relaxed and turned her gaze back toward the . . .

What was that?

She squinted at the patch of dark water where she thought she'd seen something, at the rightmost edge of the roiling wake.

There!

Molly's heart leaped as a gray shape flowed from the water, forming a graceful arc before disappearing again beneath the surface. The shape was followed by another, then another.

Porpoises. Five of them, their sleek bodies keeping pace effortlessly with the lumbering ship.

Molly leaned over the stern rail and waved frantically, then caught herself, feeling foolish.

They know I'm here, she thought. *They see everything.*

As if reading her mind, a large porpoise rose straight up, using its powerful tail to lift its head well clear of the water, dancing on the churning water. It looked at Molly, grinning, and said, "Hello."

Not in English, of course. It spoke in clicks and squeaks. But Molly had studied enough Porpoise to understand the standard greeting. Struggling to recall her lessons, Molly squeaked and clicked (the clicks were the hardest) something back, which she hoped was "Hello." What she actually said was "My teeth are green," but the porpoise was too polite to point that out.

Now the other four porpoises rose from the water, and, observing the protocol, also said "Hello." Molly told them all that her teeth were green. With the pleasantries out of the way, the lead porpoise, whose name was Ammm, made a longer series of clicks and squeaks. Molly knew just enough Porpoise to understand that Ammm was asking her if she was all right. She expected this question: it had been arranged that the porpoises would check in with Molly tonight, and the assumption had been that Molly would tell them yes, she was all right.

"No," Molly said, struggling to get the sounds right. "Trouble."

This set off a chorus of chittering and chirping among the porpoises, all still standing on their tails. Molly understood none of it, but they were clearly concerned.

Ammm turned to her again.

"Tell me," he said.

Molly had been thinking all day about how, with her very limited Porpoise vocabulary, she could say what she had to say. Leaning forward, speaking as clearly as she could—but not too slowly, as porpoises cannot understand slow talking—she said: "Message father."

"Say," said Ammm.

Molly's heart leaped: she was getting through! But now came the hard part.

"Bad man hunt ship," she said.

"Again," said Ammm.

Molly took a deep breath, then: "Bad man hunt ship."

More chittering among the porpoises. Then Ammm said: "What ship? Molly ship?"

They had understood!

"No," said Molly. "Father ship."

Ammm paused, then repeated: "Father ship."

"Yes," said Molly, thrilled they were communicating.

Urgent chittering. Then Ammm spoke again: "We go. Good-bye."

"NO!" shouted Molly, so upset that she said it in English. But Ammm understood, and looked at her expectantly. The other four porpoises resurfaced, one by one.

"More," said Molly.

"Say," said Ammm.

Molly struggled to form the sounds: "Box on Molly ship."

"What on Molly ship?" asked Ammm.

"Box," said Molly. "Box. *Box.*"

"What?"

It was no use; the sound she was making for "box" clearly

made no sense to Ammm. Molly stamped her foot in frustration, trying desperately to think of another way to say it. Maybe she could . . .

Her thoughts were interrupted by voices getting louder behind her; someone was coming her way! She gestured helplessly to Ammm, turned, and ran to the ladderway, ducking down it just as the two night-watch sailors arrived.

". . . somebody back here talking," one was saying. "Slank says we're not to allow . . ."

"There's who was talking," said the other, pointing over the side.

"Well, I'll be damned," said the first. "Porpoises making all that noise! What d'you suppose has 'em so roused up?"

"Probably saw some tasty fish."

"That's the life, if you ask me. Eat and play, not a care in the world."

"Looky this big one here! He's talkin' to us! A right speechmaker, he is!"

"Probably wants us to throw him a bite to eat."

In fact, Ammm was saying something very impolite about the sailors and their ancestors. The other four porpoises snorted, then all five turned, arced, sliced smoothly into the dark water, and disappeared.

The two sailors watched them go.

"Yes, indeed, that's the life," said the first. "Not a care in the world."

CHAPTER 12

$\mathcal{A}$NGRY $\mathcal{W}$ORDS

$\mathcal{P}$ETER AND JAMES HAD SEEN THE WHOLE THING.

They had crept aft, hoping to find some edible food somewhere, slithering silently past the two gabbing sailors on watch. They were crouched behind a barrel near the stern when they'd seen Molly emerge from the ladderway, go to the rail, and lean over.

Peter had been about to approach her when she had started making the strangest noises he'd ever heard a human make.

"Peter," whispered James. "What is she . . . ?"

Peter silenced him with quick a squeeze on his arm. He motioned for James to stay low, and the two boys slid on their bellies to a spot where they could peer through an opening in the stern rail and look down at what Molly was seeing. They emitted simultaneous gasps when they saw the five porpoises, which looked as though they were dancing on the water as they used their powerful tails to hold their heads far above the waves.

They watched, astonished, as Molly and the largest of the porpoises exchanged the odd noises, almost as if—*but that's impossible*—they were having a conversation.

To Peter, Molly's noises sounded increasingly urgent and frustrated, until finally she broke into English and shouted, "No!" Unable to contain his curiosity any longer, Peter stood to approach her, only to dive back to his belly when he heard the night-watch sailors coming. He saw Molly turn and run back to the ladderway as he and James squirmed back behind the barrel. They waited there, afraid to breathe, as the sailors commented on seeing porpoises. Sailors apparently thought porpoises brought good luck. Finally, the sailors climbed to a higher deck and disappeared.

"Peter," whispered James, "what did we . . . ?"

"Not now," whispered Peter. "Go back to our cabin, and don't get caught."

"But where are you . . ."

"Never mind," hissed Peter. "I'll be along. Just get going."

After seeing that James had crawled away safely, Peter climbed a rope and slipped under a railing that took him to the upper deck. The night-watch sailors stood talking not twenty feet away. When the nearest one turned his back, Peter edged along the rail and reached a doorway leading down a ladderway into darkness.

Peter looked around, unsure how to get to Molly's cabin from here. He waited . . . waited . . . and finally the two sailors agreed it was time for tea. They moved on. Peter slipped down the steep ladderway, into a darkened hallway. Yellow light seeped from beneath several doors in both directions. Peter moved on to the next, sticking his ear to the door. He heard loud snoring.

Assuming that it was Mrs. Bumbrake, he opened the door and slipped inside.

"Peter!" whispered Molly. "What are you doing here?"

"I must talk to you," whispered Peter.

"Now?"

"Now," he said.

Molly frowned, then whispered, "All right. But outside in the passageway." They stepped outside, and Molly closed the door.

"I saw you," said Peter.

"Saw me what?" asked Molly. She kept her voice calm, but Peter could tell he'd surprised her.

"You were talking to that fish."

"What on earth are you talking about?"

"You were talking to that fish. You were making strange noises, and it was making them back."

"Don't be silly. Fish can't talk."

"Molly, I *saw* you."

Molly stared at him for a moment, weighing something.

Then she sighed and said, "All right, listen. Those are not fish. Those are called porpoises, and they breathe air, the same as we do."

"But they look like fish."

"But they're not. They breathe air, and they make noises, just like dogs and cats and cows and other animals. I was imitating the noises they make, purely out of curiosity, to see if I could get a response. That's all you saw. It was nothing."

"That's not what it looked like," said Peter. "It looked like you were talking to them. And you were upset about something. I heard you shout 'No!'"

"I was just frustrated, because I couldn't make the noises properly," said Molly. "That's all. Nothing more."

"You ran away when the sailors came. Why?"

Molly paused, again weighing something, then answered: "Only because I didn't want them to report me to Mrs. Bumbrake. She told me to stay in the cabin. Really, Peter, you're imagining things."

She's lying.

"I am?" said Peter. "And I suppose I imagined the flying rat? And I imagined that you were in that aft hold? What's going on, Molly? Tell me what's going on."

"Nothing, Peter," said Molly. "There's nothing going on."

Why is she lying?

"Fine," said Peter. "If you won't tell me, I'll find out for myself."

"*No*," she said with sudden intensity, grabbing his arm with a startlingly powerful grip. "Peter, you must not go down to that room again. You must *not*."

Peter yanked his arm away. "Who's going to stop me?" he said.

Molly's eyes bored into his. She spoke slowly.

"I will, Peter."

"How?" he snapped.

"I'll tell Slank," Molly threatened.

"You *wouldn't*," he said.

"I will if I have to," she said.

"All right then," said Peter, his cheeks burning, his voice quivering with anger. "I see now that not all the rats on this ship are four-legged."

"*Please*, Peter," said Molly, reaching for his arm again. "You don't understand."

"Good-bye . . . *rat*," said Peter, brushing her hand away.

"Peter, *please* . . ."

He faced her. "You know," he said, "I thought you . . . I thought we . . . Well . . . I was obviously wrong."

Peter darted up the ladderway to the relative safety of the darkened deck. He crouched for a moment, breathing deeply, seething with feelings of rage and betrayal.

Thinks she can lie to me, does she? Thinks she can tell me what to do? Well, I'll show her. I can do this myself, me and Alf. I don't need her help.

Who does she think she is?

CHAPTER 13

THE LADIES

IN THE DARKNESS JUST BEFORE DAWN, Leonard Aster paced back and forth on the stern of the *Wasp*, his long legs carrying his lanky frame across the beam in just a few strides each way. Again and again he looked into the water; again and again he saw nothing.

Where are you?

Finally impatience overcame him. After checking around for observers, he leaned over the rail and made a series of inhuman noises. Almost instantly he saw the glistening silver back of a porpoise break the ship's wake. It rose on its tail, quickly joined by the other four, facing in different directions, as if keeping watch.

"Hello," said Ammm.

"Hello," said Aster, anxious to hear news, but observing porpoise protocol.

"Ammm talk Molly," said Ammm.

"What say Molly?" said Aster, leaning forward eagerly.

"Molly say three things," said Ammm.

"What things?"

"Molly teeth green."

"Molly teeth green?"

"Yes."

Aster contemplated that for a moment, and decided the problem was likely Molly's limited command of Porpoise.

"What more Molly say?" he asked.

"Bad man hunt father ship," said Ammm.

Aster felt a chill.

"Again," he said, and the response was the same:

"Bad man hunt father ship."

Bad man. Aster figured he knew who that would be. He thought for a moment, then squeaked a question to the porpoise.

"Ammm see bad man ship?"

The answer was immediate: "Yes."

"Where?"

Chittering among the dolphins, then: "Near."

Damn. Aster thought furiously. He needed to see the captain. He started to go, then remembered that Ammm had said there were three messages.

"What more Molly say?"

Ammm hesitated, as if struggling with something, then finally said: "On Molly ship."

"What?" said Aster, puzzled.

"On Molly ship," repeated Ammm.

"What on Molly ship?" said Aster.

"Not know. Molly talk sound." Ammm made a noise that sounded like an attempt at a human voice, but porpoises were ill-suited for this task, and Aster couldn't make it out.

"Again," he said, leaning forward, desperate to understand.

"Who goes there?" A sailor's voice, behind Aster.

Damn.

"Go," said Aster to the porpoises. "Go."

The porpoises turned and, in an instant, were gone.

What was on Molly's ship?

"I said who goes there?" The sailor was right behind Aster, who turned from the rail to face him.

"Ah, Mr. Aster!" the sailor said, his tone changing when he realized he was speaking to the *Wasp*'s most important passenger. "I wondered who was making them noises. Not feeling well, eh? Got the heaves, do you?"

"I need to speak to Captain Scott," said Aster impatiently.

The sailor hid a smile. "Beg your pardon, but there's nothing the cap'n can do about a sour stomach, sir."

"It's something far more urgent than that," said Aster.

"But sir, with respect, it's just past five in the morning, and the cap'n would have me keelhauled if . . ."

"Never mind," said Aster, pushing past the protesting sailor. He strode to the ladderway, descended it, and pounded on the door to the captain's cabin. In a moment the door was opened by Captain Scott, pulling his pants on over a long nightshirt, looking ready to tear the head off whoever had disturbed his slumber. His anger instantly turned to surprise when he saw who had awakened him.

"Mr. Aster," he said.

"Captain Scott. Please accept my apologies for this intrusion, but I must speak to you immediately."

The sailor clambered down the ladderway, puffing.

"I'm sorry, Cap'n," he said. "I tried to tell Mr. Aster that . . ."

"It's all right," said Scott. "Back to your watch."

"Aye aye, sir," said the sailor, leaving.

"Please come in, Mr. Aster," said Scott, stepping back so the tall man could enter his spotless, tidy cabin.

Aster shut the door behind him, and turned to face Scott. His expression was intense; to Scott, it almost looked as though the tall man's green eyes were glowing. *A trick of the lantern light*, Scott thought.

"Captain Scott," Aster began. "You know of my diplomatic status. You understand that I am on a mission for the Queen herself."

"I do, sir."

"And you understand that, as such, I am privy to certain

information that is not generally available?"

"I imagine you are, at that."

"Captain Scott, I ask that you not question how I might know what I am about to tell you, but only to trust that it is true: a pirate ship now approaches the *Wasp*, intending to do her harm."

"Approaches?"

"It is very close, I fear."

"But, Mr. Aster, that is not possible," said Scott. "Our lookouts have seen no other ship for days, save for the frigate flying the Union Jack. She may be an imposter, but even if she means us harm, she'll never catch the *Wasp*."

"I hope you are right, sir. But if an enemy should over-take us . . ."

"He will not, I assure you."

"Just so, but if he does . . ."

"Then we shall fight."

"And I trust that we shall prevail, Captain Scott. But whatever happens, understand this: the special cargo that this ship carries for the Queen must not fall into our enemy's hands. *It must not.* If that were to happen, the consequences would be dire. More dire than you can imagine."

"Then I shall make sure it is well protected," said Scott. "But I assure you that no such protection will be necessary. As I say, no ship can catch the *Wasp*."

"I pray that you are right, Captain."

"Praying will no doubt help, Mr. Aster, but so will good seamanship. I'll go topside and see to the sails."

"Thank you, Captain."

The two men climbed the ladderway, Captain Scott wondering if his distinguished passenger had lost his mind. *How would he get information out here in the middle of the ocean? And what ship could be capable of catching the* Wasp?

His answer came as soon as they reached the deck, which was washed in the blood-red light of the dawn sun creeping over the horizon. The *Wasp*'s first mate, a burly man named Romelly, came running up, breathless.

"Cap'n, sir, I was just coming to get you. We just seen it, sir, just now."

"Seen what?"

"A ship, sir, closing on us fast, and it's flying. . . ."

"But that's *impossible*," said Scott. "How can . . .

And then he saw it. Less than a mile astern was the frigate: but now she was moving faster than the *Wasp*, and faster than any man aboard had ever seen a ship move. Even at this distance they could see the two white waves of wake surging aside as the prow blasted through the water.

"What in the *world?*" said Scott, almost whispering. "What kind of . . ."

"It's flying the skull and bones," said Romelly, fear creeping into his voice. "It's pirates, sir." The word was picked up by other crewmen, and shouts of "Pirates!" rang out around the ship.

Captain Scott, usually unflappable, stood staring that the apparition bearing down on his ship. "What kind of . . ." he said. "What . . ." words failed him. He had never seen such a thing in all his years at sea.

For the attacking ship carried no sails. At least none of the ordinary kind. Instead of sheets of white canvas, the sky above the pirate ship was filled with an enormous black brassiere—an undergarment of fantastic size, as if made for a giant woman. The twin mountains of fabric, funnel-shaped, pointed and bulging ahead of the breeze.

"What is *that*?" Scott gasped.

"That," said Leonard Aster, "is Black Stache."

The crew heard that, too, and the murmur went quickly around the deck. *Black Stache.*

"He's here for the Queen's cargo," said Aster. "I don't know how he knows, but he knows. That's what he's after."

"Well," said Scott grimly, "he won't get it without a fight."

CHAPTER 14

THE ALLIANCE

PETER FOUND ALF THE NEXT MORNING. The big man was down on his aching old knees, scrubbing the deck. The wind was picking up; to the west Peter saw gathering clouds, dark and threatening, though still a good way off. They made the ship feel smaller to Peter.

Alf looked up as the boy approached.

"Hello, little friend," he said, grinning. "Seen any flying rats?"

"No," said Peter. "But I'm going back to look."

Alf's grin disappeared. He looked around the deck to be sure nobody could overhear.

"To the aft hold?" he whispered. "To the trunk?"

"Yes. Tonight."

"But there's a guard there," said Alf, "and he'll be wary. Slank was right furious at John for falling asleep last time. Had him whipped good and proper. He's put a new man on guard, an ornery old scone called Leatherface. He won't be dozing."

"I thought about that," Peter said. "I have a plan to get past the guard."

"Do you now, little friend?"

"I do," said Peter. "But I need a helper."

"I see. And you were thinking old Alf would be your helper?"

"I was."

Alf stood, towering over Peter, and put a callused hand on the boy's shoulder.

"Hear this, lad. Slank told the crew that if he found out who was in that hold, or found anybody else going in there, he'd feed 'em to the sharks."

"It's a good plan," Peter said stubbornly. "It will work."

Alf studied Peter's face for a moment.

"You really want to get into that trunk, don't you," he said.

"Yes, sir, I do."

"Bad enough to risk your life?"

"Sir," said Peter, "I don't have much of a life now, and from what I'm told I'll have even less where I'm going. If there's something wonderful on this ship, I want to know what it is. This is my only chance, sir."

Alf looked out to sea for several seconds, then back to

Peter, and Peter saw there were tears in the big man's eyes.

"Little friend," Alf said, "those words are truer of me than they are of you." He moved closer, and put his head next to the boy's. "Tell me our plan."

CHAPTER 15

The Attack

Captain Scott stood alongside the *Wasp*'s helmsman, calling out commands that were relayed to the crew via the first mate's booming voice. Leonard Aster stood just behind Scott, his attention fixed on the ship pursuing them.

The *Sea Devil* was gaining. No matter what maneuver Scott tried, the enormous black brassiere grew steadily larger, blotting out much of the sky.

For all the peril they faced, Leonard and Scott retained their British calm, sounding like two gentlemen discussing the weather.

"He will be upon us soon," Scott said.

"It appears so," Leonard answered.

"I would not have thought it possible," said Scott, shaking his head. "Those sails, I . . ." He trailed off, then added, "I assure you, sir, my men will be ready. We will repel them."

Aster was quiet for a moment, studying the *Sea Devil*,

now close enough that he could easily see the scowling faces of the pursuing pirates, waving swords and shouting vile taunts at their quarry. He turned to Scott.

"Captain," he said. "I request to be put overboard in a dory with the trunk. At once."

Scott stared at him, his composure momentarily deserting him. "Are you *daft*, man?" he said. "You can't outrun that ship in a dory!"

"No," Leonard agreed. "But it would force Black Stache to make a choice. If he chooses to go after me and the trunk—and I believe he will—then he'd turn broadside to the *Wasp*." Leonard paused a moment. "And if your cannon were made ready and waiting . . ."

". . . he'd be squarely in the line of fire," said Scott. He thought about it, clearly tempted for a moment, then shook his head. "But so would you. I'm sorry, sir, but I can't put you at risk like that. You'll stay on board."

The two men locked eyes for five long seconds, then Aster spoke again, his voice low and urgent.

"Captain, I remind you once again that I am on a mission for the Queen, and that I speak with her authority. The trunk must not—cannot—fall into the hands of this pirate. Your men are brave, but clearly outnumbered. If the enemy boards us, we will be defeated. My plan involves risks, but it is our only hope. On the authority of Her Majesty, I order you to have your men put me and the trunk over the side. *Immediately*."

Scott reddened, and appeared to be on the verge of arguing. Then, slowly, he exhaled, and turned to the first mate.

"Prepare a dory to starboard," he ordered. "Bring up Aster's black trunk. Have the men prepare the starboard cannons."

The first mate hesitated, surprised by the unexpected orders.

"At once!" Scott said.

"Aye, Captain!" The first mate relayed the orders.

"Thank you, Captain," Leonard said.

"Do not thank me, sir. I fear those orders are your death sentence."

"Well," said Aster, "perhaps we can lessen the danger."

Scott answered with a questioning look.

"I believe you have an archer in your crew," said Aster.

"I do," said Scott.

Leonard gestured up the *Sea Devil's* huge, billowing double-coned sail, now looming almost overhead. "That garment appears to be made from a fine fabric," he said. "I suspect it would burn very well."

Scott squinted up at it, then looked at Aster with a small smile. "So it would," he said. "You've seen battle, Mr. Aster."

"That I have."

Scott turned to his first mate. "Send for Jeff the archer," he said. "He'll want his bow, and some flame."

Black Stache stood at the helm of the *Sea Devil*, watching his crew work as his ship closed on its prey. The Ladies had performed as hoped; the *Sea Devil* felt almost as if it were flying across the water. The *Wasp*, sleek and fast as she was, didn't stand a chance.

Just wait 'til the Ladies are raised on that mast, he thought. *Not a ship in the world will outrun her.*

This pleasant thought was interrupted by Smee's high-pitched voice.

"Cap'n, they're getting ready to launch a dory!"

Stache snatched the spyglass and had a look. He drew a sharp breath; not only were *Wasp* crewmen getting a dory ready, but it appeared that the passenger was a man in gentleman's clothing, and the cargo was . . . a black trunk!

What trickery is this?

Stache frowned, pondering the situation. Was the trunk a decoy? If he turned to pursue it, the Ladies would lose the wind and be useless—the *Wasp* would regain the advantage and quickly put water between them. But if he let the black chest escape and it proved to be the treasure . . .

"Cap'n, should we . . ."

"Out of my way!" shouted Stache, shoving Smee aside and striding quickly amidships, stopping at the cage holding the prisoner. He knelt, reached through the iron bars, grabbed the man by the coat of his now-filthy uniform, and pulled him close, so that only the rusting cage separated their faces. The prisoner recoiled from Stache's foul breath.

Stache shoved the spyglass into the man's hands.

"You tell me, mate," Stache said. "That there trunk being loaded off the *Wasp*. Is that the treasure?"

The prisoner, weak with hunger and fear, trembled so badly that Stache had to support the spyglass for him.

"Black and shiny she is," Stache said, helping him find it, "wearing a gold emblem on her sides."

"Y—y—yes," the man stammered. "Th—that's it. Sir."

Stache leaned back, appraising the man's terrified face. "You understand, lad, if them words ain't the truth, they're your last on this earth?"

"I . . . I . . ." The prisoner tried to swallow, but could not. "I swear, sir. That's it."

"Very well," said Stache, to himself. He stood, rubbing his chin absentmindedly, wondering if . . .

"TROUBLE, CAP'N!" It was Smee hollering from the upper deck, his stubby right arm pointing up.

Stache looked up. *What NOW?*

And then he saw it—

The Ladies were burning.

———•◆•———

Captain Scott patted Jeff the archer on the shoulder.

"Good work," he said, nodding toward the *Sea Devil*. The

right cup of the enormous brassiere was afire, the flames spreading quickly.

"Stand ready, son," he said. "We'll need you again."

The archer, a thick, bald man, nodded.

Scott looked across the ship to where Leonard Aster stood, waiting as sailors lashed the trunk inside the dory. Aster was staring at the trunk.

Scott allowed himself a moment's speculation—*I wonder what's in there, to be worth dying for*—then called out to Aster.

"Good luck, Mr. Aster. God willing, we will have you back on board within the hour."

Aster looked over, his green eyes intense. He said nothing, answering only with the briefest of nods. He touched the gold chain around his neck, feeling for the locket, as if assuring himself that it was there. Then he climbed into the dory and gestured to the boatswain, who barked a command. Four sailors swung the dory out on its davits and lowered the little boat into the surging sea, carrying a passenger, and a cargo, that Scott was duty-bound to protect.

I had no choice, thought Scott. *He gave me no choice.*

Then he turned to the task of trying to save his ship.

———————

Black Stache knew when to cut his losses. Scott had a reputation as a clever sailor; the burning Ladies were proof that it was justified.

"Cut loose the Ladies," Stache ordered Smee.

"Cut them *loose*, Cap'n?" said Smee. "The *Ladies*?"

"Yes, you idjit, and NOW, before the masts and rigging catch fire," Stache said. "Attach a mooring buoy to the starboard sheet, then cut them loose. We'll come back for them later."

Smee relayed the commands, and the crew responded quickly. The flaming Ladies floated away from the ship like a gigantic kite, then fluttered and sank, falling into the sea with a loud hiss and a cloud of steam. The mooring buoy bobbed nearby, marking the spot.

No wonder he's the captain, thought Smee.

Stache looked ahead. With his sails gone, his ship was now falling behind the *Wasp*.

"FULL SAILS," he bellowed to the crew, bypassing Smee. The men scrambled to the lines, and the *Sea Devil's* regular sails were up in seconds. Stache was counting on them to steal the *Wasp's* wind, and he was gratified to see the fleeing ship's sails flutter. Now he knew he could catch the *Wasp* . . . but should he?

Or do I go after that dory?

The little boat, with the gentleman aboard, was just ahead of the *Sea Devil* now, perhaps forty yards to starboard, close enough that Stache felt as if he could reach out and touch the trunk. He could see the gentleman watching him intently, betraying no emotion, his oars idle at his sides.

As if he wants me to come for him.

Stache knew he could easily chase the dory down by tacking to starboard, but then he would lose his advantage over the *Wasp*—or, worse, expose his broadside to her cannon fire. He could pursue the *Wasp*, but it would take time overtake her, and more time to defeat her. By then he might not be able to find the dory again.

What to do?

Stache cursed a particularly foul curse, and splattered the deck with an angry gob of spit.

Nobody understands how hard it is, being captain.

———◆———

With grudging respect, Scott saw how quickly Black Stache rid himself of the burning black sail, raised new sails, and continued the pursuit.

He's gaining again. He'll have us soon.

Scott pondered his options. He could turn broadside and try using his cannons, possibly taking Stache by surprise.

But he might already be close enough to board us before we can get off a shot.

He could jibe—ducking away from the *Sea Devil's* sails— regain the wind advantage, and run for it.

But that would be leaving Aster behind.

He watched the dory, and Aster, growing smaller, now abeam of the *Sea Devil*.

I can't leave him.

He studied the *Sea Devil*.

If he turns toward the dory, we will attack.

But what if the *Sea Devil* did not turn? Could he risk his ship and its entire crew to save the life of a single passenger?

Scott felt the eyes of his men, awaiting his next command.

Nobody understands how hard it is, being captain.

⊶⊷

Smee knelt next to the prisoner's cage and fumbled with a heavy ring of keys, nervous under Stache's glare.

"Hurry it up!" Stache said, glancing up to check the *Wasp* and then the dory, now abeam of his ship and slipping behind.

The prisoner, not knowing what was happening, watched apprehensively as Smee unlocked the padlock and opened the cage door.

Stache pushed Smee away, grabbed the trembling prisoner by his uniform coat, and again pulled him close.

"You've been most helpful," said Stache, his voice oily.

"Th—thank you, sir," said the prisoner, daring to hope that his cooperation had won him freedom from the cramped cage.

"Yes," continued Stache, "very helpful. So helpful, in fact, that I've decided to let you go." ·

"Thank you, sir!" said the prisoner. "Th—NO PLEASE SIR NO . . ."

His gratitude turned to horror as Stache, in a startling display of speed and power, dragged him swiftly to the starboard rail and hurled him overboard.

"Cap'n!" shouted Smee, shocked.

"Yes, Mr. Smee?" said Stache, leaning over to watch as the prisoner thrashed, gasping, to the surface.

"But he was . . ." sputtered Smee. "I mean, I thought he had information that . . ."

"He gave us what we needed," said Stache. "And now he is providing another service."

Smee looked puzzled.

"Behold," said Stache. "As a British seaman, he knows how to swim, at least a little."

Smee remained puzzled.

"And as a British seaman in distress," continued Stache, "he must not be abandoned by the gentleman in the dory, now can he? A proper Englishman would never leave another Englishman to drown. Behold our gentleman, Smee."

Stache gestured toward the dory; Smee saw that the gentleman was reaching for his oars.

Stache said, "Have the harpooners make ready at the stern."

Smee relayed the order, noting as he did that the dory was now turning toward the drowning sailor.

His chapped lips broke into a broad smile of pleasure, both at the cleverness of his captain, and the foolishness of proper Englishmen.

———⋆———

Leonard Aster had been studying the trunk, wondering how he could get past its padlocks without tools or weapons, when he heard the scream from the *Sea Devil*, and saw the man—a man in the uniform of a British seaman—hurled overboard. He saw the man struggle to the surface, thrashing desperately to stay afloat, but clearly unable to last much longer.

With no hesitation, Aster seized the oars. He understood that the pirates had thrown the seaman overboard in the expectation that he would do exactly this. But trunk or no trunk, Leonard Aster was not going to sit by and watch an Englishman drown. He clung to the hope that, as he approached the *Sea Devil*, she would turn to him, thus exposing herself to the *Wasp*'s cannon.

But to his disappointment, the *Sea Devil* did not turn.

He's clever, he thought. *He intends to slow my escape, while he wins the* Wasp. *Then he'll come for me. For the trunk.*

Aster glanced back, and saw he was close to the sailor, still afloat, but just barely.

I can still do it, Aster thought. *With a bit of luck, I can save this man, and still be far enough away that the pirates won't be able to find this tiny boat.*

The thrashing sailor slipped beneath the surface.

Leonard pulled harder on his oars.

Scott saw now that Stache had no intention of tacking to chase the dory.

He's a clever one. He's coming for my ship first.

Scott made a decision, and gave an order, instantly repeated by the first mate.

"Hard to starboard!"

The helmsman spun the wheel and the obedient ship quickly heeled, masts creaking, lines becoming taut. The sails went slack, shifted, then filled anew with wind. The *Sea Devil* was now coming up fast on his starboard side. He had a better angle on her now—better, though far from ideal. But there was no more time; in moments the *Sea Devil* would be on them.

"FIRE!"

The cannons roared, and Scott's heart sank as he saw the balls fly over the *Sea Devil*. The cannoneers had aimed almost level, but the heeling of the ship had pointed the barrels high.

It had been gamble, tacking and firing, and now Scott was paying. The *Wasp* had lost speed; the *Sea Devil*, undamaged, was bearing down. There was barely time for another round.

"LEVEL HER OUT!" Scott roared.

This time, we must not miss.

———◆———

Leonard Aster heard cannonfire, then saw a ball, then two others, splash near him, as he shoved an oar deep into the water at the spot where he'd seen the sailor go under. He fought to hold the oar down, moving it side to side . . .

Come on . . . Take it . . .

He'd almost given up when he felt a tug. Straining, he slowly pulled the oar toward him, then grabbed the sailor's arm and heaved him up with an effort that almost over-turned the dory, which rode dangerously low in the water now from the weight of two men and the trunk. The man coughed and spat seawater, but seemed to be all right.

"Thank you," he mumbled, still coughing.

"It's quite all right," said Aster.

"That madman . . ." began the sailor, but he was inter-rupted by two loud reports. Aster spun and saw twin dark lines coming from the stern of the *Sea Devil* and streaking directly *toward the dory.*

"DOWN!" he shouted, yanking the sailor with him to the cramped bottom.

The two harpoons, well aimed and shot with gunpowder, hit almost simultaneously, their barbed heads thunking into the transom. Ten-foot chains connected the harpoon shafts to thick rope leading back to the ship. In a moment Aster felt a tug as the lines tightened. The dory began to move backward; the pirates were using winches to drag it to the *Sea Devil*.

Black Stache is having it both ways, Aster thought, with grudging admiration. *He's going after the trunk AND the* Wasp.

He lunged to the stern and tried to work the harpoons loose, but they were lodged too firmly in the transom. Desperately, he turned back and shouted to the sailor.

"Help me untie the trunk!"

"What's that?" The man was still groggy from near-drowning.

"Untie the trunk!" Leonard repeated, struggling with a thick knot. "And hurry!"

The sailor managed to sit up and reach for a knot on the other side of the trunk. After a moment he shook his head. "Wet line," he coughed. "This knot's not coming out until the line dries."

Aster yanked desperately at the rope. He looked back; the dory was almost to the *Sea Devil* now, the pirate ship's stern looming overhead. At last he managed to loosen the knot. He got his hands under the trunk and tried to lift it, hoping to work it free from the rope on the other side. He could barely budge it.

Why is it so heavy?

He tried to move it again, but could not. He looked back

again and saw that he could touch the stern of the *Sea Devil*; pirates were clambering down rope ladders to grab the dory. He gave one last desperate heave on the trunk, but it barely moved.

It's no use.

Captain Scott held off as long as he dared, waiting for the *Wasp* to level its cannons at the onrushing *Sea Devil*. When he could wait no longer, he gave the order.

"FIRE!"

The cannons boomed. One ball struck the pirate ship's prow, beheading the wooden mermaid. The rest flew wide. The *Sea Devil* came on.

We're going to be boarded, he thought. *At least Aster may escape.*

But that hope was dashed almost immediately.

"Captain Scott," the first mate said. "Lookout reports that the pirates have the dory."

"What!" said Scott. "How?"

"Harpoons, sir. They got it when Mr. Aster turned back to rescue a sailor from the sea, sir."

"One of ours? I did not hear of a man gone overboard."

"No, sir. It's Bingham, sir."

"*Bingham?*" Scott could not believe what he was hearing.

"Yes, sir. Lookout says the pirates threw him overboard, sir."

"Bingham," Scott muttered. The sailor had gone missing at the last port. Scott now understood why Black Stache had followed the *Wasp*.

He knew about the trunk. And now he has it.

He saw that the *Sea Devil* was still coming hard, pirates on the foredeck howling for blood.

He wants the Wasp, *too.*

"Archer!" Scott shouted.

"Sir?"

"Can you cut their halyards at this range?"

"A little closer, Cap'n, and I think I can."

"Then do it. Bring down as many of their sails as you can."

"Aye, sir."

Scott turned back to his first mate.

"He means to board us," he said, "but I mean to board him first. Tell the men to get swords and sabers and move to the stern. At my command, luff the sails. He'll catch us more quickly than he suspects. And when he does, we board him."

Scott knew he was taking another gamble.

I hope this one turns out better than the last.

————◆————

Black Stache could not believe how well things were working out. He had the treasure, and he was about to take the *Wasp*, which might have outrun him had Captain Scott not chosen to turn and fight.

Idjit Englishmen, always doing what was right.

"Dory's aboard, Cap'n," Smee informed him.

"Excellent," said Stache, glancing back. He saw the retaken prisoner and the idjit Englishman who'd rescued him. The trunk had been hoisted onto the deck.

"TWENTY LENGTHS AND CLOSING FAST!" came the shout from the crow's nest.

"Prepare to board!" Stache shouted, his excitement building. This was the moment a pirate lived for.

His men readied their swords, knives, and guns. Stache estimated that the two ships would come together in about five minutes. Glancing around the deck, he was seized by an impulse.

"Open the trunk!" he shouted.

"FIFTEEN LENGTHS AND CLOSING."

"But, sir," said Smee, "perhaps we should wait until after . . ."

"NOW!" Stache roared. "OPEN THE TRUNK!"

The greatest treasure ever sent to sea. Stache meant to see it *now*, in his moment of glory.

Two sailors fired pistols at the locks. The chains fell away. Stache saw the idjit Englishman move forward, staring intently at the trunk lid.

"What's that look in your eye, Englishman?" Stache thundered. "You think a genie's going to jump out and save you?"

"Something like that," the Englishman answered, and something in his voice unsettled Stache for just a moment. As he watched, the Englishman's hand reached inside his shirt.

"Grab his arms," Stache shouted.

A burly sailor quickly pinned Aster's arms behind his back.

"TEN LENGTHS!"

"Cap'n," said Smee, "we . . ."

"Quiet!" said Stache, striding over to the Englishman and ripping open his shirt. A bright gold locket sparkled in the sun.

"What have we here?" said Stache. He reached for the locket, and as his fingers touched it, he felt the strangest feeling, as if . . .

"FIVE LENGTHS!"

"Sir!" shouted Smee. "I think *they're* going to board us!"

The Englishman pulled back, drawing the locket from Stache's grasp. Stache shook his head, as if awakening from a dream. He saw that the *Wasp* was less than three boat lengths away, its aft deck swarming with armed sailors.

He turned, stared for an instant into the intense green eyes of the Englishman, then leaned over to open the trunk. Time seemed to stand still as the lid slowly came up; a smile of formed on Stache's lips as he readied himself to gaze upon the greatest treasure ever sent to sea.

"*WHAT?*" he screamed. He looked up, his face twisted with fury. "What trickery is *this*, Englishman?" He grabbed Aster by the coat and dragged him around the trunk lid so he could see inside.

The trunk was filled with sand.

The Englishman gasped, snapped his head up, and looked out to sea, suddenly remembering Ammm's message: *On Molly ship* . . .

Black Stache followed the man's gaze. *He's as surprised as I am*, he thought.

And then Stache remembered: there had been a second ship leaving port on the day he'd been watching the *Wasp*. It, too, had taken many trunks aboard.

"They pulled a switch, didn't they, Englishman?"

Aster stared defiantly at the pirate.

"It's on the other ship, isn't it?" said Stache.

Aster's jaw clenched, but he remained silent.

"TWO LENGTHS!"

"It seems you've been had, Englishman," said Stache. "And so have I. But unlike you, I can do something about it, as soon as I have the *Wasp*."

"BRACE YOURSELVES!" came the shout from above. "WE'RE GOING TO RAM!"

Stache gestured to the burly sailor. "Take the Englishman below and lock him up," he said. "I'll deal with him later."

The burly sailor reached for Aster, but just as he did the

prow of the *Sea Devil* struck the stern of the *Wasp*. The deck shuddered violently, and the sailor fell.

Before he could get up, Leonard Aster had leaped overboard.

Stache cursed and raced to the rail. Looking over he saw nothing at first, and then . . . *was that the back fin of a porpoise?*

There was no time to look further. An arrow whizzed overhead, and the *Sea Devil's* mainsail came cascading down on Stache and his crew.

The battle had begun.

———

It took only a few bloody minutes for Captain Scott to understand the awful truth: his second gamble had also failed. His men fought courageously, but the pirates outnumbered them two to one. He could not stomach watching his men be slaughtered in a hopeless cause.

Despair seeping into his soul, he tied his white handkerchief to the tip of his sword and gave the signal for surrender. The flag was greeted by sullen acceptance from his brave crew, and howls of triumph from the pirates. Scott's last, desperate hope now was that he could bargain, somehow, for the lives of his men.

But he held no hope for himself. He was the captain, and he had lost his ship.

The *Wasp* now belonged to Black Stache.

CHAPTER 16

BAD NEWS

MOLLY CROUCHED ON THE AFT DECK of the *Never Land*, watching the water, waiting. The hours had crept by with agonizing slowness. But it was almost time.

At least tonight she didn't have to worry about the men on watch. They'd found some rum somewhere, and when Molly crept by them earlier, they'd both been flat on their backs, snoring.

Heaven help this ship if we ever face any real danger.

Her thoughts were interrupted by the welcome sight of a dorsal fin breaking the surface, followed by the sound of a cheerful chitter. Molly leaned over the stern rail and, despite her anxiety, smiled broadly as a familiar silver shape appeared.

"Hello," said Ammm.

"My teeth are green," replied Molly.

"Yes," agreed Ammm, politely.

With the formalities concluded, Molly clicked and chirped the message she'd been practicing all day.

"Ammm see Molly father?"

"Yes."

Thank goodness.

Carefully, Molly chirped: "What news?"

Ammm hesitated, then: "Bad man have father ship."

Molly's heart froze. "Molly father . . ." She struggled to make the sounds. "Molly father . . ."

"In water."

Molly could barely breathe. "Molly father . . ." she began, but Ammm mercifully cut her short.

"We swim Molly father," he said. "Swim to island."

Molly almost collapsed from relief. *The other porpoises are taking father to land. That's why Ammm came alone. But . . .*

"Molly father message," said Ammm.

"What message?" said Molly.

"Bad man hunt Molly ship."

Fear stabbed at Molly. *The trunk. Somehow, Black Stache knows about the trunk. Father must know as well, so he . . .*

Ammm chittered again: "Father come. Soon."

But would he be soon enough?

Molly took a deep breath, fighting to control her feelings of panic, to form the right sounds.

"Message father," she said.

"What message?"

"Hurry."

"Hurry," repeated Ammm.

"Yes."

And with a brief farewell chitter, Ammm was gone, leaving Molly staring at the water, wondering how long it would take her father to reach land, to find a new ship, to set out to find her . . .

Meanwhile, the world's most vicious pirate is hunting us down in the fastest ship afloat.

Molly had never felt so alone in her life. If Black Stache arrived before her father did, she had no choice: she would have to deal with the situation herself. She *had* to. And she could not fail.

She needed an ally. Someone she could trust.

She turned from the rail, to go looking for him. As she entered the ladderway, she cast one last glance back at the sea.

Please hurry.

CHAPTER 17

THE NEXT TARGET

THE SEA DEVIL AND THE WASP, tied side by side, rolled in the dark waves as Stache's crew, working by torchlight, finished the hard labor of moving barrels and crates from the conquering ship to the conquered one.

Belowdecks on the *Wasp*, Black Stache surveyed the tidy cabin that had once belonged to Captain Scott.

"A fine cabin, Mr. Smee, is it not?" he said.

"Aye, Cap'n, it is," said Smee, thinking, *and it smells much better than your old one.*

"Have the prisoners been dealt with?" asked Black Stache.

"Aye, sir, as you ordered. Captain Scott and the others you wanted kept for ransom and barter are locked below. The rest will be set adrift in the *Sea Devil*, once we've moved her sails and provisions to the *Wasp*."

"D'you think it'll hurt me reputation, Smee? Allowing

them to die of thirst, rather than slitting their throats?"

"No, Cap'n," said Smee. "I think it's a grand humanitarian gesture."

"Well, tell our boys to hurry, before I change my mind," said Stache. "It's turning to daylight, and I want to get after that other ship—the one with me treasure—the . . . what's it called again?"

"The *Never Land*, sir."

"Stupid name," said Stache.

"Yes, Cap'n."

"I don't much like *Wasp*, either."

"No, Cap'n."

"A wasp is an insect."

"It is, Cap'n."

"We're *pirates*, Smee. Not insects."

"No, Cap'n. I mean, yes, Cap'n."

"A pirate ship needs a name that inspires fear in the heart of every sailor who hears it," said Stache. He drummed his bony fingers thoughtfully on the desk that once belonged to Captain Scott.

Smee said, "What about the *Jellyfish?*"

Stache turned and stared at Smee with a look that Smee, unfortunately, mistook for encouragement.

"I mean the stinging kind," Smee continued brightly. "I've seen grown men cry when they—"

"SHUT UP, YOU IDJIT," thundered Stache, slamming the

desk with his fist. He took a long, deep breath, then continued in a calm voice: "You don't name a pirate ship the *Jellyfish*."

"I just thought . . ."

"Shut up, Smee."

"Yes, Cap'n."

"Sailors will not feel fear in their hearts at the approach of the *Jellyfish*."

"No, Cap'n."

"I shall give this ship a *pirate* name, Smee."

"Yes, Cap'n."

"I shall give it the name of the most feared flag on the seven seas. The *pirate* flag, Smee."

"That's a fine name, Cap'n."

"What is?"

"The *Pirate Flag*, Cap'n."

Black Stache pressed his face into his hands.

"Smee," he said, through splayed fingers. "You have seaweed for brains."

"Yes, Cap'n."

"The name of the ship will be the *Jolly Roger*."

"But you just said . . ."

"THE JOLLY ROGER *IS* THE PIRATE FLAG, YOU KELP-BRAINED IDJIT."

"Yes, Cap'n."

"Now, get out of my sight, and send in Storey. We've work to do."

Storey, who'd been waiting outside to be summoned, entered the cabin.

"Yes, Cap'n?"

"Have you found the Ladies?"

"Yes, sir. Wimple went out in a boat and got 'em back."

"Good. We raise sail as soon as we're done offloading the *Sea Devil*. We're after the *Never Land* next."

"Yes, Cap'n."

"One of the prisoners was kind enough to tell me a few things about the *Never Land*," said Stache, not bothering to mention that the officer had been staring at the point of Stache's cutlass, an inch from his right eyeball. "He says she left port the same day the *Wasp* did, and she's bound for Rundoon, same as the *Wasp* was. She's a fat sea cow of a ship that can't make better than five knots. So she's well behind us."

"Aye, Cap'n.

"I want you to do your figuring, and put us on zigzag course back in her direction, twenty mile tacks 'til we spot her masts. Understand? We'll be flying Her Majesty's colors. She'll sail right to us, thinking we're the *Wasp*. And then she's ours. Get to it."

"Aye, Cap'n," said Storey, leaving. Stache drummed his fingers on the desk for another minute, wondering if he should go up and make a few prisoners walk the plank. He was tired, but it was important to keep up appearances. He was still pondering when there was a rap on his door; it was Storey again, looking ashen-faced.

"What is it?" said Stache.

"Cap'n . . . it's . . . I think you need to come on deck and see for yourself, Cap'n."

Following the navigator to the deck, Stache saw it instantly: a dark roiling mass of clouds spreading across the horizon, already huge, and . . . *growing*. Growing *fast*.

Black Stache had spent his life at sea; he had long believed that he'd faced the worst that the sea could hurl at him, and that he had nothing more to fear.

But seeing this thing coming toward him now, Black Stache, for just a moment, was afraid.

$\mathcal{T}$HE $\mathcal{P}$LAN

$\mathcal{P}$ETER'S PLAN TO GET PAST THE GUARD named Leatherface was simple, but effective.

It involved rum. Peter was still not sure exactly what rum was, but he knew two things about it, from watching the *Never Land* crew.

The first was that the sailors loved to drink it, and gulped it down whenever they had any. The second was that it made them sleep. Sometimes it made them do strange things first—laugh, cry, sing, fight, talk about their mothers—but in the end, it always put them into a deep slumber, from which it seemed nothing could awaken them for hours.

Peter had also learned, from his many secret food forays around the ship, that the cook kept a barrel of rum in the galley. This was one reason why the *Never Land*'s food was so bad: the cook spent far more time drinking rum than cook-ing. He guarded his rum supply from the rest of the crew by sitting on the barrel virtually all the time, day and night. But much of the time, because of the rum, he was slumbering, which presented an opportunity for a small, clever person to creep up, quietly open the barrel's spigot, and fill a jar. And that is what Peter had done.

The other part of the plan involved the foul pot of revolting "food" that Hungry Bob brought each morning in the crockery pot. Most days the boys left it untouched, which was fine with Hungry Bob, who collected it each night and happily downed its contents, wriggling bits and all.

But not this day. This day, Peter had taken the pot and dumped the rum jar into it. Both the food and the rum smelled foul to Peter; the mixture smelled no different.

He'd waited until dusk, then carried the crockery pot to a secluded spot on the forward deck, where Alf was waiting, as they'd arranged.

"Try to hurry," Peter said. "Hungry Bob will be coming for this soon."

"Right, little friend," said Alf, taking the pot and heading aft. At the ladderway, he glanced around, then ducked down the ladder and scuttled along a dim passageway, and down a second ladder.

"Who's that?" came a gruff voice. It was Leatherface, a tall, rawboned man whose skin had been ravaged by too many years in the wind and the weather. He stood in front of the door to the hold where the trunk was kept, his hand holding a club.

"It's me," said Alf. "Alf."

"Nobody's allowed down here," barked Leatherface. "Slank's orders."

"But it was Slank who sent me," said Alf. "He sent you this here grub." He held out the pot.

Leatherface eyed it suspiciously. "I already had me grub," he said.

"I know, I know," said Alf. "It's extra rations, for the extra work you're doing."

Somewhere deep in Leatherface's brain was the beginning of a thought—that it was very much unlike Slank to make thoughtful gestures to the crew. But Leatherface was not one to encourage thoughts, and, like the rest of the underfed sailors on the *Never Land*, his instinct was to eat whatever there was to be eaten. He leaned the club against the hold door and took the pot from Alf.

"I'd be grateful if you'd finish it off now," said Alf. "Save me a trip back down and up these ladders. Hard on me old knees."

Leatherface grunted, raised the crockery pot, and began to swig the contents down. It tasted a bit unusual to him, but he'd had worse. At least most of the lumps were still.

A half dozen gulps later, the pot was empty. Leatherface

handed the pot back to Alf, picked up his club, and issued a massive belch. "Now, get out," he said.

"My pleasure," said Alf, as foul burp fumes filled the passageway.

A few moments later, Alf was back on the foredeck, handing the pot to Peter, who peered inside.

"He ate it all," said Peter.

"Like a bird eating a worm," said Alf.

"How long, d'you think?" said Peter.

"If there's a jarful of rum in there," said Alf, "he'll be sleeping like a babe in an hour's time."

"Right," said Peter. "So we'll meet here?"

"We'll meet here."

Peter hurried the crockery pot back to the boys' cabin, where in a short while it was retrieved by a disappointed Hungry Bob.

"What's this?" he said, examining the empty pot. "Have you lads taken a fancy to the cook's grub?"

"No!" chorused the boys.

"Yes," said Peter, casting a sharp look at the others. "I mean, no, but today we were . . . very hungry."

"You're not giving the grub to another sailor now, are you?" said Hungry Bob.

"No, sir."

"You better not be," said Hungry Bob, "after all I do for you, carrying this pot down here every day."

When he was gone, James said, "Peter, what *did* you do with the food?"

"Never mind what I did with it," said Peter. "You're better off not knowing."

"It's that trunk, isn't it?" said Tubby Ted. "It's got something to do with that stupid trunk, right?"

"I said *never mind*," Peter snapped.

"Creeping 'round the ship all the time," muttered Tubby Ted. "He'll get us all in trouble, he will."

"You don't seem to mind eating the food he gets from creeping around," retorted James, drawing smiles from Prentiss and Thomas.

James turned to Peter. "Are we going out tonight, then?"

"*I* am, yes," said Peter. "But I want you to stay here."

James's face fell. "But . . . but I thought I was helping. I thought . . ."

"You *have* been helping," said Peter. "You're a great help. But tonight I . . . it needs to be just me. You can help by keeping an eye on this lot. All right, mate?"

"All right," said James, his eyes downcast.

"That's a good man," said Peter. "I'm off, then."

In a moment he was on deck, where he found Alf waiting. Together they crept aft in the darkness, easily avoiding the two bored, gabbing sailors on watch. With Peter in front, they crept down the first ladderway and along the passageway. They stopped at the top of the lower ladderway, cocking their ears downward. There was a noise coming from below, a deep, irregular rumbling. . . .

Snoring.

Peter glanced back at Alf, who nodded, and the two moved quietly down the ladderway. As their eyes adjusted to the gloom, they saw the dark form of Leatherface sprawled on his back in front of the hold door, right hand still curled around his club. Alf leaned over and took hold of the snoring man's heels, then gently pulled him clear of the doorway.

Peter, heart pounding, reached for the door handle, and . . .

The door was locked.

It was a padlock, passed through a hasp. Peter's heart sank. He hadn't thought of this; the last time, the door had been open.

But of course; Slank wasn't taking any more chances.

"It's locked," Peter whispered.

"What?" whispered Alf. "But you said . . ."

"I know," whispered Peter. "It wasn't locked before."

Alf bent over and, in the dim-yellow light of the passageway lantern, peered at the door. He saw that the padlock and hasp, like all the iron objects on the *Never Land*, were old and rusted.

"Here," he whispered. "Gimme that club."

Peter bent down, gently pulled the club from Leatherface's fist, and handed it to the big man. Alf slid the handle end of the club down behind the hasp, then took hold of the fat end with both hands.

"Be ready to run," he whispered to Peter.

Alf heaved back on the club. Peter heard the hold door creaking, then a pop, then another. The hasp bolts were breaking. Another heave; two more pops. A final heave, and . . .

CLUNK CLUNKETY-CLUNK

. . . the hasp and padlock, suddenly yanked free, bounced across the floor. For a moment, neither Alf nor Peter moved a muscle. Then Peter glanced down at Leatherface; he continued to snore. Peter and Alf remained motionless for perhaps a minute, listening. They heard no steps running, no stairs creaking. Nothing. Slowly, they began to breathe normally again, and their attention returned to the hold door, now unlocked.

Alf tugged on the handle, and the door swung open. Peter and Alf peered in, seeing nothing at first in the pitch-black hold. Wishing he'd thought to bring a candle, Peter took a tentative step forward. Still he saw nothing. He felt Alf behind him. Again he slid his foot forward.

"*Stop.*"

Alf and Peter froze. The hissing voice had come from behind them, on the ladderway. Heart thumping, Peter turned and . . .

Molly.

"Get away from the door," she whispered. "Both of you, get out of here *now*."

"Miss," said Alf, "we don't mean no . . ."

"You don't know what you're getting into," she said. "You must leave here this instant."

Alf, his face worried, said to Peter, "Maybe we should . . ."

"No," said Peter, furious. "We've come this far, and we're going to go in there, and she can't stop us."

"Yes I can," said Molly, her voice dead calm.

Peter and Alf both looked at her.

"I can scream," she said.

"You wouldn't," Peter said.

"Yes I would."

"You don't dare," said Peter. "You're not supposed to be here, either. You'd be in as much trouble as us."

"I could say I heard a noise," she said. "I heard something fall." She pointed to the padlock. "I came to investigate. And when I saw you, I screamed."

"All right, miss," said Alf. "No need for that." He put a hand on Peter's shoulder. "Come on, lad."

"No," said Peter, shrugging off the hand, glaring at Molly. "You go, if you want. She doesn't scare me."

"I'm going to count," said Molly. "If you're not gone when I get to ten, I *will* scream."

"You're bluffing," said Peter.

"One," said Molly.

On the floor, Leatherface stirred, rolled over, resumed snoring.

"Little friend," whispered Alf, his tone urgent now. "I'm going."

"Go, then," said Peter.

"Two."

"Please, little friend."

"*No.*"

"Three."

"All right, then," said Alf, shaking his head. "Good luck, then."

"Four."

Alf was up the ladder, and gone.

"Five."

"Why are you doing this?" hissed Peter.

"Six. Because I have to." Her face was grim.

"But *why?*"

"Seven. I can't tell you."

"Tell me *what?* Why can't you tell me?"

"Eight. You wouldn't believe me anyway."

"How do you know if you don't try?"

"Nine. Because I . . . Because it . . . it's so . . ." Molly's voice broke. Peter saw she was crying.

"Molly, please, whatever it is, *just tell me.* Maybe . . . maybe I can help you."

For several seconds, Molly looked at him, a look of lonely

desperation, tears brimming in her luminescent green eyes. Then she made a decision—Peter saw it happen—and her expression was grim again.

She's going to say Ten, thought Peter. *She's going to scream.*

Molly opened her mouth.

"All right," she said. "I'll tell you."

CHAPTER 19

THE WITCH'S BROOM

THE WIND WAS MUCH STRONGER NOW. Not full-force yet; no, it was still a long way from the fury that every man on the *Jolly Roger* could see was coming. But it was strong enough to make the rigging shriek; strong enough to rip the hat from Black Stache's head and send it tumbling across the aft deck, with Smee's blubbery body scuttling after it.

Stache seemed not to notice. As the gusts tossed his long, greasy curls, he stared back toward the storm. Dwindling rapidly astern was the *Sea Devil*—barely a speck, now—manned by the sailors he'd thrown off his new ship. When the *Jolly Roger* had cast them off, they'd been frantically trying to jury-rig sails from whatever scraps of canvas they could find, hoping desperately to somehow outrun the black, boiling clouds bearing down on them.

Not bloody likely they'll make it, thought Stache. *It'll be dicey enough for us.*

The last of the *Jolly Roger's* sails had just gone up, full and billowing; the masts groaned and the rigging creaked as the sleek ship, propelled by the mighty following wind, surged forward, sliding down the face of a great wave, then climbing the next. Stache grabbed a stout line to keep his balance, and looked up at the rigging, a rare expression of respect on his face. He was feeling more confident now.

"She's a fine ship, this one!" he roared to the helmsman. "Have you ever *seen* such speed?"

The helmsman could only nod; even with his massive arms, he had to fight the wheel with all his strength to hold the course.

Smee, clutching Stache's hat, staggered back across the sloping deck, casting a worried look at the storm. Most of the sky was now black; it was daytime, but the pirates below were using lanterns.

"Can we outrun it, Cap'n?" Smee asked, clutching the captain's hat as if it were a baby blanket.

"Outrun *that*?" Stache laughed. "No, Smee, she's a witch of a storm, and this here"—he waved at the wind—"is her broom. She flies too fast for us, Smee. She'll be on us in a few hours. We'll be reefing every sail we got and dragging sea anchors before this one's through with us. But before that happens, we'll ride this witch's broom ourselves, Smee. We'll fly straight to the *Never Land*. She's out there, and we need to reach her before the witch herself does." Stache looked again at the sails, then turned to the helmsman.

"I think we can coax another knot or two out of her," he shouted. "Let's put her on a broad reach, eh?"

The helmsman knew better than to question an order from Black Stache, but he shot him a glance. Putting the ship at a sharper angle to the wind would, indeed, increase its speed; but in this ferocious gale, it would also cause the ship to heel steeply, and put a massive strain on the sails, masts, and rigging.

Catching the helmsman's look, Stache bellowed: "DO IT, MAN!"

The helmsman heaved on the wheel. The black ship slowly turned, groaning, and heeled hard to starboard. The crew grabbed for handholds as water crashed across the decks.

"HAUL IN THEM SAILS!" bellowed Stache. "GIVE ME MORE SPEED!"

Despite the fearsome angle of the deck, crewmen clambered to the winches and, working furiously, managed to take in a few more feet on the sheets, which were taut as piano wires from the massive strain of holding the sails. As the ship gained even more speed, the starboard rail went under, and from below came the crashing sound of unsecured cargo tumbling into the side of the holds.

"SMEE!" shouted Black Stache.

"Aye, Cap'n?" answered Smee, who was clinging to a

mast, his chubby arms wrapped around it, holding the captain's hat in front.

"Are the uniforms ready?"

"Aye, Cap'n." Stache had ordered all the *Wasp* crewmen, including Captain Scott, stripped of their naval uniforms; they'd been left in their long johns.

"Good. Get below, and have the men come down one at a time and change into the uniforms. When those idjits on the *Never Land* sees Her Majesty's fine ship coming their way, we'll want them to see fine British seamen on deck, coming to their rescue."

"Aye, Cap'n," said Smee, grateful for the chance to get out of the weather. He released the mast and lunged for a ladderway, staggering two steps before falling belly-first on Stache's hat.

"I'm all right!" he called, crawling the rest of the way to the ladder. "I'm all right."

Ignoring him, Stache turned to the helmsman, who was straining every muscle to keep the ship steady. Leaning close to the man's ear, Stache said, "A gold piece to you, lad, if we reach the *Never Land* before the full weight of this storm reaches us."

The helmsman glanced back at the rolling waves and punishing wind, then up at the straining sails, then forward into the stinging sea salt spray. "We'll do it, Cap'n," he said. "If these sails hold."

Stache grinned a wide, yellow grin. The ship groaned as it rose to the top of a giant swell, then seemed to fly down the other side. The masts bowed and looked as if they might snap. At that moment sheets of rain poured from the sky, soaking both men and beating the ocean into a furious froth.

Stache, his long, wet locks streaming rainwater, tossed his head back and laughed.

He hadn't had this much fun in years.

CHAPTER 20

MOLLY'S STORY

PETER'S SHOULDERS SAGGED WITH RELIEF. "Good," he said. "I knew you—"

"Not here," said Molly, gesturing toward the snoring Leatherface. "We'll go to my cabin. Mrs. Bumbrake shouldn't be back for an hour, at least." Mrs. Bumbrake had taken to spending most of her evenings in Slank's cabin, which was fine with Molly.

"All right," said Peter, heading toward the ladderway.

"One thing first," said Molly. She picked up the padlock and hasp. "We need to find the other pieces to this."

"Why?" said Peter.

"Just do it, please," she said.

Sighing, Peter joined Molly in searching the floor by the dim lantern light. In a minute or so they'd found the four rusty bolts Alf had broken.

"Close the door," whispered Molly.

Peter, having decided it was no use to question her, obeyed. Molly held the padlock and hasp up to the door and inserted the broken bolts into their former holes. Carefully, she let go; the hasp and padlock remained in place. It looked as though the door were still securely locked. Peter was impressed.

"Come on," said Molly.

Peter followed her up the ladder. She motioned him to stay in the passageway while she looked inside her cabin; seeing that it was, as she had expected, empty, she motioned Peter inside and closed the door.

"Please sit," she said, pointing to one of the cabin's two narrow cots. "This will take some time."

Peter sat. Molly remained standing, facing Peter, silent for a long moment, thinking. Finally she spoke.

"I shouldn't tell you any of this," she said.

"But you . . ."

"Just listen," she said. "I shouldn't tell you, but, given the circumstances, I've decided I have no choice."

It sounded to Peter as though Molly was talking to herself, more than to him.

"I'm not sure how much to tell you," she continued. "There's much that I don't know myself. But if I'm to ask for your help, if I'm to ask you to risk your . . . I mean, there is terrible danger, and it would be wrong if you . . . that is, if you didn't . . ."

"Molly," said Peter, exasperated. "Just *tell* me."

"All right," she said. She took a deep breath. "Peter, have you ever seen a shooting star?"

"Yes," said Peter. It had been at St. Norbert's, an eternity ago. The other boys had been asleep; Peter was lying on the narrow wooden platform that served as his bed, staring through the slit of a window at the night sky. He'd almost not believed it, the first time—the startlingly sudden, eerily silent flash of brilliant, streaking light, there for an instant and then . . . *gone*. But then he'd seen it again, and again, and again.

The next day he'd asked Mr. Grempkin what the streaks were, and Mr. Grempkin had said they were shooting stars. So Peter asked what shooting stars were, and Mr. Grempkin said they were meteors. So Peter asked what meteors were, and Mr. Grempkin said they were rocks that fell from the heavens. So Peter asked if that meant that the heavens were made of rocks, and why were the rocks so bright? Were they on fire? How did rocks catch fire? And Mr. Grempkin clouted Peter on the ear and told him not to ask so many questions. And that had been the end of it.

"Do you know what they are?" said Molly.

"They're rocks," said Peter. "That fall from the heavens."

"That's true of most of them," said Molly. "Almost all of them, in fact. But not quite all."

"What do you mean?" said Peter.

"I mean some shooting stars are not rocks. Some—a very few—are made of something quite different. It's called starstuff. At least that's what we call it."

"Starstuff? You mean pieces that fell from a star?"

"We don't know what it is, truthfully," said Molly. "But it's not rocks, and it comes from the heavens, and sometimes it comes to Earth. And when it does, we have to find it, before the Others do."

Peter shook his head. "Who d'you mean by 'we'?" he said. "Who are the others? What does this have to do with . . ."

"*Please*, Peter," she said. "I'm explaining it as best I can."

"Sorry," he said. "Go on."

"All right. First, what I mean by 'we.' Peter, I'm part of a group, a small group of people. Well, mostly people. We're called"—Molly's hand went to the gold chain around her neck—"the Starcatchers."

"Starcatchers."

"Yes. My father is one, as was his mother, and so on. Most of us are descended from Starcatchers, but not all. There have been Starcatchers on Earth for centuries, Peter. Even we don't know how long. But our task is always the same: to watch for the starstuff, and to get to it, and return it, before it falls into the hands of the Others."

"Return it where?"

"That's . . . difficult to explain."

"Well, then, who are the 'Others'?"

"They're . . . people, too, or most of them are. And they've also been around for a long time. They are our—that is, the Starcatchers'—enemy. No, that's not quite right: we oppose them, but in truth they are mankind's enemy."

"Why? What do they do?"

"They use the power. They take it, and they . . ." Molly saw the puzzlement on Peter's face. "But you don't know what I mean, do you? I need to explain, about the starstuff."

"Is that's what's in the trunk?" said Peter.

"Yes," said Molly. "That's what's in the trunk. It has amazing power, Peter. Wonderful power. Terrible power. It . . . it lets you do things."

"What kind of things?"

"Well, that's one of the mysteries. It's not the same for everybody. And it's not the same for animals as for people."

"The rat," said Peter. "The flying rat."

"Yes," said Molly. "That's one of the powers it can give. Flight."

"To rats," said Peter.

"Not just rats," said Molly. "People, too."

Peter's eyes narrowed. "It makes *people* fly?"

"It can," said Molly.

"Can *you* fly?" asked Peter.

"I have," said Molly.

"Prove it," said Peter.

"What?"

"Prove you can fly."

"Peter, this isn't the time or the . . ."

Peter was on his feet now. "Listen," he said. "You're asking me to believe . . . I mean, it all sounds like nonsense, really. This 'starstuff,' and these 'others,' and . . . and I don't know why I should believe any of it."

"Peter, you saw the rat."

"I don't know what I saw. I mean, I saw a rat in the air, yes, but what if it was a trick? What if, I don't know . . . what if you tied a string to it?"

"There was no string, Peter. The rat got into the starstuff somehow. It was flying."

"Prove it."

"Peter, please, you must . . ."

"*Prove it.*"

Molly took a deep breath, exhaling slowly. "All right, then," she said. "I really shouldn't do this, but if you're going to be stubborn . . ."

"I am," said Peter.

"Then sit down."

Peter sat. Molly reached her hand to her neck, put her finger under the gold chain, and from under her blouse pulled out a small golden five-pointed star. She placed this on the palm of her left hand, which she held at neck level.

"What's that?" said Peter.

"A locket," said Molly.

With her right hand, she opened the lid of the locket. As she did, it was suffused by light, so that Peter couldn't see the locket, only a small, glowing sphere of golden light. Molly's face, and the cabin ceiling above her, were bathed in the glow. Peter had the strangest sense that he could *feel* the light, as well as see it.

"Is that—" he began.

"Quiet," said Molly. Slowly, carefully, she touched her right index finger into the sphere.

"Unhh," she moaned, leaning her head back, her eyes closed, her expression calm, blissful. She remained that way for perhaps five seconds, and then there was the *click* of the locket closing, and the glow was gone.

Peter wanted it back.

Molly's head came forward, and she opened her eyes, which to Peter looked unfocused, and more luminescent than ever.

"Are you all right?" Peter said.

Molly blinked, then looked at Peter. "Yes," she said. "I'm all right."

"What was—"

"*Shhhh.*" Molly said. "Watch."

She stared at Peter, and he stared back into her startling green eyes. After a few moments Peter said, "I don't see anything."

"Peter," she said. "Look at my feet."

He looked down and gasped. Then he jumped up from the cot and dropped to his hands and knees, his cheek pressed to the floor, looking to see how she did it, what the trick was. But there was no trick.

Her feet weren't touching the floor. They were at least two inches above it. And as Peter looked, the distance grew; Molly was rising, her head now gently touching the cabin ceiling. As it did, her body began to pivot, until she was completely horizontal, facing the floor, her back pressed to the ceiling, as though she were sleeping up there. She smiled down at Peter.

"Now do you believe me?" she asked.

"Yes," said Peter.

"Good," she said. Her legs swung back down to the vertical, and she descended gently to the floor.

For a moment Peter was speechless. Then questions came flooding out.

"Can you . . . can you do that any time?" he began. "I mean, could you just fly around whenever you want? Like a bird?"

"No," said Molly. "To fly, I must use the power of the starstuff, and I . . . that is, we, the Starcatchers, carry only a limited amount. In time, it wears off. We're supposed to use it only in an emergency. I really shouldn't have used it just now. It's precious, and I really don't know how much I have in here." She tapped her locket, and tucked it back into her blouse.

"But can't you just get more?" said Peter. "From the trunk, I mean. There must be lots in there."

"Yes, there is," said Molly. "There's enough in that trunk that I could fly forever, and do many other things besides."

"Is that why you're so concerned about it?" said Peter. "Because you want to get it?"

"No, Peter. I told you before. Our task is to get the starstuff before the Others do, and return it."

"But why don't you just keep it?" said Peter.

"Because of the power," said Molly. "The power is too great. There's too much danger that it can be used for evil."

"But the Starcatchers—*you're* good, aren't you?" said Peter. "If *you* have the power, why don't you just use it to control these . . . these others?"

"Because it doesn't work," said Molly. "Because if people have the power, even if they start out using it for good, in time they will use it for evil."

"How do you know that?"

"Because that's how it all started, this business of the Starcatchers and the Others. It has been going on for thousands of years, Peter. Nobody knows precisely when it started, but in the beginning, somebody must have stumbled across some starstuff that had fallen to Earth. And whoever that was touched it, and felt it—it's a *wonderful* feeling, Peter. Not just the flying. That's the most obvious, but there's *much* more . . ."

"Like what?"

"Intelligence, for one thing. It's not so much that you become smarter, as that you feel as though you can really *use* your mind. You can see things you couldn't see before, understand things that others can't. Sometimes you even know what other people are feeling—you can *feel* it. And sometimes, if you're close enough, you can change the way they feel—make them afraid, or happy, or sleepy . . ."

"The guard," said Peter. "The night I saw you in the room with the trunk, and the rat—the guard fell asleep that night. Slank thought he was drunk. But you made that happen."

"Yes," said Molly. "I made that happen. I'd begun to suspect that the trunk . . . but I'm getting ahead of my story."

"You were talking about the first person who found the starstuff," prompted Peter.

"Right. Well, whoever that was had suddenly become the most powerful person on earth. And he must have shared it with some others, probably his family, his descendants. Because in time there came to be legends—stories of beings who had incredible powers, who could fly, who could control others. You've heard of those legends, Peter."

"I have?"

"Yes. In fact, I'm sure you studied them. The legends of Zeus, of Apollo . . ."

"You mean mythology? The Greek and Roman gods? But Mr. Grempkin said that was just . . ."

"*That was all true*, Peter. Except that they weren't gods. They were people who'd found the starstuff. But to ordinary people, they appeared to be gods; they inspired fear; they were worshipped; they were obeyed absolutely. In time they learned to guard their secret better, to use the power more subtly; instead of gods, they were called royalty. But they ruled just the same. They grew in power; they prospered; they had families; there came to be more of them. And they all wanted the power; they all needed the starstuff.

"But as I said, it only lasts for a while, and then you need more. From time to time, more falls to Earth, but nobody knows when it will fall, or where, or how much there will be. And so there came to be struggles, desperate struggles, over the starstuff that was known to exist, and the new batches that fell to Earth. *Wars* were fought, Peter. In the history you were taught, the wars were caused by disputes over land, or trade, or religion. And some of them were. But in truth, much of the death and misery visited upon mankind over the centuries was the result of a secret, vicious struggle, among a very few people, over starstuff."

"And were the Starcatchers part of that struggle?" asked Peter.

"No," said Molly. "They were a response to it. As the struggle became more violent and widespread, a few of the people who knew the secret of the starstuff began to see how dangerous it was—how there could never be enough of it, and how easily it could be turned to evil purposes. Those few formed a secret society—a secret society within a secret society, really. They swore an oath that they would dedicate their lives to ridding the earth of the starstuff, except for the small quantities they would need to carry out their mission. Their strategy was simple. They would not try to get the existing supplies of starstuff away from the Others; in time, they knew, those supplies would be used up. Instead, they would focus their efforts on new batches of falling starstuff. They would get to these first, and capture them. And so they called themselves the Starcatchers.

"And their strategy worked, Peter. It took time, but it worked. For years the Others didn't realize what was happening—only that it was more and more difficult to replenish their starstuff supplies. By the time they found out about the Starcatchers, they had been greatly weakened, and most of the starstuff was gone."

"Where did it go?" asked Peter. "What do the Starcatchers do with it?"

"I don't honestly know," said Molly.

"What do you mean, you don't know?" said Peter. "You're one of them, aren't you?"

"Yes," said Molly, "but I'm still only an apprentice. It takes a great deal of training to be a senior Starcatcher. And one of the last things we learn is how to return the starstuff, once we've captured it."

"But what do you mean *return?*" said Peter. "Return it *where?*"

"That's what I'm telling you," said Molly. "I haven't learned that yet. However the process works, I think it's dangerous, because there are . . . *forces,* I think, and . . . they're not all good. This is probably a crude way of putting it, but: just as we have the Others and the Starcatchers here on Earth, there seems to be something similar going on up there." She pointed toward the sky. "And you must be very, very careful when you deal with these forces, or . . ." She shook her head.

"But here on Earth—the Starcatchers are winning here, aren't they?" said Peter. "You have the upper hand?"

"Well," said Molly, "in recent times, yes. We're better organized than the Others, by our very nature—we're working for a common cause, while they're every man for himself, and quick to stab the other one in the back for a bit of starstuff. So we've got quite an organization, and plenty of observers, counting people and porpoises."

"The porpoises!" said Peter. "So you *were* talking to them!"

"Yes," said Molly, blushing. "Sorry about the lie. We've been working with the porpoises for many years. Extremely intelligent, they are. More intelligent than many people, if you ask me. Anyway, there's more sea than land, so as you'd imagine a fair amount of starstuff lands in the water, and the porpoises have learned, much as we did, that it's best to get rid of it."

"What do you mean?"

"It's very odd, what it can do to animals. Some of them hardly seem to be affected by it. But some of them change in the *strangest* ways. Horses, for example. It's very bad to let a horse near starstuff."

"Why?" said Peter.

"Back to your mythology," said Molly. "Have you ever heard of a centaur?"

"The thing that's half man, half horse," said Peter. "But Mr. Grempkin said that was . . ."

"It was real, Peter. And not very pleasant, either. Something quite similar happens with squid."

"What's a squid?"

"An ugly, slimy, ill-tempered beast that lives in the sea, with lots of long arms," said Molly. "Some time ago, some of them got hold of a large batch of starstuff and . . . well, the porpoises were *years* sorting all that out, not to mention all the problems that human sailors had with what they called 'sea serpents.'"

"Oh," said Peter.

"But, as I was saying, with the porpoises helping us, the Starcatchers have been able to deal with the starstuff situation most of the time, over most of the earth. The problem is that, every now and then, a new batch falls, and we're not always able to get there before somebody finds it. Often, no harm is done; in fact, the results can be quite nice. Not so many years ago, some starstuff fell in Italy. Our agents got there soon enough, and thought they'd retrieved it all, but apparently they missed some, and some young men found it. Fortunately, they were not inclined toward evil. Have you ever heard of the artists da Vinci and Michelangelo?"

"No," said Peter."

"Well," said Molly, "they were quite good. But we've not always been so lucky. I don't suppose you've heard of Attila the Hun?"

"Was he an artist?"

"He most certainly was not. He was a very bad man who found a very big bit of starstuff and did some very bad things."

"Oh."

"Occasionally," Molly continued, "*very* occasionally, even one of the Starcatchers succumbs to the lure of the starstuff, and has to be . . . dealt with. But for the most part, the Starcatchers have done their job, and done it very well. I don't mean we've eradicated evil from the world, of course—the world will always have evil—but because of the Starcatchers, it has been a good long time since any *widespread* evil has been the result of starstuff. So to answer your question: Yes, for the moment, the Starcatchers have the upper hand. But only for the moment."

"What do you mean?"

"I mean at the moment, the situation is a bit . . . unbalanced."

"Unbalanced?"

"Yes. About two months ago, a very large quantity starstuff fell to Earth, in Scotland. A *very* large quantity. Father says it's the most that has fallen in his memory, and perhaps in centuries. The Starcatchers knew it was coming; I don't know why, but we *feel* it when it falls. And, as I say, this was an unusually large amount—we had people see it as well as feel it. They were headed to the landing place on horseback immediately. It was a remote spot, no towns around, and our men got there quickly. But the starstuff was gone."

"Somebody found it first."

"Yes," said Molly, "but that has happened before. And usually whoever it is is still there when our agents arrive. In fact usually they're floating at treetop level, happy as birds, and it's easy enough for our agents to retrieve the starstuff from them, and help them to forget all about it by . . . well, it's a technique I haven't learned yet. But when it's used, they fall asleep; and when they wake up, they've forgotten all about it, no harm done. But this time there was nobody there, and no starstuff. And that was the odd part. This was a large and powerful supply, Peter. It can be moved, but it takes skill and knowledge to handle it, and a proper container to put it in. So it wasn't moved by some local folk who happened across it. Whoever took it knew what it was, and knew how to handle it."

"The Others."

"Yes. Somehow, they got there first, and now they have more starstuff than they've had for centuries."

"And you . . . the Starcatchers . . . you don't know what they've done with it?"

Molly laughed, but not happily. "Oh, I know exactly what they've done with it."

"What, you . . . you mean . . . You mean *the trunk on this ship?*"

"Yes," said Molly. "That trunk."

"But how . . . I mean, who . . ."

"Bear with me just a little longer," said Molly. "We're almost there. The Starcatchers have always had spies among the Others. After the starstuff went missing in Scotland, we had our spies poke around, and they found out quickly enough what had happened to it. It had been placed in a trunk and taken to a castle in a little town called Fenkirk."

"Couldn't the Starcatchers fetch it from there?" asked Peter. "Using those, what did you call them, techniques?"

"Unfortunately, no," said Molly. "For two reasons. One is that those techniques are not effective against people who know how to use the starstuff power. The other is that, in addition to the Others, the castle was heavily guarded by soldiers."

"Soldiers?"

"Soldiers of the Queen of England."

"The *Queen*?" said Peter. "Are you saying the Queen is one of the Others?"

"No," said Molly. "At least we don't think so. The Starcatchers have people who know the Queen—my father is one of them—and they're quite certain she is not in league with the Others. But apparently somebody close to the Queen is, and whoever that person is has made it impossible for our agents to get near the trunk. After a week in the castle, it was moved under heavy guard to London, where our spies learned that it was to be loaded onto a ship called the *Wasp*. And that was a very bad sign indeed."

"Why?" said Peter.

"Because the *Wasp* was bound for Rundoon," said Molly, "which is ruled by His Royal Highness, King Zarboff"—she held up the three middle fingers of her right hand—"the Third."

"Oh my," said Peter. "He's one of them, isn't he."

"Yes," said Molly. "Zarboff is one of the Others. He's perhaps the most evil one there is. The Starcatchers could not allow him, of all people, to gain possession of the trunk."

"That's why you're on this ship," said Peter. "To stop it."

"No," said Molly. "My father put me on this ship precisely because he believed the trunk was *not* here. It was for my safety. He sailed on the *Wasp* because our spies said that's where the trunk was. Obviously," she added bitterly, "they were mistaken."

"What was your father planning to do on the *Wasp?*" asked Peter. "I mean, how was he going to get the trunk away from the others, if there was only one of him on the ship?"

"It wasn't going to happen on the *Wasp*," said Molly. "It was going to happen when they got to Rundoon. There would be other Starcatchers waiting. They had a plan to get the trunk, and capture Zarboff, who'd become a problem. It was quite a brilliant plan, really, except that . . ."

". . . except that the trunk isn't on the *Wasp*."

"No," said Molly. "They switched it. I suspected it the first day, when I saw how that sailor reacted when he touched it. I should have tried to get word to Father then, but, stupidly, I didn't. Then that night—the night you saw the flying rat—I went down there to check, and as soon as I walked into the hold, I knew it was the trunk. I could *feel* it, the immense power, like nothing I've ever felt. So I tried to send a message to father, using Ammm . . ."

"Who?"

"The porpoise, Ammm. But I'm not very good at porpoise, and I thought I'd muddled it, and then Ammm came back and told me . . . he told me . . ."

Molly pressed her face into her hands, sobbing. Peter wanted to do something, pat her shoulder, perhaps; but he was terrified she would take it wrong. So he stood helplessly and watched her sob for a minute or so. Finally she raised her face, showing him reddened eyes and tear-wetted cheeks.

"Sorry," she said.

"It's all right," said Peter, feeling like an idiot.

"Anyway," Molly said, "Ammm said, at least I *think* he said"—she fought down a sob—"that Father's ship has been sunk by pirates."

"Molly, no!" said Peter.

Molly shook her head. "But Ammm also said, I think, that the other porpoises had rescued Father."

"Thank goodness," Peter said.

"Yes," said Molly. "But Ammm said something else."

"What?" said Peter.

"He said, 'Bad man hunt Molly ship,'" said Molly.

"Bad man?" said Peter. "What bad man?"

"Peter," she said, "have you ever heard of a pirate called the Black Moustache?"

"Yes," said Peter. He'd heard the crew talk, heard the fear in their voices.

"I think he's after the *Never Land*."

Peter felt a chill. "After *this* ship? But this is just an old . . . Wait—are you saying he knows about the trunk?"

"He must, Peter. He must have been after the *Wasp* for that reason. He was fooled just as Father was. But now Father's lost at sea somewhere, and the Black Moustache is coming for the trunk. He's *coming*, Peter."

"Molly," said Peter, "if *he* gets that trunk . . ."

"I know," she said. "I know. Peter, we must stop him."

Peter nodded. She was right. They had to stop him.

But how?

CHAPTER 21

THE SIGHTING

BLACK STACHE CUPPED HIS HANDS and screamed through the rain toward the crow's nest. "Anything?"

"Not yet, Cap'n!" returned the lookout from the top of the mainmast.

"Not much chance of seeing her in this swill, Cap'n!" shouted the helmsman, over the roar of the storm.

"She's out there!" Stache shouted back. He rubbed the end of his spyglass on a wet bit of his jacket, but still had no luck looking through the thing.

One by one, his crewmen were returning to the deck, having changed into British naval uniforms. Stache smiled at the look of it—cutthroat pirates, dressed as Her Majesty's sailors.

Just then he caught sight of a porpoise off to starboard. *Good luck*, he thought.

"Strange to see a porpoise in a storm, don't you think?" Stache shouted to his helmsman.

"Where, Cap'n?" the helmsman shouted.

Stache pointed. The helmsman gaped.

"Strange don't begin to capture it," he said. "Porpoise is too smart to get caught in a blow. Never seen nothin' like it."

"I've got it! I've got it!" It was Smee, now dressed in a British uniform that barely contained his belly. He'd given up trying to button the pants, and as he held up the British flag—the Union Jack—his pants sank to his knees, drawing laughs from the crew. Smee tried to pull up his pants, but in doing so almost lost the flag to the howling wind.

"Bring it here, you idjit!" Stache yelled.

The distraction had taken his attention off the porpoise. He looked back, but it was gone. He felt a twist in his belly—*That was my luck*—then forced the thought from his mind.

Smee staggered over and presented the Union Jack to Stache, his pants again dropping in the process.

"Hoist her high!" Stache ordered, handing the flag to a sailor. "And you, Smee, hoist your britches." This drew another laugh from the crew, interrupted by a cry from the crow's nest.

"SHIP HO!"

Rain stinging his eyes, Stache looked in the direction of the lookout's gesturing arm. He couldn't see it, not yet, in

the swirling storm. But the direction was right, and he had a
feeling about it.

The *Never Land* . . .

It had to be.

CHAPTER 22

BLACKNESS ON THE HORIZON

PETER HADN'T CLOSED HIS EYES ALL NIGHT. For one thing, the weather had steadily worsened; the ever-larger waves kept the *Never Land* in constant, sickening motion, and the groaning and creaking of the ship's ancient timbers—much louder now—made sleep difficult.

But Peter couldn't have slept anyway. Not when his mind was still trying to absorb what Molly had told him. The thoughts swirled in his head . . . falling stars, centaurs, a trunk with the power to change the world . . . It was an incredible tale.

But it's not a tale. It's all true.

When he'd returned to his tiny sleeping space, Peter had wanted to tell the other boys, or at least James. But he'd decided it would be best, for now, not to. For one thing, he doubted that they'd believe him. For another thing, he didn't want to run the risk that one of the boys would spoil whatever plan he and Molly came up with for the trunk.

That was the question: what *would* they do about the trunk? Peter and Molly had just started to discuss it last night when they'd heard Mrs. Bumbrake clunking noisily down the ladder. Peter had barely managed to dart out of the room and hide on the lower ladder before Mrs. Bumbrake had reached the passageway. Molly's last whispered words to him, as she pressed the door shut, had been: "We must act soon. Find me in the morning."

We must act soon. Yes, certainly; if what Molly had told him was true—and he believed her now, absolutely—they had to do something. But what? What could two children do on a ship full of men?

So Peter's night had been sleepless. At the first dim light of morning, he crept out of the boys' cramped hole and made his way to the foredeck. The sky was a dull gray, and the wind was flicking foam off waves far bigger than any Peter had seen. He'd adjusted to the steady swells of the open sea, but these waves were much more menacing; some of them, as they swept toward the *Never Land*, looked taller than the masts. Fear tightened Peter's chest, and he felt no better when he turned to the horizon astern; the sky there was black as night, a vast swirling darkness

The deck of the *Never Land* had never been busier. Slank bellowed orders, and the usually turtle-paced crew now scurried around urgently. Peter started aft and immediately encountered Alf, who was trotting forward, a barrel on his right shoulder. Seeing Peter, he glanced back to see if Slank was watching, then quickly set the barrel down and knelt next to the boy, as if scratching his foot.

"Ahoy, little friend," he said. "Looks like you got out of there all right last night. Missy decided not to scream, eh?"

"Yes," said Peter. "She didn't . . . I mean, she was . . ." He trailed off, wanting to tell Alf more, tell him about the trunk, maybe enlist his help. . . .

"Not now, little friend," said Alf. "No time to talk. Big storm coming. Slank's turned us around, but there's no chance this tub will outrun it." He put his big hands on Peter's bony shoulders, and looked into the boy's eyes. "We're in for a bad one, little friend. When it gets here, make sure you're holding on tight to something."

Peter looked at the horizon. The blackness looked distinctly closer now. Alf was on his feet again, hoisting the barrel to his shoulder.

"Remember, little friend," he said. "Hold on tight." And he left.

Peter headed aft, unnoticed in the confusion of shouting, bustling crewmen. To his relief, he found Molly immediately; she was standing on the aft deck, looking back at the approaching storm. He called her name, and she turned. Peter's heart fluttered when he saw in her eyes how glad she was to see him.

"Peter," she said. "There's a storm, a bad one. It's . . ."

"I know," he said. "Alf says it's going to get us soon."

"I fear he's right," she said, looking back at the horizon.

"What about the trunk?" Peter said.

Molly looked around before answering, though in this wind there was no chance that anyone could overhear them.

"I don't think there's anything we can do now," she said. "But as soon as the storm is over, we need to move it."

"Move it where?" said Peter.

"I'm not sure," Molly said. "But we have to hide it somewhere else on the ship, so that when Black Stache catches us—*if* he catches us—it won't be easily found. Perhaps we can trick him into thinking it's been thrown overboard, or was never on the *Never Land* in the first place."

"Why don't we just throw it overboard ourselves?" said Peter. "He'd never get it, then."

"No, *he* wouldn't," said Molly. "But we'd have no control over who *would* find it. It would be terrible, Peter—you've no idea how terrible—if it were to fall into the wrong hands. Or tentacles." She glanced into the dark water, and shuddered. "If we absolutely *must* throw it overboard—if there is no other way to keep it from Black Stache—then we shall. But for now, we must try to guard it, keep it safe, and hope that we can gain enough time until my father can get to us."

"You're sure your father's coming?" Peter asked, and instantly regretted it, seeing the worry in Molly's eyes.

"Father will come," she said. "He *has* to."

"Right," said Peter. "So we move the trunk. But first . . ." He gestured at the approaching storm.

"Right," said Molly. "First we get through this."

If *we get through this*, thought Peter.

"MOLLY ASTER! WHAT ARE YOU DOING OUT THERE!"

Peter and Molly turned to see the formidable form of Mrs. Bumbrake, one hand on a rail, the other gripping an umbrella.

"Mrs. Bumbrake!" Molly said. "I was just . . ."

"AND WHAT IS HE DOING BACK HERE?" shouted Mrs. Bumbrake, attempting to point at Peter with her umbrella hand, only to see a fierce wind gust grab the umbrella and send it flying forward, darting this way and that like a giant disturbed bat, before narrowly missing a ducking sailor and hurtling overboard.

"MY UMBRELLA!" shrieked Mrs. Bumbrake. "WHAT ARE YOU TWO LAUGHING AT?"

"Nothing, Mrs. Bumbrake," said Molly, forcing her face to frown.

"Nothing, ma'am," said Peter, hand over mouth.

"DON'T YOU MOCK ME, YOU LITTLE URCHIN," said Mrs. Bumbrake. "YOU'RE NOT SUPPOSED TO BE BACK HERE, AND I INTEND TO TELL MR. SLANK. AND AS FOR YOU, YOUNG LADY, I HAVE TOLD YOU A HUNDRED TIMES THAT . . ."

But Mrs. Bumbrake did not get her chance to tell Molly for a hundred-and-first time. She was interrupted by a shout from the *Never Land*'s lookout, echoed by a chorus of shouts from the men on deck. A crowd of sailors joined Molly, Peter, and Mrs. Bumbrake at the stern; they were looking and pointing at the cause of the lookout's shout: an approaching ship, between the *Never Land* and the storm. The sailors babbled excitedly, speculating on its identity, then fell silent when Slank appeared on the aft deck, holding a spyglass.

Peter ducked behind a sailor, but Slank's attention was focused on the following ship. The men grew silent as Slank raised the glass to his eye and focused it. He grunted, lowered the glass, shook his head, blinked, then looked through the glass again. Finally, he spoke.

"I'll be hanged," he said. "It's the *Wasp*."

CHAPTER 23

ANY MINUTE NOW

SMEE PULLED HAND-OVER-HAND, hoisting the Union Jack high on the *Jolly Roger's* mainmast, as Black Stache watched approvingly. Stache's men were all now wearing British uniforms. Stache glanced down at his own uniform—a *captain's* uniform—and felt particularly handsome.

Stache peered through the glass at the *Never Land*. His swift ship had turned downwind and was now closing quickly on the old cargo hulk.

Any minute now . . .

"READY, MEN?" he called out, and he was answered with a roar, as his men thrust their swords into the air.

"Keep those blades hidden!" shouted Stache. "Wait for my command!"

He raised his glass again. The *Never Land* was very close now; he could see the storm was treating her badly. Stache grinned.

They don't stand a chance. . . .

CHAPTER 24

OVERBOARD

THE GOOD NEWS SPREAD QUICKLY on the *Never Land*.

"It's the *Wasp*! The *Wasp* is coming!"

More sailors gathered at the stern, watching Slank as he raised the glass to his eye again.

"She's changed course," he said. "She'll be coming alongside, to port. It's Captain Scott. He must have turned to run from the storm. Now he's come to stand by us."

The crew was delighted. Instead of facing a monster storm alone at sea in a decrepit barge, they now would be escorted by the finest ship in His Majesty's navy.

"All right, you bilge rats," shouted Slank. "We hold steady until the *Wasp* is alongside, then we . . ."

"NO!"

Slank looked down, startled, into the frightened but determined face of Molly Aster.

"What did you say?" he said.

"You can't let that ship get close to us," she said. "That ship is under the command of Black Stache."

The sound of the dreaded name drew a nervous murmur from the crew, quickly silenced by a laugh from Slank.

"Back Stache?" he said. "Young lady, with all due respect, Black Stache commands a ship called the *Sea Devil*. That there"—he pointed at the approaching ship—"is the *Wasp*. I know her well. We was in port with her. And that's her."

"Yes, yes," said Molly. "But Black Stache . . ."

"Molly Aster!" Mrs. Bumbrake elbowed her way past the sailors and took Molly by the arm. "You stop this silliness this *instant.*"

"Let *go*," said Molly, yanking her arm free.

"Well, I *never*," said Mrs. Bumbrake. "Young lady, when your father . . ."

"Oh, be *quiet*," said Molly, startling Mrs. Bumbrake so much that she actually became, for a moment, quiet. Turning to Slank, Molly took a deep breath to calm herself, and said: "Sir, you must believe me. That is the *Wasp*, yes. But it was captured by Black Stache, and he's coming for this ship now."

"And how do you know that?" asked Slank. "Did a seagull tell you?" This brought chuckles from the crew.

Something like that, thought Peter.

"Please," said Molly, desperation in her voice, "I can't

explain how I know, but I *know*. That ship is commanded by Black Stache."

Slank's smile wavered for an instant, then returned.

"Young lady," he said, "even if that was Black Stache, which it ain't, it's only the finest ships he's after. He wouldn't waste his time on an old bucket like this, especially not with that storm closing on him."

"MOLLY ASTER," said Mrs. Bumbrake, having recovered the ability to speak, now tugging at Molly's arm again. "YOU LEAVE OFF THIS SILLINESS AND COME WITH ME THIS . . ."

"Please," Molly begged Slank, her eyes welling with tears of frustration. "You must *not* allow that ship to reach us."

Slank turned and raised the spyglass to his eye again, taking a moment to find the following ship. He took the glass away and looked back at Molly, smiling again.

"Young lady," he said, "that ship this is manned by sailors of the British navy." He held the glass out toward her. "Look for yourself."

Molly took the glass, peered through it, then handed the glass back.

"It's a trick," she said. "It has to be. Please, *listen* to me! You can't—"

"THAT'S QUITE ENOUGH, YOUNG LADY," bellowed Mrs. Brumbridge, moving in.

"All right then," said Slank, visibly relieved, as he turned to the sailors who'd been watching the little drama. "WE GOT A STORM COMING!" he shouted. "BACK TO WORK, YOU BILGE RATS!"

"And *you're* coming with me, young lady," said Mrs. Bumbrake, towing Molly toward the ladderway.

As Molly was pulled away, she caught Peter's eye, and pointed downward. Her meaning was clear: *Meet me below.*

Peter nodded. Dodging among the bustling crewmen, he found a relatively quiet place along the starboard rail where he could wait for a chance to go below. From time to time he glanced back at the following ship, growing steadily larger, as was the roiling mass of clouds behind it. He didn't know which he was more nervous about: Black Stache, or the storm.

I guess we're going to get both, he thought.

In a few minutes he saw his opportunity and ducked, unobserved, down the aft ladderway. He rapped softly on Molly's door, and she opened it immediately. Peter was momentarily startled to see Mrs. Bumbrake on her bed, snoring; then he understood. *Molly had put her to sleep.*

"Hurry," Molly said, brushing past Peter and heading for the lower ladderway. He followed, and they descended to the hold level, where they had their first piece of good luck: there was no guard. Evidently Slank had decided that, for the moment, preparing for the storm was more important than protecting the trunk.

Their second stroke of luck came when Molly pulled on

the padlock. It came off easily in her hand; their ruse had not been detected. She opened the hold door and, with Peter behind her, stepped inside. At first he saw nothing in the darkness, though Molly seemed to know exactly where she was going. He heard her footsteps, then a rustling sound.

"Help me get the canvas off," she said.

Holding his hands in front of him, Peter inched forward until he felt his knees bump into a solid bulk. He reached down, felt the rough canvas covering the trunk.

"There's a rope," said Molly.

Peter's eyes were adjusting to the darkness. He saw the rope, and helped Molly work the canvas free. It dropped to the floor, exposing the trunk, and . . .

UHHHH

Moaning, Peter staggering back, momentarily blinded by a brilliant golden light filling the hold. He closed his eyes, but could still feel the light, a powerful, wonderful warmth flooding into his body, feeling *so good*. And there was more— *bells*, it sounded like, making some kind of fantastic music . . .

"Peter! Peter!"

Molly was shaking Peter's arm. He opened his eyes to find the hold suddenly dim again.

"The light," he said. "What did . . ."

"There are cracks in the trunk," said Molly. "It's not made right; I think the cracks are getting bigger. I've put the canvas back on."

Peter's eyes were readjusting. He saw the trunk now; the canvas was over it once again, tucked loosely into the rope. But now the whole bulk, canvas and all, was glowing faintly. Peter stared into the glow, feeling lightheaded, euphoric. Feeling *wonderful*.

Molly's hand was on his arm again.

"Peter," she said, "I know this is difficult for you. It's difficult for me, and I'm used to it."

Peter struggled to speak. "What?" he said, his own voice sounding distant to him. "I mean, what shall we . . ."

"Help me lift it," she said. "Take that end."

Following Molly's lead, Peter bent and, reaching under the canvas, took an end of the trunk. Immediately he heard the music again, and felt the wonderful warmth, surging through his hands, his arms, into his body. He fought to keep his mind on what Molly was saying.

"All right, then," she said. "Lift it."

They rose, and to Peter's surprise the trunk rose with them as if it weighed nothing. Fascinated, Peter let go of his end of the trunk; it hung in the air for a moment, then slowly, slower than a falling feather, began to descend. He caught it again, and raised it with just the barest effort. He heard the music again, the bells, and the warmth spread through his body. He felt peaceful, relaxed, yet at the same time completely very aware of his surroundings, of Molly, of *everything*.

"This way," said Molly, holding her end of the trunk as she backed through the hold door, Peter following. They easily maneuvered the trunk to the ladderway, and Molly began to climb the steps, guiding her end of the trunk with one hand; Peter, on the bottom, pushing the almost-weightless bulk upward with his fingertips.

They paused at the top of the ladderway, Peter again becoming aware of the creaking and rocking of the ship—he'd almost forgotten the storm raging outside.

"Where are we taking it?" he asked.

She pointed up. "To the main deck," she said.

"But they'll see it!" said Peter.

"By the time they do," she said, "it will be in the sea."

"*Overboard?*" said Peter. "But I though we were going to hide it!"

"There's no time," said Molly. "Black Stache will be here in minutes."

"But what if it's not him?" said Peter. "How do we know it's him?"

"Because Ammm told me," said Molly. "And because there is no other reason why that ship would be coming for us now, in this storm. It's not a rescue, Peter; it's an attack. And this trunk is what he wants."

"But . . ." said Peter, "but . . ." He tried to think of an argument, but the only one that came to mind was: *But I want to keep touching the trunk.*

Molly studied his face for a moment.

"I know," she said, softly. "I know. I feel it, too. More than you. But we must do this, Peter. Now."

She started forward again, and Peter, sighing, followed. They guided the trunk to the upper ladderway, and, again with Molly leading, they ascended the steps. The wind was shrieking outside now; through the opening, Peter saw rain flying past sideways in dense gray sheets.

At the top of the ladderway, Molly stuck her head out and looked around. She ducked back down, her hair now wet and in wild disarray.

"There are some men over there," she said, pointing to the ship's port side. "I think they're shouting to the other ship. It's very close. When we get the trunk onto the deck, we'll go that way"—she gestured to the starboard side—"and throw it overboard directly. All right?"

Peter nodded.

"Peter," Molly said, "if anybody sees us, if anybody tries to stop us, we must keep going, do you understand? We must not fail."

"All right," said Peter.

"Let's go, then," said Molly, and, grabbing the end of the trunk, stepped onto the deck. Peter followed, and in a moment found himself drenched with wind-driven rain. As Molly had said, a knot of sailors was at the port rail, shouting; in the swirling gloom beyond them, Peter saw the shape of a large, long, black ship, very close now; Peter recognized it as the ship he'd seen the day the *Never Land* left port, what seemed like years ago. Its crew was lowering sail, apparently preparing to come alongside.

On the raised deck at the black ship's stern, Peter saw a stocky helmsman, fighting to control the wheel as the two ships drew together. Next to him, partially hidden by a mast, was a tall man, wearing an officer's uniform, apparently the captain. Peter noticed—even with the storm and confusion, Peter was noticing *everything*—that the tall man seemed to be deliberately using the mast to conceal his face. He looked at Molly, and saw that she had spotted the tall man, too. She caught Peter's eye.

"It's him," she said. "Come on."

Stepping carefully on the wet, pitching deck, they guided the trunk toward the starboard rail. The yelling from the port side was louder now, some of the shouts turned to cries of alarm as the two ships converged. Molly and Peter reached the starboard side, and Molly raised her end of the trunk over the rail.

"Now!" she shouted, over the wind.

Peter braced himself to shove his end and push the trunk into the sea. But as he did the hulls of the two ships, riding different parts of different waves, slammed together. Peter felt his feet slide out from under him as he fell backward, slamming the back of his head onto the deck. He heard a cry from Molly and saw that she, too, had fallen, almost landing on him; he was dimly aware of the trunk settling gently onto the deck a few feet to the other side of her. From the port side of the ship Peter heard shouts, and now some screams.

Head throbbing, Peter struggled to his knees.

"Molly!" he said. "Are you all right?"

"Yes, yes, I'm all right," she said, sitting up. "The trunk! Peter, hurry!"

Struggling to their feet, Molly and Peter staggered on the lurching deck to the trunk, Molly reaching it first, leaning down and . . .

"PUT THAT DOWN!"

Molly screamed as Slank, grabbing her by her hair, yanked her away from the trunk. Peter lunged forward, grabbed Slank's arm, and sank his teeth into it, tasting blood. Now it was Slank's turn to scream as he spun away from Peter, releasing Molly—all of them crashing to the rain-slicked deck.

"PETER, THE TRUNK!" Molly shouted. Peter rolled, stood, got his arms around the trunk, and felt it come up easily from the deck. He turned toward the rail, *just two steps now* . . .

"GET HIM!" roared Slank, struggling to his feet, and in that moment Peter felt a massive hand on his shoulder, felt himself yanked back and slammed to the deck, the trunk again slipping from his hands. Through the throbbing haze of his pain, Peter heard more screams. Looming above him, he saw the giant form of Little Richard, holding Molly, and now the fury-twisted face of Slank.

"*BITE ME?*" he shrieked. "YOU DARE TO *BITE ME?*"

Peter saw it all slowly, as if in a dream—the face coming closer, the hamlike fists closing violently on his shirt. He felt himself lifted high in the air, and he had a momentary glimpse of the horror on Molly's face as Slank hurled him, with all his strength, over the side of the *Never Land*, toward the raging sea.

CHAPTER 25

A Fly in a Spiderweb

Black Stache's plan was going perfectly. The crew of the *Never Land* had shown no sign of alarm as the disguised pirate ship came alongside.

While the pirates were approaching, they'd heard some kind of commotion—shouting, then screams—coming from the deck of the *Never Land*. But whatever it was, it had not caused the old freighter to change course. Now the two ships were side by side; sails had been lowered, lines tossed to secure the ships together, fenders positioned to keep the hulls, which had slammed into each other, from colliding again.

Stache kept his face hidden behind a mast, though he knew his ruse would not fool the *Never Land* sailors much longer. *They're bound to notice that my entire crew is barefoot.*

Stache had a single-shot flintlock pistol in his right hand, held to his side, out of sight. He liked the idea of a bloodless coup, with no sword soiled. The sight of pirates generally put such fear into merchant sailors that they often surrendered immediately.

He waited, relying on Smee to be his eyes.

From the corner of his mouth, Smee said, "They's tied up to us now, Cap'n."

Like a fly in a spiderweb.

"How many on deck?" said Stache.

"A dozen or so crew. A few passengers, including some children."

"Armed?"

"The *children?*"

"No, you idjit! The *crew.*"

"A few knives," Smee said. "A pistol or two."

"Our crew?"

"Ready and itching to go." The pirates had gathered along the rail, their blades concealed in their uniforms.

"Good," said Stache. "Now, call for the captain."

"AHOY THERE! *NEVER LAND,*" shouted Smee, to the other ship. "WHO'S IN CHARGE THERE, IS IT?" He knew this didn't have the right ring to it, but there was no taking it back.

"THAT WOULD BE ME!" a deep voice thundered back. The owner of the voice, a big man, stepped to the rail; Smee saw that the man's arm was bleeding.

"ARE YOU THE CAP'N THEN, MATE?" Smee said,

then cringed. He wasn't getting any of this navy talk right.

"THE CAP'N IS . . . INDISPOSED," the other man said. "I'M THE FIRST MATE, SLANK." His eyes were on the half-hidden form of Black Stache. "IS THAT CAP'N SCOTT?"

"NO, I . . ." stammered Smee. "I MEAN, YES, BUT . . . I MEAN . . ."

"You *idjit*," hissed Stache.

Slank, suddenly suspicious, scanned the hard, unshaven faces of the men lining the rail of the dark ship, then glanced down, and noticed the bare feet.

"CUT THE LINES!" he bellowed. "CUT THE LINES!"

But before the crew could act, Black Stache was out from behind the mast.

"NOW!" he roared, and before the sound had died from his lips, two dozen pirates had drawn their blades and leaped onto the deck of the *Never Land*, whose crewmen froze in terror.

Stache, moving calmly, deliberately, followed his men over to the *Never Land* deck. He sauntered up to Slank and pointed his pistol directly into his face.

"Mr. Slank, is it?" he said. "Black Stache, at your service."

Some *Never Land* crewmen whimpered at the name. Slank, on the other hand, stared coolly at Black Stache for a moment, then—in a reaction that Stache found odd—

turned and looked back over his shoulder, toward a young girl who was standing by the far rail, sobbing, as a huge man held her arms, as if keeping her from jumping over the side.

Slank turned back to Stache, again meeting his eyes. Stache was impressed by how little fear the man showed. *I might have room for a man like that*, he thought. But what he said was: "If you wants to keep breathing, Mr. Slank, you'll tell your men to disarm."

Not taking his eyes away from Stache's, Slank shouted to his crew: "Put them down, men!"

The relieved *Never Land* sailors, who'd had no intention of trading steel with the pirates, hastily dropped their weapons to the deck.

"Very good," Stache said, stepping closer to Slank, his pistol barrel now almost touching the space between Slank's eyes. "Now, we ain't got much time with this storm, so I'll make this quick. You have something I want. Where is it, Mr. Slank?"

Slank took a moment to answer. Again, Stache was impressed by the man's calm in the face of a loaded pistol.

"We have a few women," Slank said. "And plenty of rum. But if you think there's treasure on this old scow, I'm afraid you'll be disappointed."

Stache's finger tightened slightly on the trigger, then he eased off. Was Slank bluffing? Or could it be that he didn't know what he had on his ship? Stache thought about it for a moment, then decided that, for now, Slank was more useful alive than dead.

"Mr. Slank," he said, "if I don't find what I'm looking for, it's you who'll be sorry. Now, step aside."

Stache turned to a knot of pirates nearby, raising his voice over the wind.

"YOU MEN COME WITH ME," he shouted. "WE'RE LOOKING FOR A TRUNK."

CHAPTER 26

INTO THE SEA

PETER COULD NOT SWIM, so he knew, even as he felt Slank lift him, felt his body being hurled over the side of the *Never Land*, that he was going to die.

He was terrified, of course, but at the same time, as he felt himself tumble in space, he was acutely *aware* of his terror, as if it were somebody else's; he was also acutely aware of the pain in his head, of Molly's anguished screams from the deck, of the sound of the wind, of everything around him.

It seems to be happening so slowly.

But it wasn't happening slowly; it was happening very quickly; Peter was aware of that, too. It was only that, since he'd touched the trunk, he could *think* about it so much faster than he usually thought about things. He could even think about how fast he was thinking about things.

But I'm still about to die.

Peter saw he was going to land in a trough between two waves.

Should I hold my breath?

He noticed that one of the waves was slightly higher than the other, and had some seaweed in its churning foam.

If I hold my breath, it will take me longer to die. Is that good or bad?

He decided to hold his breath, and to try to twist his body so he could look up at the ship as he entered the water, in case somebody tried to throw him a rope.

Though I doubt Slank will throw me a rope. . . .

He held his breath, and he got his body twisted around just as he reached the water, so he was looking up at the ship as he felt his left leg plunge into the sea.

It's cold.

And then his right leg, and then his waist, and then . . .

What?

He felt it in his back, a sudden pain, as if he'd landed on something blunt, and . . .

What's happening to me?

Peter felt his body rising with the swell of the wave, and then, as the wave receded, he felt himself *rise out of the wave*, all the way out, back into the wind.

I'm . . . like the rat. Like Molly . . .

He twisted around and saw that he was several feet above the water now, drifting across the tops of the waves, the wind pushing him away from the *Never Land*. He heard an odd sound beneath him, looked down, saw the familiar rounded snout.

The porpoise. It pushed me up out of the sea.

It was chittering at him, but he had no idea what it was saying. Peter was sure it was the large porpoise, the one Molly had been talking to.

Ammm, that's what she called him.

The porpoise began to swim toward the *Never Land*, now receding in the distance, then back toward Peter, then toward the ship again, then back. More chittering.

He wants me to follow.

Tentatively, Peter waved his arms; the wind was carrying him away, but he found that his arm motion had turned his body, so that he was horizontal, with his head pointing toward the ship. He waved his arms some more; nothing. Then he heard Ammm squeaking urgently, now from directly under him. Peter looked down, and . . .

Whoa.

His body suddenly swooped forward, against the wind, gaining speed. . . .

I'm going into the sea!

Peter raised his head; instantly, his body swooped upward, into a vertical position. He stopped moving forward, and found himself again being carried back by the wind. More squeaking from below. Tentatively, Peter leaned his body toward the horizontal again, and again he started moving forward, more slowly this time.

Ammm is teaching me to fly.

Peter began to experiment, cocking his head at different angles, shifting his body, his shoulders, his arms, his legs, noticing how the movements affected his direction and speed, caused him to rise and fall. The wind was howling, the rain pelting his face; but Peter felt himself gliding through the storm almost effortlessly. He was far above the waves now, perhaps fifty yards, perhaps more. He felt increasingly confident, then excited, then almost joyful.

And then the thought struck him.

The ship. Where's the ship?

Peter squinted into the storm, but saw only darkness, and towering waves. He wasn't sure how far he'd flown; wasn't sure what direction. His exhilaration was gone, replaced by the cold squeeze of fear in his gut.

I'm lost out here.

And then he heard it, above the roar of wind and wave; the high-pitched sounds, calling from somewhere in the darkness below. Carefully, Peter angled himself down through the swirling gloom, descending slowly toward the menacing wave tops, following the sounds, until finally he saw the ghostly gray snout of Ammm.

"I'M HERE!" Peter shouted, relief cracking his voice. "HERE!"

Ammm rose high on his tail, dove forward, then rose again, looked back at Peter, turned and dove again. Understanding that he was to follow, Peter leaned toward Ammm's ghostly form as it plunged swiftly through the waves, until . . .

There's the ship.

Two ships, in fact; Peter saw, in the gloom ahead, that the *Never Land* was now tied to the black ship. *The pirate ship.* Peter slowed himself, and angled toward the starboard side of the *Never Land*, the side Slank had thrown him from, away from the pirate ship. As he drew near, he heard shouting, and saw that the decks were swarming with unfamiliar men—men wearing uniforms, carrying swords. Peter glided close to the hull, keeping his head just below deck level, trying to decide what to do.

It was then that he noticed something disconcerting: he was starting to sink toward the water. It was gradual, and with an effort, he was able to pull himself up again. But it was definitely getting more difficult to stay aloft.

I'm going to have to get back onto the ship, he thought. *Soon.*

Then he heard Molly's voice, shouting, from nearby on the deck.

And then he heard the screams.

$\mathcal{T}$HE $\mathcal{R}$ETURN

BLACK STACHE WAS FURIOUS.

He and his men had searched belowdecks on the *Never Land*, looking for the treasure trunk. They'd had no luck in the main holds. There were a few trunks, which they'd smashed open with an ax; but these contained only clothing and household goods.

They'd also gone through the cabins, finding a few small pieces of jewelry in one, but nothing else of value. In the captain's cabin they'd found a confused man talking gibberish. There had been one moment of hopeful excitement, when they'd found an aft hold that apparently had, at some point, been padlocked shut. But it was empty.

Now they were back on the main deck. Stache, quivering with rage, wished he could make somebody walk the plank; this usually had a soothing effect on him. But plankwalking, done right, took time, and Stache did not have time: from the look of the approaching storm, he had only minutes to get off this wretched bucket and make his run.

So, once more, he pressed his pistol to Slank's forehead.

"Mr. Slank," he said, "I have no more patience. *Where is the trunk?*"

Slank glared back at him. But Stache caught something in his look . . . a wavering, perhaps. He curled his finger on the trigger, making the motion elaborate, so Slank could see it. Stache saw a flicker of fear in Slank's eyes. *He's about to crack . . .*

"Cap'n!" It was Smee, stumbling across the pitching deck, his ill-fitting British uniform trousers falling to his knees.

"NOT NOW, SMEE!" shouted Stache. "CAN'T YOU SEE I'M ABOUT TO BLOW THIS MAN'S BRAINS OUT?"

"Sorry, Cap'n," said Smee, yanking his pants up practically to neck level. "But you said you was looking . . ."

"I SAID *NOT NOW!*" bellowed Stache, turning his attention back to Slank. "Now, Mr. Slank, I'm going to count to three, and if you don't tell me where the trunk . . ."

"Yes!" said Smee. "A trunk!"

Stache whirled to Smee. "YOU FOUND THE TRUNK?"

"Over there, Cap'n! By the starboard rail! There was a canvas over it, and the wind tore it off, and we seen it."

Stache glanced at Slank, and saw in the man's eyes that this was, indeed, what he was after.

"I'll deal with you in a moment, Mr. Slank," he said, and strode to the starboard rail.

There he saw it: an old trunk, its wood rough and scarred, nothing like the elegant black trunk he'd found on the *Wasp* filled with sand.

Clever, he thought. *Put the treasure in an old box, and leave it out on deck, where nobody would think to look.*

A few feet from the trunk stood a huge man, who was warily watching, and being watched by, a semicircle of pirates, their swords ready. The giant held a young girl— *pretty young thing,* thought Stache—by her right arm, as if restraining her.

Restraining her from what? Stache wondered. *And why is she looking at me that way?*

But he had no time for the girl, not now, not with the treasure, finally, at hand. His men had left it alone, not daring to approach it before he did.

Stache stepped forward and looked down at the trunk, savoring the moment. *The greatest treasure ever to go to sea.* And it was about to be his!

He leaned forward and touched the trunk lid. As he did, he felt a strange tingle in his hand, then his arm—strange but not unpleasant. He grabbed the latch holding the trunk lid and . . .

"NO!"

The shout came from the girl, who had managed, somehow, to twist herself free from the grasp of the giant. She lunged toward Stache, her green eyes blazing with fury. Before Stache could react, she had knocked him away from the trunk, her hands clawing at his face. As he tripped and fell onto his back, he screamed in rage, in pain, his screams mingling with the roars of the giant, who had lunged forward to grab the escaping girl, only to be attacked by the pirates who'd been watching him.

Now there were bodies sprawling all over the pitching, rain-slicked deck: Stache, on his back, with the relentless girl still clawing at his face; the giant, beaten to the deck but still fighting, his massive thrashing arms and legs knocking down his pirate attackers like bowling pins. More pirates ran toward the commotion, slipping and falling as they came.

Slank, temporarily unguarded, also moved toward the starboard rail, and he was among the first to see it—a sight so stunning that, for a moment, all the fighting stopped, as all eyes turned to watch, and there was no sound except the storm.

It was a boy. It was—*But that's impossible*—the boy Slank had thrown overboard. He was coming back aboard the ship. But he wasn't climbing the rail; he was *floating*, a good ten feet over the men's heads as he swooped onto the deck.

The boy was flying.

MOLLY'S TURN

MOLLY RECOVERED FIRST. While the others—pirates and non-pirates alike—were momentarily paralyzed by the astonishing sight of the flying boy, Molly rolled away from Black Stache and got to her feet, pointing to the trunk and shouting: "PETER! THERE!"

Peter saw it and swooped, landing hard on the deck next to the trunk. He stumbled, then found his feet and threw his arms around the rough wood.

"STOP HIM!" screamed Slank and Stache both, almost with one breath, and a half dozen pirates lunged toward Peter across the rain-slicked deck. But they were just a bit too far away, and Peter was just a bit too quick; he had the trunk on the rail now, and as the closest pirate got to him, he gave it a shove.

"NO!" screamed both Slank and Stache, again sounding almost like one man, as the trunk toppled off the rail and . . .

. . . and it did not fall. Instead, it hung in the air next to the ship, then lazily, pushed by the wind, began to drift forward, and ever so slightly downward. . . .

"AFTER IT!" shouted Stache, scrambling to his feet and lunging to the rail, only to find his way blocked again by Molly.

Who IS this infernal girl?

Hurling Molly aside, Stache ran along the rail, chasing the trunk, reaching his hand out to grab it, and . . .

UNNH

Peter, having made a leap that covered twenty feet of deck, slammed into Stache from behind, slamming him forward onto the rail. His hand slapped the trunk, sending it into a lazy spin, the wind carrying it faster now as it twirled gently forward and down, down, to the waiting waves.

With a roar of fury Stache turned and grabbed for Peter, meaning to wring this little flying pest's neck, for starters. But Peter was again too quick, seeing the pirate's hands coming and springing backward, his momentum carrying him over the rail, over the side, off the ship. He twisted in the air, angled his body forward, and . . .

UH-oh.

Peter felt it immediately: He could no longer make himself rise.

Molly said it wears off.

He was sinking. Not quickly, but there was no question:

He was falling gently back into the sea. He had time to look back to the deck of the *Never Land*, at Black Stache, screaming in fury; at the pirates, still battling to subdue the giant Little Richard; at Slank, glaring at Peter with what looked like hatred; and at Molly, at the rail, her wet hair matted down, her dress torn, watching Peter intently until she knew he saw her, then mouthing something. . . .

Fly, she was saying. *Fly.*

"I CAN'T," Peter shouted, moving his arms helplessly. "I CAN'T, MOLLY!"

And as he shouted those words, he felt his feet touch the crest of a wave. It passed, but Peter looked down, and saw he would be in the sea soon. He scanned the waves, hoping, desperately, to see the familiar round snout. But Ammm was not there.

Another wave crest, this one hitting his knees, tossing him sideways. The next wave would take him down with it.

Peter looked back up at the *Never Land*, hoping for a last look at Molly. But she wasn't where she had been. Frantically, Peter ran his eyes along the ship. Then he saw her: she was at the bow. She had climbed up on the rail, and was balanced, precariously, as the ship tossed. Behind her, Mrs. Bumbrake was shrieking; men were running toward Molly. But it was too late.

Molly jumped into the sea.

CHAPTER 29

ABANDON SHIP

BLACK STACHE WAS IN A DARK RAGE. The treasure had been in his hands—*in his hands*—and now it was in the sea, thrown there by a boy. A *boy*. Stache had always disliked boys, and the fact that this one had appeared to be flying made him even more unappealing in the pirate's eyes. Stache had seen many things in his pirate career, but never a flying person, and, even in the wild confusion on the wave-washed deck of the *Never Land*, it nagged at him.

Maybe he wasn't really flying. Maybe it was a trick played by the wind.

Whatever the explanation for the boy, Stache was sure it had something to do with the trunk. Which was now in the sea. This fact made Black Stache so angry he could barely think. He wanted very much to soothe his nerves by killing somebody, perhaps several people, ideally including a boy. But there simply wasn't time. The *Never Land* was pitching and heaving in twenty-foot seas, riding up one gigantic wave and then slipping down the backside only to be caught by the next and lifted again. Towering walls of foaming seawater crashed over both ships from all directions; Stache knew he had to cut the *Never Land* loose from the *Jolly Roger* before the ships smashed each other to bits.

"Back to the *Jolly Roger*, men!" he shouted over the roar of the wind. The pirates, eager to escape the *Never Land*, began leaping from one pitching deck to the other, taking whatever valuables they'd been able to scrounge from the *Never Land*, including a very alarmed pig.

"Cap'n," shouted Smee. "What about prisoners?"

"We'll take the giant," replied Stache, gesturing to the Little Richard, who'd finally been subdued by six pirates and was lying, beaten and bound, on the deck. A man like that could be useful, once he'd learned to obey.

"Take the woman, too," said Stache, pointing to Mrs. Bumbrake. It was Stache's policy always to take women, although this one was quite large. But a woman was a woman, the way Stache looked at it. The large woman had been sobbing uncontrollably since the girl had jumped into the water. Stache wondered about that, too—why a girl would do such a thing.

It had something to do with that trunk, he thought, and that reminded him of something.

"Take Mr. Slank as well," he shouted. He had noticed

how eager Slank had been to protect the trunk. As he was shoved toward the *Never Land*, Slank gave Stache a cool look, and then glanced into the water, where the trunk had gone over.

He knows something about the trunk, thought Stache. *And I aim to find out what it is.*

Stache had not given up on the treasure, not at all; in fact, now that he'd had it in his hands, he was more determined than ever to have it. The trunk was made of wood, and it was clearly not heavy; the boy had lifted it easily. It would float. It was in the sea, somewhere, nearby. The storm would pass. And Stache would find it.

"And the others, Cap'n?" shouted Smee, pointing to the rest of the *Never Land*'s crew and passengers—a wretched, drenched lot of bedraggled sailors and small boys. Some were screaming, begging to be taken aboard the *Jolly Roger*, having decided it was better to be prisoner on a ship full of vicious pirates than to be left aboard the *Never Land*. The pounding, crashing waves were sweeping across the old ship's deck, breaking off pieces of wood; the *Never Land* was starting to fall apart. It would not be long now.

"LEAVE 'EM TO DIE," shouted Stache, and he was gratified by the looks of terror on the faces of those he had just doomed. Especially the boys.

"REEF HO!" shouted the lookout from the crow's nest of

the *Jolly Roger*. This got Stache's attention; if the lookout could see a reef in this weather, it was very close.

"CUT 'EM LOOSE," bellowed Stache, and his men cut the lines holding the *Jolly Roger* to the *Never Land* and its wailing occupants.

If the storm don't get 'em, the reef will, he thought happily.

Stache watched as the *Never Land* separated and, grabbed by a wave, rose up impossibly high, then slipped over the far side of a monstrous mountain of seawater. As it disappeared from his view, he heard the wails of men mixed with the high-pitched screams of boys. A moment later it was the *Jolly Roger's* turn to be lifted. As the ship settled, Stache cleared his eyes of the rain, and saw that the *Never Land* had vanished in the spray and gloom.

"Smee," shouted Stache.

"Aye, Cap'n."

"A reef ain't out here on its own," he said. "There'll be an island nearby, and maybe a harbor or cove where we can ride out this blow. Tell the lookout to find that island. And tell him—tell *all* the crew—that there's ten gold pieces and a bottle of grog for the man who spots that trunk that went overboard."

Smee's eyes widened.

"*Ten* gold pieces, Cap'n?"

"Twenty, if he spots that boy, too."

"The boy that was flying, Cap'n'?"

"He wasn't flying, you idjit," roared Stache. "That was a trick of the wind."

"Aye, Cap'n. Well, if he can't fly, I reckon he's gone for sure now, in these seas."

"Stop reckoning," shouted Stache, "and give the crew me orders."

"Aye, Cap'n," said Smee, stumbling away on the pitching deck, leaving Stache staring into the raging sea. The trunk was out there, he was sure; and somehow he knew that the boy was out there, too.

I'll find them both, he thought. *And when I do, that boy will walk the plank. Let's see how high he can fly with cannonshot lashed to him.*

CHAPTER 30

A Helping Hand

THE THIRD WAVE GRABBED PETER high on his chest and yanked him down in its cold, relentless grip. As his head went under, he grabbed a breath of air, wondering if it was his last, but the churning of the water brought him up again for a moment, and he managed to get another. Then the massive weight of the wave drove him deep, tumbling him, so he no longer knew which way the surface was. Seconds passed, then more seconds, and as his body continued to tumble, his chest began to burn, to ache, and as the ache turned to agony, he knew that soon he would not be able to hold his breath any longer.

That was when he felt a hand grab him by the hair.

Molly.

He felt himself being pulled up, up, but before he reached the surface, his desperate lungs gave out and he felt seawater rushing into his mouth, and then for a while he didn't know

what was happening, and then he was gagging and coughing up seawater, and he was cold, but he was also breathing, which meant he was still alive.

"Peter, are you all right?" Molly was shouting into his ear. He wanted to tell her he was all right, but he couldn't talk, because of all the water coming out of him.

"Peter," shouted Molly, "you must hold on to me, do you understand? I can't keep us up much longer."

That was when Peter noticed he was flying again. Actually, Molly was flying, and somehow holding Peter up, having draped his right arm around her shoulder. They were perhaps twenty-five feet above the sea now, and Peter could see that just ahead of them, the towering waves were crashing, with an ungodly thunder, onto what appeared to be jagged rocks.

He could feel that Molly was struggling to hold him; her voice was strained.

"Put your arms around my neck," she shouted. "There's rocks here. There might be an island. But the starstuff is wearing off."

Her locket, thought Peter. *She used her locket.* Still choking up seawater, he managed to drape his arms around her neck, locking his hands together as tightly as he could. He felt Molly lean forward, and felt them glide downward a bit, then swoop up. The thundering of the waves on the rocks grew louder, deafening now. Peter, trying not to think about what lay below him, concentrated on holding on to Molly. But his arms were getting weary; his hands were beginning to slip apart.

Molly felt it. "Don't let go!" she shouted.

But Peter couldn't help it; he felt his grip weakening.

"Hang on!" shouted Molly. "Just a bit more!"

But Peter couldn't hang on. He felt his cold fingers separate, and suddenly he was falling again. He heard Molly shout his name, but before she got it all out he was plunged into the cold sea again. He managed to struggle to the surface and get his head up for an instant, then felt himself hurled violently forward, tumbling like a leaf in a windstorm, over and over, and then he slammed into something, then again, then again, scraping against his face. . . .

Sand.

He got his feet under him, only to be knocked down and rolled by another wave, then another and another. On hands and knees now, he crawled forward, until finally, *finally*, he escaped the clutching waves. Still on hands and knees, he heaved up what seemed to be an impossible amount of seawater. When he could heave no more, he tried to stand, but found that he was too weak. He put his head down on the sand and, as the surf thundered behind him and the wind howled above, Peter fell asleep.

CHAPTER 31

THE LAGOON

NOT FAR FROM WHERE PETER LAY UNCONSCIOUS, a lagoon connected to the sea. It was, in good weather, a beautiful place—a near-perfect semicircle of flawless white sand, perhaps a mile across, bordered by a curtain of tall, graceful palms. In the center of the curved beach lay two dozen or so massive, sea-smoothed boulders, some of them the size of a sailing ship, forming a hulking jumble of rock that stretched from the trees into the blue-green water. Behind the beach the island rose steeply to a ridge several hundred feet high, jungle-thick with vegetation, forming a curved green wall that cut the lagoon off from the rest of the island.

The lagoon teemed with life—turtles, jellyfish, crabs, and vast schools of lavishly multihued fish. Normally these creatures were sheltered from the surge of the sea by a coral reef; it ran across the mouth of the lagoon from one side to the other, with only a small break in the center, through which the tide flowed in and out.

But the low reef was no match for the waves churned up by this storm. Every few seconds, a towering wall of wind-driven water rose high over the reef and broke upon it with a thunderous crash, sending a surge of churning, foaming water rushing high onto the beach, then back toward the sea, leaving the surf-scrubbed beach empty for a few seconds, awaiting the next incoming surge.

But one of the waves left something behind: the trunk. It happened to tumble ashore in the center of the beach, becoming wedged in the sand at the base of one of the massive round boulders. The waves had taken their toll on the old wooden box: there were several cracks now, one perhaps a quarter-inch wide. As the waves washed over the trunk, water seeped into the cracks, and then back out.

The water seeping out was glowing—a soft, greenish-gold glow, the color of fireflies. The glowing water behaved oddly; it remained next to the trunk, swirling and spiraling around it, somehow unaffected by the push and pull of the raging wave-water rushing past.

In time, as the storm began to subside, a large, sleek fish with a silver body and a bright green tail glided near, and then into, the glowing seawater. It stopped there, hovering; it did not leave. Soon it was joined by another, similar fish, and then another; they, too, remained in the glowing water, unable, or unwilling to leave. They stayed there for hours, their fins barely moving, their gills working. At times the water changed colors that changed and shifted—now one color, now another, now many colors, an underwater rainbow.

And then . . . the fish began to change.

CHAPTER 32

THE WRECK
OF THE Never Land

ON THE HEAVING DECK of the *Never Land*, James, huddled with the other boys, watched in despair as the pirates leaped back onto their sleek black ship, taking a few prisoners—*the lucky ones*, thought James. Then the pirates cut themselves loose from the old tub.

As the ships separated, the *Never Land* was seized by a huge wave and heaved violently skyward. James felt the deck tilt sharply. He then fell, hearing the screams of the other boys—Prentiss, Thomas, and, loudest of all, Tubby Ted—as they, too, lost their footing on the sloping, slippery deck.

Grown men screamed as well, as the ship reached the top of the mountain of water and began to slide down the other side, faster and faster, tilting now at an impossible angle. The *Never Land* broke apart, whole sections of the deck tearing loose, the masts splintering like twigs. A crewman was pitched, screaming, into the sea; he was followed by another, and then another. James felt himself sliding, with the other boys, toward the ship's downside rail, toward the angry sea, all of them flailing desperately, trying to grab on to something. By the look of things, James knew that soon enough there would be no ship at all.

"Here, lad!" boomed a voice from behind him. "Over here!"

James turned his head and saw the big crewman—Peter's friend, Alf—holding out a massive hand. James grabbed hold of it, and felt himself hauled away from the rail. The big man managed to rescue the other boys as well, hauling them toward him, somehow keeping them all from sliding off the ship.

"Hold on to each other, lads!" he shouted. "There's a dory this way!" He jerked his head toward the stern. "Hurry!"

Clinging to each other, Alf and the boys half-crawled, half stumbled to the stern, where a battered dory tumbled back and forth on the deck, held tenuously on to the deck by a frayed line.

"Get in, lads!" shouted Alf, untying the line. "I'll put you over the side!"

Prentiss and Thomas clambered into the dory, but Tubby Ted pulled away, screaming, "I'm not getting in that little boat!"

"HURRY!" bellowed Alf. "The next wave puts us on the reef!"

"GET IN!" shouted James, grabbing Tubby Ted's shirt and yanking him, so that they both fell backward into the dory. James's head slammed against the side. Momentarily stunned, he felt Alf shoving the dory, then heard shouts and screams as another huge wave rose high over the ship and crashed onto the deck, sending the dory shooting overboard, and at the same time dashing the *Never Land* against the reef, instantly splintering the old ship into hundreds, *thousands*, of pieces.

The dory capsized the instant it hit the water, but somehow the four boys managed to hang on, scrambling out from under, clinging to the little boat's rough bottom. James looked frantically around for Alf, but saw only barrels and pieces of wood, shards of the ship, tossing in the churning sea.

For an hour, two hours, they clung to the side of the little boat as the sea swept it one way, then another, rain pounding down on them; the smaller boys crying; James trying to comfort them. At last the rain stopped, and the waves diminished, although the sea was still rough. The sky began to clear, first to gray, then to a bright blue. And still the little boat drifted, drifted . . .

And then . . .

"What's *that?*" Prentiss said.

James looked where Prentiss was pointing, and saw it, looming on the horizon. "Something big," he said.

"That's a *mountain*," said Prentiss.

"Land!" shouted Thomas.

"Is there food?" asked Tubby Ted.

"Start kicking!" James ordered.

And they kicked, their excitement momentarily driving the fatigue from their limbs. They kept kicking, but after a few minutes their exhaustion started to return as it became clear they weren't making much progress. The mountain looked as far away as before—maybe farther. The random, powerful thrusts of the sea were far more powerful than their puny legs.

"We'll never get there," said Prentiss, sniffling. "We're going to drown out here."

"No we're not!" reprimanded James, but he feared Prentiss was right. He kept kicking, but, one by one, the others quit, too tired to continue. James saw now that it was no use: the mountain was at a different angle now; the sea was going to carry them past it. James closed his eyes, fighting tears, fighting despair.

"Need some help, lads?"

The boys spun their heads so fast they almost lost their hold on the dory. There, behind them, clinging to a barrel, was Alf. *Smiling.*

"What d'you say we go ashore, lads?" he said.

"We can't, sir," said James. "We've been trying, but we can't."

"Let old Alf give you a hand," said the big man, letting go of the barrel and swimming to the bow of the dory. "Where's that line . . . ah, here we go."

With practiced sailor's hands, Alf quickly tied the line around his chest.

"Hang on," he said, pushing off and swimming, with clumsy but strong strokes, toward the island. The boys felt the dory moving, and hope returning.

It took a good hour more; Alf had to stop and rest repeatedly. But finally they were close enough to the island to see trees, and then a beach; and in another few minutes Alf put his feet down and stood, and the boys cheered in gratitude— to Alf and the Almighty, in that order—as he dragged the tiny boat across a shallow lagoon to the edge of the beach.

James jumped off and ran onto the sand, falling on his knees.

"We're safe!" he shouted.

"I hope you're right," said Alf.

The boys looked at the big man.

"What d'you mean?" asked Prentiss. "Aren't we safe here?"

"That depends," said Alf.

"Depends on what?" asked James.

Looking off into the dense jungle, Alf said, "On who else is here."

CHAPTER 33

LAND HO!

THE JOLLY ROGER PITCHED AND HEAVED in the rolling seas as sunrise broke in a cloudless sky, the storm now past. A shifty fog had settled in the wake of the storm. The *Jolly Roger* cut in and out of it, like ducking behind a curtain.

Black Stache, still wearing the British captain's uniform, climbed onto deck, with Smee following closely behind. Stache rubbed the weariness out of his eyes and released a ferocious belch. Then he froze as an opening in the fog gave him a clear view starboard. At that moment, the shout came from the crow's nest.

"LAND HO!"

"ALL HANDS ON DECK!" Stache hollered, and the disheveled crew, sleepless after a nerve-wracking, storm-tossed night, stumbled onto the deck in ones and twos. They smiled at the welcome sight of the mountainous island, its lush greenery beckoning.

"HEAVE TO, MEN!" shouted Stache. "HOIST THE MAIN AND HARD TO STARBOARD! FRESH WATER AND COCONUTS WITHIN THE HOUR!"

The sailors cheered, setting eagerly to work as Smee, needlessly, repeated the orders.

The *Jolly Roger* quickly drew close to the island, rounding a point of land that opened onto what looked like a fine lagoon anchorage. Stache raised his spyglass, scanning for rocks or reefs ahead, and saw none; he then aimed the glass at the beach.

A line of footprints in the sand!

"Smee," he said. "Ready a landing party at once."

<hr />

"Shut up, so I can hear!" Slank kicked Little Richard, who was snoring at the top of his sizeable lungs.

Little Richard snorted awake, a line of drool from his chin to the floor of the cage where he and Slank were locked in the lowest hold of the *Jolly Roger*. The cage was the ship's brig, but it had also been used as a livestock cage; in fact, Slank and Little Richard were sharing it now with a pig and a cow, neither of which seemed happy with its new cellmates. The two animals huddled together by the cell door, opposite the two men.

Because of the livestock, the brig had reeked when the men were thrown inside; but the stench was even worse now, because Little Richard had been sick in the storm.

"What is it?" said Little Richard, sitting up.

"Quiet," said Slank. "They're shouting." He pressed his ear to the low, damp ceiling, concentrating, then: "They've spotted land!"

"Land?" said Little Richard. "But we're a thousand leagues from nowhere."

"Must be an island," said Slank. "Time for us to get off this ship."

"How?" said Little Richard, looking at the iron bars surrounding them. "We can't bend these."

They'd tried that during the night—both of them gripping a bar and straining against it all their might. But even Little Richard's massive muscles were no match for the brig's bars.

"I've got an idea," said Slank. "Give me your belt."

"My *belt?*" said Little Richard.

"Just give it to me," snapped Slank, taking off his own belt. He joined the two belts, then, standing next to the cow, passed the belts around two of the iron bars of the cell door. The cow shifted nervously, trying to move away, but Slank grabbed the rope around its neck and quickly tied it to the belts.

"Do you see now?" Slank asked.

"All's I see is a cow tied to the cage," said Little Richard.

"To the cage *door*," corrected Slank. "When the cow jerks away, it'll yank the door open."

"But what's going to make the cow jerk away?" asked Little Richard.

"You're going to milk it," said Slank.

"But I don't know how to milk a cow!" said Little Richard.

"Exactly," said Slank.

CHAPTER 34

REUNITED

PETER AWOKE FACEDOWN, with sand in his mouth and a bird on his head. When he spat out the sand, the bird squawked and fluttered into the air, landing a few yards away on the beach, disappointed at having lost its comfortable perch in Peter's thick red hair.

Still spitting sand, Peter stood unsteadily and looked around him, blinking, almost blinded by the glare of the bright sun on the white sand. The beach, curving gently around a deepwater lagoon, stretched out several hundred yards in each direction; ahead of him, maybe fifty yards away, was a line of palm trees; beyond that, the land rose steeply, thick with green vegetation.

He looked at the bird, which was looking back at him.

"Can you tell me where I am?" Peter asked.

The bird said nothing.

"I didn't think so," said Peter.

He itched all over; he was hungry; his throat burned from swallowing seawater. He began trudging toward the trees. His plan was to climb into the hills, looking for a stream; there had to be water, he figured, with all this greenery.

But he was still weak from his ordeal at sea, and when he reached the palms, he decided to rest a bit. He sat beneath a tree, his back against its rough gray bark, and closed his eyes.

He opened them when he felt a shadow fall on his face.

"Hello, Peter," said Molly.

"Molly!" said Peter, scrambling to his feet. "It's you!"

This immediately struck Peter as an exceptionally stupid thing for him to have told Molly, but she didn't seem to notice.

"Yes," she said. "It's me. Are you all right?"

"Yes," said Peter, brushing some sand off his clothes. "I'm fine. And I . . . That is, you . . . I mean, you . . ." He stammered to a stop, his face red.

"What is it, Peter?"

"I mean, thank you, Molly. For saving me."

Molly took a step forward and put her hand on Peter's arm. This felt absolutely wonderful to Peter; he cast his eyes down, lest she see the effect she was having.

"Peter," she said. "It's I who should be thanking you. You helped me when I desperately needed help. You got the trunk off the ship. You risked your life for me. The least I could do was try to keep you from drowning. I'm only sorry I let you fall . . ."

"That wasn't your fault!" said Peter. "I couldn't hold on any longer."

"After you fell," she continued, "I began to descend, and fortunately the wind drove me onto this island, not far from here. I've been searching since then, hoping that you were . . . I mean, I was *so* worried, Peter, and when I saw you against the tree, I . . ."

Now it was Molly's turn to cast her eyes downward.

After an awkward silence, Peter said: "Have you seen a stream? I'm awfully thirsty."

"No stream, not yet," said Molly. "But I think I've found water."

"What do you mean?"

"On the beach, just a bit that way," said Molly, pointing. "There's a barrel; it looks like a water barrel from the *Never Land*."

"The *Never Land*," said Peter, suddenly remembering. "Do you think it was . . . I mean, James and them, do you think . . ."

Molly's look was somber. "I don't know, Peter," she said. "All we can do is hope they're all right. But for now we need to look after ourselves."

"What d'you mean?"

"Well, for starters we should get that water barrel off the beach, before the tide takes it back out to sea. We'll need it if we can't find any other water. We'll also need to find food, sooner or later. And most important, we need to look for the trunk."

"Really?" said Peter. "You think it could have ended up on this island?"

"The barrel ended up here, didn't it?"

"True," said Peter.

"Let's go get that barrel," said Molly. "Then we'll climb this hill and have a look 'round at what else is on this island."

The barrel was heavy; it took all their strength to roll it up the beach. It was sealed with a thick cork stopper, which Peter managed, with considerable effort, to dislodge by banging it with a sharp piece of coral.

The water was warm and brackish, but they both drank greedily. Then, at Molly's insistence, they dragged the barrel into a depression in the land, and covered it with fallen palm fronds. Then she made them back away from the hidden barrel, using fronds to sweep away their footprints.

"Why are we being so careful?" Peter asked. "There's nobody here but us."

"That's true now," said Molly. "But somebody may come, and I don't want them taking our water."

When she was satisfied that the barrel was hidden, she and Peter set off inland. They soon found themselves struggling up a steep mountainside, thick with vegetation—trees, vines, bushes bearing large, sweet-smelling yellow flowers.

Insects hummed around their ears; birds twittered and screeched in the tree canopy above them. At times the vegetation was so thick Peter couldn't see Molly a few feet ahead of him; at times he couldn't even see his feet. He wondered if there might be snakes—it certainly *looked* as though there might be snakes—but he did not voice this thought, as he didn't want Molly, forging resolutely ahead, to think he was scared.

After about forty-five minutes of hard climbing, they emerged onto an open, rocky plateau, from which they could look back and see where they'd been. They were several hundred feet up now, looking down on the lagoon where Peter had come ashore; Peter could see the gouge in the sand they'd made when they dragged the water barrel up the beach.

To the far right-hand side a ridge jutted into the sea, separating Peter's lagoon from another, shallower one, with a wide beach that . . .

What was that?

"Molly!" said Peter, pointing toward the far lagoon. "Look!"

Molly squinted, shading her eyes.

"It's a boat!" she exclaimed. "A little boat, and . . . people! I see three . . . four . . . five of them!"

Peter strained to make out the distant, dark shapes on the white beach. "It looks like four smallish ones, and one

biggish one!" he said. "Oh, Molly, d'you think it's James and them?"

Molly studied the shapes some more.

"Yes, she said, "it's definitely them, and a crewman—I believe it's your friend, the big one."

"Alf!" said Peter, his heart soaring. *Even Alf was alive!* "Let's go down to meet them!"

"Yes," said Molly, suddenly serious. "And we had better hurry."

Peter, hearing the change in her tone, looked at Molly, and saw alarm in her face.

"What is it?" he said.

"See for yourself," she said, pointing off to the left.

Peter looked, and saw it instantly: a ship, heading straight toward the lagoon where he'd come ashore.

A black ship, flying the Jolly Roger.

CHAPTER 35

INTO THE JUNGLE

"C'MON THEN, LADS," said Alf, trudging up the beach. Behind him, walking single file and glancing nervously at the line of palm trees ahead, were James, Prentiss, Thomas and Tubby Ted.

"Sir," James asked, "what're we going to do?"

"We're going to look for water," said Alf.

"And food?" said Tubby Ted.

"Water first," said Alf. "We can go days without food."

"We can *what*?" shouted Tubby Ted.

"Keep your voice down," said Alf. "We might have company on this island."

"Wh . . . What kind of company?" asked Prentiss.

"I dunno," said Alf. "But some of these islands is inhabited by savages."

The word hung in the air. *Savages.*

"Sir," Thomas said, "are savages bad?"

"Not all of 'em, no," Alf answered. "Some are just, what's the word, primitive. Like big children."

"What about the others?" said Prentiss.

"Well," said Alf, "I've heard stories about sailors who were shipwrecked on islands just like this, and the savages come and grabbed 'em and put 'em in a big pot."

"Wh . . . Why did they do that?" asked Prentiss.

Alf stopped, looked back. "Why d'you think?" he said.

"Y . . . you mean they . . . they *ate* them?" said Prentiss.

"Like a Christmas pudding," said Alf, resuming his trudge toward the tree line. The boys were quiet now, thinking unpleasant thoughts, except for Tubby Ted, who was torn between unpleasant thoughts and pudding.

They reached the palm trees and explored the area a bit—that is, Alf explored the area, with the boys staying as close as possible to his reassuring bulk. They found nothing of interest: no water, no food, no footprints.

"That's it, then," said Alf. "We'll have to go in there." He nodded toward the green wall of vegetation covering the mountainous slope rising away from the beach. The boys peered apprehensively at the impenetrable façade of the jungle.

"But, sir," said Thomas. "What if there's savages in there?"

"We got to chance that," said Alf. "If we don't find water, we'll die, and then the crabs'll eat us just as sure as savages would." He started forward, shoving his big frame through a thick mass of vines. They closed behind him like a green curtain, and suddenly he was out of sight. His muffled voice came back to the boys.

"You lads coming?"

The boys looked at one another, all thinking the same thing: they didn't want to go into the jungle, but they also didn't want to be separated from Alf. James, grimacing, pushed his way through the vine curtain, followed reluctantly, but very closely, by Prentiss, Thomas, and Tubby Ted.

As the vines closed behind them, they found themselves in a world quite different from the brilliantly sunlit beach. The sun barely pierced the thick tree canopy above them, its light weakened to a kind of green dusk. The vegetation around them was so thick that they could see no more than a few feet in any direction, and sometimes not even that. There was no path, no opening, only the random riot of the vines and trees, and within a few steps James could not be sure which way they had come from, and which way they were going.

What was more alarming was that he also did not see Alf.

"Sir?" said James. "Sir?"

"This way!" came Alf's voice, even more muffled now, more distant.

"Coming, sir," said James, pushing in the direction he thought the voice had come from.

Behind him, Prentiss said, "I can't see anything."

"Nor I," said James.

From the rear, Tubby Ted said, "There could be anything in here with us, and we wouldn't see it. There could be lions."

"Don't be stupid," said James. "There's no lions."

"How d'you *know* that?" said Tubby Ted.

"'Cause it's an *island*. Lions don't live on islands."

"There could be gorillas," said Tubby Ted.

"What's gillas?" said Prentiss.

"Gorillas," said Tubby Ted. "Big hairy jungle things. They swing through the trees and grab you and take you to their nests."

"Gorillas don't have nests," said James.

"*Course* they do, you git," said Tubby Ted. "Why d'you think they live in trees?"

James could not think of a good answer to that. He glanced up at the tree canopy, thick and dark and close.

Prentiss caught the glance, and his eyes followed it. "Why do the gil . . . *gorillas*, why do they take you to their nest?" he said.

"You don't want to know," said Tubby Ted, meaning, of course, that he was about to tell them. "They crack open your head like a coconut. Then they feed your brains to the baby gorillas."

Prentiss and Thomas looked horrified.

240

"They do *not*," said James.

"Yes they do," said Tubby Ted. "And then they take your eyes and they . . ."

"Shut *up*," said James.

"I want to go back to the beach," said Prentiss.

"Me, too," said Thomas.

"We're not going back there," said James. "We're staying with Alf."

At that moment, all the boys had the same thought: *Where was Alf?*

"Sir?" called James. "Sir!"

There was no answer.

"SIR! CAN YOU HEAR ME, SIR?"

Nothing.

Now they were all shouting, as loud as they could, but nothing came back to them but the hum and whine of unseen insects.

"I want to go back to the beach," repeated Prentiss.

"All right, then," said James. "We'll go back to the beach, and we'll . . . we'll wait for Alf. When he sees we're missing, he'll come back and find us."

"If the gorillas don't get him," said Tubby Ted. "Or us."

"Shut *up*," said James. "All right, we'll . . ."

James looked around him. In every direction, he could see perhaps six feet; in every direction, everything looked the same.

Which way is the beach?

James looked around for a moment, feeling the weight of the other boys' eyes on him.

"All right, then," he said, shouldering his way through the vegetation. "This way."

The unyielding jungle made the going tiring. The weariness James felt in his arms and legs was worsened by the feeling—growing stronger in his gut each minute—that he had gotten them seriously lost. He couldn't tell if he was going in a straight line; he sometimes had the feeling he was walking somewhere that he'd already been, but there was no way to be sure in the unrelenting sameness of the jungle. Behind him, he heard Prentiss and Thomas crying softly, and Tubby Ted's labored breathing as he struggled to keep up.

Tubby Ted's too tired even to talk, James thought. *That's one good thing come of all this*.

As they walked, James regularly shouted for Alf, but there was no response. Every few minutes the boys stopped to rest, and James would try to cheer up the others. But more and more he saw hopelessness on their faces, as well as growing exhaustion on Tubby Ted's. More and more, James had to speak sternly to get them moving again.

He struggled to stay calm, but, as he stumbled forward through the clinging vines, the fears were multiplying in his mind: what if they were still lost when night fell? It was dark enough now, but . . . he shuddered at thought of being surrounded by this jungle in pitch blackness.

"ALF!" he shouted, for the hundredth time, and for the hundredth time he got no answer.

"All right, then," he said, stopping again. "Let's rest here for a bit."

He turned reluctantly, not wanting to see the disheartened faces of the others, but feeling the burden of command. *I wish Peter were here.*

Behind him, Prentiss and Thomas were sitting in a dense growth of low ferns on the jungle floor, their heads down. Tubby Ted was . . .

Tubby Ted wasn't there.

"Ted?" said James. "TED! D'YOU HEAR ME? TED?"

Nothing.

"Wasn't Ted right behind you?" James asked Thomas, fighting to keep the panic he was feeling out of his voice.

"He was, last I looked," said Thomas.

"When was that?" said James.

"I dunno," said Thomas. "A few minutes ago."

"You didn't hear anything?" said James.

"No," said Thomas, sobbing now. "What if a gorilla got him?"

That got Prentiss crying, too.

"Stop it, you two!" said James. "Now, listen. It wasn't any gorilla. Tubby Ted probably tripped and fell, is all. We have to go back and find him."

"I don't want to go back," said Prentiss. "I just want to get out of here."

"Me too," said Thomas. "I'm not going back where there's gorillas."

"There's no gorillas!" said James.

"You don't know that," said Thomas. "You don't even know where we are. I'm not going back."

"Me neither," said Prentiss.

"All right then," said James. "All right. You stay here. I'm going to go back just a few steps and have a look."

"No!" said Prentiss. "You'll get lost!"

"I won't," said James. "I'll be careful. Just a few steps. Stay right here. *Don't move*, you understand?"

Prentiss and Thomas nodded. James edged past where they were sitting and pushed his way back in the direction they'd come from. He followed the broken leaves and branches, walking for perhaps a minute. Then he paused and shouted: "TED! TED! ANSWER ME, TED!"

Nothing.

James looked back and called: "PRENTISS! THOMAS! CAN YOU HEAR ME?"

"Yes!" The two voices were muted, but not far off.

James decided to backtrack a little farther. *Just a few more steps.* He pushed on a short distance, then shouted again.

"TED! TED, IT'S JAMES! CAN YOU HEAR ME? ANSWER ME!"

Nothing.

Not daring to venture any farther away from Prentiss and Thomas, James turned back. He trudged a few yards and shouted: "PRENTISS! THOMAS!"

Nothing.

James's spine went cold.

"PRENTISS! THOMAS! THAT'S NOT FUNNY! ANSWER ME!"

Nothing.

Now James was running, stumbling forward, shouting. In a minute he reached what he judged to be the place where he'd left them.

There was nobody there.

Maybe it's the wrong place.

But it wasn't the wrong place. He could see two flattened areas in the fern patch, where Prentiss and Thomas had sat. This was where they'd been.

"PRENTISS! THOMAS! ANSWER ME!"

Where had they gone?

Alone now, no longer trying to hide his fear, James whirled in circles, shouting, looking, shouting, looking, but seeing only the dark green blur of the jungle. Finally, exhausted, he dropped to his knees, then onto his stomach in the thick, soft ferns. Then he put his face in his hands and cried—big, chest-wracking sobs—until he couldn't cry anymore.

He lay there, face in hands, trying to imagine that he could wish everything away, so that when he opened his eyes, it would all be gone—the pirates, the shipwreck, and especially this awful jungle. Gone. Everything gone but his friends.

But when he opened his eyes, the jungle was still there, surrounding him with its ominous, gloomy silence.

Now, as James's eyes adjusted, as he raised his face from the ferns, he saw that there was something else, right there in front of him.

Two pairs of very large, very brown bare feet.

CHAPTER 36

GETTING CLOSE

MOLLY AND PETER FOUND IT TOUGH GOING; the lower they descended on the mountain slope, the denser the vegetation, until they almost felt as though they were swimming in it, rather than walking through it.

With visibility limited to only a few feet, and with no way to take their bearings, they couldn't be sure if they were still going in the right direction. As the mountain slope became more gentle, they had trouble determining which way was downhill. They found themselves stopping more and more, unsure which way to go.

"Let's yell for them," said Peter. "They can't be far off now."

"No yelling," Molly said. "There are pirates about, and for all we know there may be others here as well."

"What others?" said Peter.

"I don't know," said Molly. "But I'd prefer to find out about them before they find out about us."

And so, having determined—they hoped—which way was downward, they pushed on. Impossibly, the jungle grew even thicker; there were times when Peter, only two steps behind Molly, could not see her. That was why, when he pushed through a particularly lush curtain of hanging moss, he bumped into her back.

"Oof," he said. "Sorry. I . . ."

"*Shhh*," she said, putting her hand on his arm. "Listen."

Peter listened. He heard nothing.

"What?" he whispered.

"I heard somebody shouting," she said. "From that way." She gestured in roughly the direction they'd been walking.

"Shouting what?" said Peter.

"I couldn't make it out," she said. "But it wasn't a man's voice. It was a *boy's*."

"That's them!" said Peter. "H—"

He was stopped from shouting by Molly's hand clapped over his mouth.

"*Shhh*," she said, then removed her hand.

"But why?" whispered Peter.

"Because," said Molly, with exaggerated patience, "as we were discussing one minute ago, *there are pirates about*."

"But they're nowhere near *here*," said Peter.

"You don't know that," said Molly.

Peter, unable to think of a good answer, settled for looking annoyed.

"All right, then," said Molly. "We'll go toward the shout, but we'll go quietly. Agreed?"

Peter said nothing. He wasn't sure about taking orders from her.

"Good," said Molly, moving again.

"You worry too much," Peter said to her back.

She stopped, turned and faced him, her index finger pressed to her lips. And then he, too, heard it: voices in the distance . . .

But speaking a language he'd never heard before. *Grunts* and . . . *clicks*.

Whoever they were, they weren't pirates.

Peter wasn't sure they were human.

CHAPTER 37

HEAVY LIKE A TRUNK

THE TOWERING MOUNTAIN OF ROCK AND JUNGLE, engulfed in soft white mist, rose before Stache's vision like an altar.

"Beautiful, ain't she?" Stache said, in a moment of uncharacteristic reverence. He jumped from the longboat into the now-gentler surf and trudged to the beach, his boots squishing wetly. Behind him, Smee and a dozen of Stache's best men hopped out as well, and dragged the longboat up onto the white sand.

Stache, followed by the others, strode quickly to the line of footprints he'd seen from the deck of the *Jolly Roger*.

"Here they are," he said. "Smee! What do you make of this?"

Smee came puffing up and examined the sand.

"Footprints," he said.

"I *know* they're footprints," said Stache. "What's *between* the footprints, Smee?"

"Ah," said Smee, squinting. "Something's been dragged."

"Very good, Mr. Smee," said Stache. "And how much does this something weigh?"

"Heavy," said Smee.

"Yes, heavy." Stache smiled, his twisted black moustache turning at the edges with the grin. "Heavy like a trunk."

"A trunk!" said Smee. Then, after a pause, he said: "Say, Cap'n, wasn't you *looking* for a trunk?"

"OF COURSE I AM, YOU SEAGULL-BRAINED CRETIN," bellowed Stache. "THE TRUNK IS WHY WE'RE ON THIS BLEEDIN' ISLAND!" Then, calming somewhat, he turned to the pirates and said, "Looks like we'll be taking a walk through the jungle, men."

"It looks a might thick, don't it, Cap'n?" asked one the pirates, hesitantly. "Could be all manner of snakes in there, waitin' to chomp on our legs."

"An excellent point," said Stache. "That's why *you* shall go first."

The pirate's face fell, but he dared not say any more.

"Now," said Stache, looking at another of the men, and pointing to the footprints. "How many d'you figure?"

The man dropped to one knee and studied the sand.

"A bit confusing, it is," he said. "Might be two. Might be four. And"—he turned and pointed to the pirates' prints in the sand—"I'd say they ain't half the weight of us, neither, Cap'n. Children, I'd say."

"Children," said Stache, his face darkening. "That cursed *boy.*"

"But, Cap'n," Smee said, "I don't see how . . . In that storm . . ."

"It's HIM," thundered Stache. "Him and that girl. They're on this island."

"Yes, Cap'n," said Smee.

Stache pointed to the man he'd designated as snake bait.

"Get moving," he said, pointing up the beach at the waiting jungle. "We've got a trunk to find. And a boy to kill."

CTHE CTRANSFORMATION

*I*N THE LAGOON, THE FISH WERE STILL HOVERING. There were nine of them, all females, and for hours they had barely moved, other than to make small, efficient motions with their bodies to counteract the ebb and flow of the wave-surge, and thus keep themselves bathed in the glowing, green-gold water.

They hadn't moved much, but they were *changing*. And *fast*. They still had their tails, though these had grown longer and more graceful. In their midsections, their bodies narrowed and their skin changed abruptly, from rough green scales to a white, fleshy smoothness. This fleshy, forward section now grew larger; a distinct head appeared, separating from the trunk by a slender neck. The eyes, originally on opposite sides of the head, moved closer together. The mouth became smaller, and a bulge of flesh started to protrude above it; ears were sprouting on each side of the head.

On the trunk, the dorsal fin now shrank, absorbed by the body, while the pectoral fins stretched longer, with the ends splaying into distinct fingers of tissue.

These creatures were not human; their features were still crude, their flesh startlingly white, their eyes, huge, shining, almost luminescent.

No, they weren't human. But they were no longer fish, either. And with each moment, as their bodies became less fishlike, so did their brains. No longer were they "thinking" only in simple survival urges—*move, eat, fight, flee*. Now their thoughts were far more self-aware and complex. And, more and more, these thoughts centered on the cause of their wondrous transformation.

They were thinking about the trunk.

CHAPTER 39

$\mathcal{E}$SCAPE

Little Richard was drenched in milk, and the cow was none too happy. But the iron brig door hung open.

"Good job," said Slank.

"Next time, you milk the cow," said Little Richard.

Slank led the way quietly out of the cell. A few yards away was another cell; in it lay Mrs. Bumbrake, sound asleep, snoring. Slank barely glanced at her as he led Little Richard through the ship's stores. They entered a narrow corridor, where Little Richard's huge bulk touched both walls; then they came to a ladder, which led up to the *Jolly Roger*'s galley.

The ship's cook never saw them coming. He became aware of them only when he felt Little Richard's enormous paw pick him up by the neck and toss him casually down the ladderway, like a sack of flour.

With that taken care of, Little Richard, always hungry, grabbed a loaf of bread and stuffed it, whole, into his mouth.

Slank, meanwhile, looked for weapons, grabbing several knives, and handing Little Richard a massive iron skillet.

Thus armed, they headed back toward the ladderway. Slank knew that, with Stache gone, the crew would be slacking. Most likely the only man awake would be the lookout.

"You head straight to the crow's nest," he whispered to Little Richard. "Bonk him on the head quietly."

Little Richard nodded. They poked their heads out into the fresh salt air. Sure enough, the crew was sprawled helter-skelter on the deck, snoozing in the sunshine. Nothing moved but a scrawny red chicken.

Little Richard pushed past Slank, and, with astonishing stealth for his bulk, slipped over to the mainmast and began to climb. A minute later, Slank heard the *thonk!* of the skillet. The lookout was now napping as well.

With a kitchen knife, Slank quietly cut some strips of sailcloth and lengths of rope. Then he and Little Richard took care of the rest of the crew, one by one: the big man would clap his huge hand over a sleeping pirate's mouth, holding him firmly while Slank quickly gagged and bound him.

When the pirates had all been subdued, Little Richard, feeling prankish, hoisted and slung them over the main boom, like human laundry hung out to dry. There was dark fury in the eyes of the pirates, thoroughly humiliated by being taken prisoner, without a fight, on their own ship, *by two men.*

But there was nothing the pirates could do. They weren't

going anywhere, and Black Stache no longer had any back-up from his ship.

While Little Richard was hanging the laundry, Slank located four pistols and two swords. Then, with the pirates watching sullenly, Little Richard single-handedly lowered a dory—normally the job of four men—over the starboard rail, where it couldn't be seen from the island.

Little Richard climbed over the rail and slid on a rope down to the boat. As Slank prepared to do the same, he turned toward the glaring pirates, blew them a dainty kiss, and shouted, "Ta ta, ladies!"

Turning his back to them, he reached beneath his shirt and pulled out a gold locket, checking to be sure the chain was intact. He replaced it, grabbed the rope, and slid down to the boat, where Richard was already at the oars. Slank cast off; Little Richard dug the oars into the water and gave a mighty backward heave; the dory shot forward. Slank reached down and touched the blade of his sword; a thin line of blood instantly appeared on his thumb.

Nice and sharp.

As they rounded the stern of the *Jolly Roger*, the island came into view. The longboat Stache had used to go ashore was pulled up on the beach, but there were no men in sight.

"Take us straight in," Slank commanded, his hand on the sword handle. "We have an appointment with Mr. Stache."

CHAPTER 40

CAPTURED

JAMES STARED, FEAR-FROZEN, at the feet in front of his face. They were like no feet he'd ever seen before: sun-bronzed, callused, with long, curling yellow toenails. Not Alf's feet. Not pirate feet, either.

Savages.

For several eternal seconds, James kept his eyes on the feet, too terrified to lift his head and look at their owners. His body was rigid with terror as he waited for the savages to something horrible to him—bash his head with clubs, or stab him with spears, or . . .

. . . or tap him on the shoulder.

James flinched violently when the finger touched him. From above, he heard chortling.

They're laughing.

Slowly, James raised his head, taking in two pairs of sturdy brown legs, leading up to two filthy loincloths made of some kind of woven fiber; then two muscular torsos, and, finally, the faces of his captors.

They were young men, in their mid-twenties, one slightly taller than the other. Their faces, framed by shoulder-length jet-black hair, were enough alike that the men could have been brothers: both had high cheekbones, jutting angular noses, and dark, deep-set eyes.

They did, in fact, have spears—dark wooden shafts topped with bright-pink tips, apparently fashioned from sharpened shells. But they held the spears upright, and their bemused expressions told James that they weren't planning to stab him.

Not right now, anyway.

For a moment James regarded the savages, and they him. Then the taller one made a lifting gesture with his nonspear hand, which James understood to mean that he was to stand. Legs trembling, he stood. Immediately, the shorter man turned and slipped into the jungle. The taller one gestured that James was to follow his companion. James stumbled forward, trying to keep up with the shorter man, who seemed to move effortlessly through the thick vegetation. The taller man followed close behind James, occasionally prodding him with a finger when they fell too far behind.

They walked in silence, not stopping, for maybe fifteen minutes; James couldn't tell how the savages knew where they were going, but clearly they did, because suddenly they came to a large clearing, roughly circular, easily two hundred feet across. In the center of the clearing was a cluster of enormous trees, unlike any James had seen. Their stout branches, extending outward horizontally, were supported by thick, rootlike shoots that reached down to the ground, forming a labyrinth of columns that surrounded the massive main tree trunks.

James could see people moving around in the shadowy interior of the tree fortress; there appeared to be dozens of them, dark-haired and brown-skinned like his captors, men and women, some of them children. They were speaking, but in a strange language that consisted of mostly of guttural sounds, and a strange clicking noise.

As James neared the trees, his attention was drawn to a place at the far end of the clearing. There a half dozen men holding spears were loosely gathered around a small group of people seated on the ground.

One large person, and three small ones.

Alf and the boys.

James's knees went weak with relief. Prodded, unnecessarily, by the savage behind him, he stumbled toward his mates, who turned toward him as he approached. He saw worry on Alf's face, and fear on those of Prentiss, Thomas, and Tubby Ted. James, suddenly aware of his exhaustion, plopped down next to Prentiss.

The two savages who'd captured him exchanged a rapid

series of odd sounds with the others in the circle. Then they fell silent, watching the captives, expressionless.

Alf glanced up at the men, then turned to James. "You all right, lad?" he whispered.

"Yes, sir," said James. He turned to the other boys. "You all right?"

"I'm sc—scared," said Prentiss, his voice shaking. "When you left to look for Ted, they c—came out of nowhere, and th—they . . ."

He stopped, his shoulders shaking with sobs. James put his arm around Prentiss and said, "It's okay. We'll be okay."

"Oh, *right*," sneered Tubby Ted. "We'll be just *fine*."

James shot Tubby Ted a be-quiet look, but Ted wasn't finished.

"*You* got us into this," he said. "*You* said we should go into this stupid jungle. And *now* look where you've got us. Captured by savages. Thanks to you we'll be killed and *eaten*."

Now Prentiss and Thomas were both sobbing.

"Ted," said James, his voice low but furious, "if you keep that up, I'll kill you myself, you understand? We don't know what they plan to do. So far they haven't done anything to us. They may be friendly. Right, Alf?"

The boys looked at Alf.

"Erm . . . *right*," said Alf, not at all believably. "They could be very friendly."

"Then why did they capture us?" whispered Prentiss. "Why are they watching us like this? What are they going to *do?*"

"I dunno," said Alf. "But I aim to talk to them."

"But how, sir?" said James. "They make those . . . those *noises.*"

"I know," said Alf. "But I've heard some tales in my time about how you talk to a savage. The trick is, keep it simple."

"What do you mean?" said James.

"Watch," said Alf. Slowly, he got to his feet; the savages shifted a bit, getting closer to him, but not stopping him. Alf faced the savage closest to him, an older man, perhaps in his forties. Solemnly, Alf raised his right hand, palm out.

"How," he said.

The savage studied Alf for a moment, then turned and grunt-clicked something to his comrades, who laughed. Then the savage turned back to Alf, and, transferring his spear to his left hand, raised his right hand, and said: "How."

Alf looked quite surprised.

"Now, what?" whispered James.

"I dunno," said Alf. He hadn't really planned it out. His mind raced frantically, but nothing came. Finally he decided to stick with what had been working so far. He raised his palm again.

"How," he said.

This elicited more grunts and clicks from the older savage to his co-savages, who responded with more laughter. The older savage then turned to Alf again, and again raised his hand and uttered another solemn "How."

Alf pondered his next move. On the one hand, the savages seemed to be responding reasonably well to "How." On the other hand, they really weren't making much progress.

At least they're not eating us, he thought.

Ten seconds went by, then twenty, as Alf looked at the older savage, and the older savage looked at Alf. Finally, out of sheer nervousness, and unable to think of what else to do, Alf raised his right hand again. But this time, just as Alf began to speak, the savage rotated his spear from the vertical to the horizontal, pointing it toward Alf's chest. Alf stopped in mid "How," staring at the sharp pink spear tip, inches from his heart.

And then the savage spoke.

Poking his spear tip against Alf's chest, he said: "Can we move this conversation along, old chap? I'm getting frightfully tired of 'How.'"

CHAPTER 41

"WE'LL THINK OF SOMETHING"

PETER WAS BARELY BREATHING NOW. He was right behind Molly, the two of them moving slowly, slowly, through a thicket of vines, placing each footstep with excruciating care, lest they break a fallen branch and give themselves away.

They were very near the voices, which were coming from a clearing just ahead. Mostly it was the strange grunts and clicks, but twice there had been another low, distinct voice, and both times Molly had turned back and mouthed the name: *Alf*.

Now Molly stopped. She'd reached the edge of the thicket, and was carefully pushing some vines aside, making a slit to see through. Peter moved close, looking over her shoulder, careful not to touch her, but very aware of the fact that he liked the way her neck smelled.

As the vines parted, Peter's attention was drawn from Molly's neck to the clearing, which was dominated by a huge tree—actually, a group of trees—in the center, protected by a thicket of odd vertical polelike growths descending from the branches. Moving among these poles were brown-skinned, black-haired people—the men wearing only loincloths, the women in slightly more modest loose shifts, the smaller children happily naked.

"Peter," whispered Molly, nodding toward the right. "*Look.*"

Peter looked, and his heart jumped. There, perhaps fifty feet away, a half dozen spear-wielding men were surrounding his mates—James, Prentiss, Thomas, and Tubby Ted. Alf was there, too, but the big man was standing, holding his right hand up, speaking to the oldest-looking of the men. Whatever he said, it apparently was the wrong thing, because suddenly the savage was pointing his spear directly at Alf's chest.

"He's going to kill Alf!" whispered Peter. "We've got to stop him!"

"How?" said Molly.

"I don't know," said Peter, moving toward the right, keeping just outside the clearing. "We'll think of something."

We'd better think of something.

CHAPTER 42

"It's Here"

Little Richard slipped into the waves without a splash, a difficult job for a man so big, and dragged the dory ashore alongside Stache's longboat.

Slank, a sword and two pistols stuck into his belt, waited for the boat to hit sand, and then hopped out into the shallow water. He strode to the sand, knelt on one knee, and studied the pattern of prints in the sand.

"Two . . . maybe four, children. Black Stache and his men behind them." He pointed out the thick groove in the sand. "Somebody was dragging something heavy."

"The treasure?" said Little Richard.

"The treasure ain't heavy," said Slank. "And it *floated*, don't forget."

"But if not the treasure . . ."

"Wreckage from the *Never Land*, I'd venture to guess. Dunno why they'd be dragging it up the beach." He looked up toward the jungle, and Little Richard followed his gaze.

"We're going *in* there?" he asked.

"A big ape like you . . . afraid?" said Slank.

"Spiders," said Little Richard, sheepishly. "I hates 'em."

"I reckon there's spiders in there big as your fist," teased Slank. "Hairy spiders. Spiders that need a shave."

Little Richard shuddered, then saw something in the sand. "Look here!" he said.

Slank came over to see what Little Richard was pointing to. It was an indentation in the moist sand, with parallel bands running left to right. Between the bands was a pattern of wood grain.

"Water barrel," Slank said. "Whoever was dragging it stopped to rest here. Mr. Black Stache might be a fearsome pirate, but he's not much of a tracker, is he? He's chasing a *water barrel*." Slank barked out a laugh.

"What's more," he continued, "the fool's left his longboat unguarded. We'll tow it around that point"—he indicated a curving spit of sand in the distance—"so when Mr. Stache returns from his water-barrel chase, he'll find he has a nasty long swim to reach the *Wasp*. Meanwhile, we'll be locating that treasure."

"How d'you know it's here?" said Little Richard. "How d'you know the storm didn't carry it off?"

"Oh, it's here, all right," said Slank, his hand going to the chain at his neck. "I can feel it. It's here, and it's going to be mine."

CHAPTER 43

𝒱ISITORS

𝒜LF GAPED AT THE SAVAGE FOR SEVERAL SECONDS before he could get the words out.

"You . . . you speak English," he said.

"Yes," said the savage. "So, apparently, do you."

The savaged grunt-clicked something to the others, who chuckled.

"B—But how?" said Alf.

"Oh, English is easy," said the savage. "You want a difficult language, try this one." He rattled off a bizarre-sounding sequence of grunts, clicks, and pops, culminating in a low whistle. This got another big laugh.

"Yes," said Alf, "but what I mean is, how did you *learn* English?"

"The same way you did, I assume," said the savage. "From listening to Englishmen. I spent thirteen years on ships of the British navy."

"You was a sailor?" said Alf.

"I think a more accurate word is *slave,*" said the savage, "although the term the navy used was *pressed into service.* Twenty years ago they landed here and took me. And my two brothers."

The savage's tone remained conversational, but his eyes had turned cold.

"My brothers responded to captivity less well than I," he continued. "They were both gone within a year. But I was . . . *adaptable,* and quite good at languages. Thirteen years I spent in the company of—doing the bidding of— Englishmen. Thirteen years, until the kindness of fate, and a shipwreck, brought me back home, to Mollusk."

"Mollusk?" said Alf.

"The name we call this island, our home," said the savage. "Actually, our word for it is . . ." He uttered a strange sound, from somewhere deep in his throat. "We call ourselves the Mollusk people. I have the honor of being our leader. My name—or the English version of my name—is Fighting Prawn."

"Fighting *Prawn?*" said Alf.

"Does my name amuse you, Englishman?" said Fighting Prawn.

"No," said Alf, his grin evaporating.

"If I may ask," said Fighting Prawn, "what is *your* name?"

"Alf," said Alf.

"Alf," repeated Fighting Prawn. He said something to the other Mollusks, which included "Alf." They roared with laughter. Fighting Prawn turned back to Alf.

"In our language," he said, "Alf means squid poop."

"Ah," said Alf.

"Now, *Alf*," said Fighting Prawn, getting a chuckle from the men, "these boys"—he gestured to James, Prentiss, Thomas, and Tubby Ted—"are they your children?"

"Oh, no," said Alf. "Them's orphans, from the ship.

"I see," said Fighting Prawn. "And where is your ship at present?"

"Bottom of the sea, I reckon," said Alf. "Storm broke her to pieces, it did. We barely got off with our skins."

"Pity," said Fighting Prawn. "And were there any other survivors?"

"Dunno," said Alf, shaking his head. "It was terrible rough out there. A bloody miracle we found this island, it is."

"Oh, you'd be surprised," said Fighting Prawn. "We get visitors here every year or so. Some arrive through misfortune, as in your case; others arrive with a purpose. At one time, the Mollusks welcomed these visitors. We have learned better."

"Wh—what do you . . . mean?" said Alf.

"I mean," said Fighting Prawn, "that we have learned that things seem to work best on Mollusk when the only inhabitants are Mollusks."

There were a few moments of silence, broken by James.

"Sir, if you please," he said.

"Yes, boy?" said Fighting Prawn.

"What happened to the other, uh, visitors? Do they still live here?"

Fighting Prawn regarded James for a moment, his black eyes impassive. "No," he said, finally. "They no longer live here."

"So," said James, "wh—when visitors come, you let them go?"

"I didn't say that," said Fighting Prawn.

CHAPTER 44

$\mathcal{P}$ARTING $\mathcal{W}$AYS

$\mathcal{P}$ETER STOPPED, HOLDING UP HIS HAND. Molly paused a foot behind him.

They'd moved along the edge of the clearing, following the sound of voices. Mostly they'd heard two—Alf, and another man—*both* speaking English, which puzzled Peter, as the only men he'd seen other than Alf were savages.

Now, approaching the voices, separated from the clearing by only a few yards of thick vegetation, Peter turned and leaned in close to Molly, speaking in the barest whisper.

"How much of that stuff have you got left in your locket?"

"I don't know," she whispered back. "Why? What are you thinking?"

"I'm going to run out there and start yelling," said Peter. "I'll get the savages to chase me into the jungle. Then you can run over to the boys and Alf, and fly them out of there. We can meet on the beach."

Molly shook her head. "No, Peter," she said. "I don't know if I've got enough starstuff left for that. Besides, they would likely catch us both before we took two steps."

"Then what's *your* plan?" said Peter.

"We go find the trunk first," said Molly. "With more starstuff . . ."

"No," Peter interrupted. "They could be . . . dead . . . by then. We don't know where the trunk is. We don't even know if it's on this island."

Molly reached up, wrapped a hand around her locket and said, "It's not far off. I can *feel* it. We *must* find it. It's our only hope to help the boys."

"You don't care about my mates," Peter said. "You just want your trunk."

"That's not true," she said. "Of course I care about them. But, yes, the trunk is more important than any of us . . . than all of us combined. And right now it's also our only hope to help the boys, and ourselves. *Please*, Peter."

Peter shook his head. "I won't leave my mates," he said. "I can't."

"All right," said Molly. "Fine, then. I'll find the trunk on my own."

"Seriously? You won't help me?"

"Help you get yourself killed? No, I won't."

Peter drew back, his expression hurt and angry. "Fine, then," he said. "Good luck finding the trunk . . . *without* me."

Not waiting for her response, he turned and crept closer to the clearing. As he reached its edge, he stopped and looked behind him.

Molly was gone.

Fine, then.

On his stomach now, Peter inched forward until he could peer into the clearing. There were savages standing only a few feet in front of him; beyond them he saw his mates. Alf stood with them. Although he'd heard talking as he crawled forward, there was only silence now, and a fearful look on Alf's face.

Peter patted the ground around him; his hand closed on a rock, and he tugged it out of the damp, spongy soil. His plan now—it was the best he could come up with, under the circumstances—was to create a distraction. He would hurl the rock at the savages, yell, and then retreat into the jungle, hoping they'd chase after him. That would give Alf and the boys a chance to run off.

Holding the rock, Peter slowly rose to his feet.

Here goes nothing.

He took aim at the older savage, who appeared to be the leader. He drew his arm back . . . judged the distance . . . then brought it forward, hard.

Nothing happened. His hand was empty.

Where's the rock?

Peter whirled, then gasped; behind him, nearly on top of

him, towered a large savage, holding Peter's rock up next to his face, smiling broadly.

From the clearing, the older savage spoke: "Ah, I see Fierce Clam has found yet another visitor. Welcome, boy. Come join your friends. I was just about to explain our policy regarding strangers on this island."

CHAPTER 45

THE WATCHERS

BLACK STACHE AND SMEE STRUGGLED to the top of a steep ridge, breaking out from jungle to a thick green, slippery moss, laid like a carpet over a black, gnarly volcanic rock.

They were lost. They'd followed the tracks from the beach into the jungle and almost immediately became confused and frustrated by the suffocating vegetation. For the past hour they'd been thrashing around almost at random, until finally Stache had decided to climb the ridge and get his bearings. He'd taken Smee, leaving the rest of their raiding party at the base of the mountain, with strict orders to keep alert, though Stache was sure they'd fallen asleep within minutes of his leaving them.

Looking down at the menacing green carpet below, Stache held out his right hand, palm up. Smee studied it for a moment, then, concluding they were celebrating their successful climb, reached out his hand and shook Stache's.

"I DON'T WANT YOUR BLEEDIN' HAND, YOU IDJIT!" bellowed Stache, startling a bright-green bird into flight from its perch in the trees just below. "I WANT THE BLEEDIN' SPYGLASS."

Smee quickly tugged the brass spyglass from his waistband and handed it to Stache, who held it to his eye and began a slow, methodical sweep of the island below, left to right. About two-thirds of the way across, he stopped the glass.

"Aha!" he said.

"Geseundheit," said Smee.

"No, you fool, look there!" Stache said, pointing. "At the edge of that clearing. D'you see it?"

Smee peered downward, but saw nothing at the edge of any clearing. He didn't even see a clearing.

"It's a camp," said Stache, still looking through the glass.

"A camp?"

"Savages," said Stache.

"*Savages?* The kind that, that . . ."

". . . that eats people, yes," said Stache. "Cannibals, by the look of them."

"So we'll be getting off this island now, Cap'n?" said Smee. "We'll be getting back on the ship and sailing right . . ."

"No, Smee," said Stache, with a grim smile.

"No? But, Cap'n, them cabinals . . ."

". . . they have the boys," said Stache.

"The boys from the *Never Land*? Alive?"

"No, chewed to the bone," Stache snarled, lunging at Smee, who jumped back. "Of *course* they're alive! It's the same boys, including that cursed little devil who stole the trunk when it was in me grasp. And there's a sailor with 'em, from the *Never Land*. He looks to be talking to an old savage with white hair."

"Talking? To a savage?"

"I'm wondering about that meself," said Stache. "I don't like this, Smee. I don't like it a bit. I'm wondering if the boys still have that trunk, and are using the treasure—*my treasure*, Smee—to negotiate with them savages."

Stache handed the glass to Smee, and stood for a moment, staring toward the clearing, thinking. "Smee," he said. "Fetch the men."

With the telescope now held to his own eye, Smee said, "But them cabinals have *spears*, Cap'n. Lots of spears. Lots of cabinals, far as that goes."

"It's *cannibals*, idjit," said Stache. "Now, shut up, and do as you're told. Them boys down there . . . Mark my words, them boys is still mixed up with that trunk, with *my trunk*. And if them boys is working with the savages, I intend to find out about it. We're going down there, quiet-like, see what's what. Fetch the men *now*."

As Smee, grumbling, started down the mountainside,

Stache turned his gaze back toward the clearing, and spoke softly to himself.

"And if it comes to cutting," he said, "they'll learn that spears is no match for pirate steel."

CHAPTER 46

SOMETHING IN THERE

PETER, PROPELLED BY A SHOVE from the big man behind him, stumbled into the clearing. The big man grunted something to Fighting Prawn, who nodded, then said to Peter, "Fierce Clam thought he heard you whispering. Was there someone with you, boy?"

"No," Peter answered quickly. Then, frowning, he said: "You speak English."

Fighting Prawn sighed. "I'm growing tired of having people point that out to me," he said. *"Préférez-vous que je parle français?"*

"What?" said Peter.

"Never mind," said Fighting Prawn. He grunt-clicked something, and Fierce Clam melted into the jungle, followed by two other Mollusks.

"If there are others," said Fighting Prawn, "we'll find them."

Peter thought of Molly, alone in the jungle, hunted. *Maybe I should have gone with her.*

He shook his head, turning his attention to Alf and the boys, who looked tired and scared, but relieved to see him.

"Are you all right, lad?" said Alf. "When you went overboard, we was so worried. . . ."

"I'm all right," said Peter. "How 'bout you?"

Alf, nodding toward the Mollusks, gave a *Who knows?* shrug.

"We're all right," said James.

"Oh, yes, we're *fine*," hissed Tubby Ted, "except for the part about being captured by savages."

"Savages?" said Fighting Prawn. He stepped toward the seated Tubby Ted. "You think we're *savages*, boy?"

Tubby Ted, whimpering, scooted back a foot on his bottom.

"We're not savages here," continued Fighting Prawn. "I know. I've seen savagery. I saw it often when I was a . . . *guest* of the British navy. I experienced it many times myself, at the wrong end of a whip. Oh yes, boy, I know what savagery is, and it's not to be found here. *Except* when we have visitors."

"Sir," said Alf, "if you please, we ain't savages neither. I'm just an old sea dog, with no great love of the British navy myself. And these here is just boys."

"Yes," said Fighting Prawn. "*English* boys. Who will grow to be English men."

Alf started to answer, but Fighting Prawn turned away, and began walking toward the mass of trees at the center of the clearing. The Mollusks who'd been surrounding Alf and the boys stepped forward, tugged the seated boys to their feet, and began herding the group after Fighting Prawn.

As they walked toward the trees, Mollusks emerged from the labyrinth of vertical branches to watch their approach; by the time they reached the tree complex, the crowd had grown to at least a hundred men, women, and children, staring at Alf and the others, who walked in a close, nervous little clot.

Peter whispered to Alf, "What d'you think they're going to do to us?"

"We'll be fine, lad," whispered Alf, though his eyes betrayed his misgivings.

"They're *savages*," said Tubby Ted. "They live in a *tree*. They mean to eat us. Look."

Coming into view ahead, just past the tree complex, smoke was rising lazily from a large fire pit.

Prentiss and Thomas clutched at Peter, whimpering.

"It's all right," said Peter, putting his arms around the smaller boys, one on each side of him. "Nobody's going to eat us." *I hope*.

They were at the edge of the trees now. Peter tried to peer into the labyrinth of branch-poles, but no matter which opening he looked in, he saw only a few feet before the passageway twisted out of sight, into the gloomy interior.

They moved along the edge of this strange tree fortress until they came to a section where the exterior branch-poles had been fortified with horizontal logs, lashed to the uprights with thick rope made from braided vines. These logs formed a wall easily ten feet high and forty feet wide; Peter could see that the wall curved inward at each end, continuing into the fortress.

Like a cage, Peter thought.

Fighting Prawn stopped next to this wall, and the little procession stopped with him. Now the rest of the Mollusks gathered around in a semicircle, staring at Alf and the children, who faced the tribe, their backs to the logs.

Fighting Prawn began talking to the throng in Mollusk, the tribe listening in motionless silence. His speech dragged on for five minutes, then ten. When he stopped, one of the other Mollusk men spoke, then several of the women. Then Fighting Prawn spoke again, at length; then some others. It seemed to be a debate of some kind—serious, but not heated.

Peter noticed that the bright tropical light had faded slightly. Soon it would be dusk; then night would come to the jungle. He wondered how Molly was doing out there. *I hope she's all right.* He realized that, aside from being scared, he was tired and hungry; it had been a long, foodless day. He leaned back, propping himself against the log wall.

Suddenly, he jerked forward. There was something moving

behind him, inside the wall; he had not so much felt it as *sensed* it. He turned to see what it was, but there was very little space between the logs, and all he could see in the cracks between them was darkness.

But there was something in there.

Staring at the wall, Peter realized that the Mollusks had stopped talking. He turned and saw that the tribe was again staring silently at the prisoners. Fighting Prawn stepped forward.

"Englishmen," he said. "We have made our decision. It was more difficult than usual, because some of you are children. But we have a law for visitors. We have learned that this law is the only way we can ensure the survival of the Mollusk people. We have made exceptions in the past, and we always regretted it. We have since decided that there can be no exceptions, even for children. The law must be applied to you as well. I am sorry."

Fighting Prawn grunt-clicked something. A dozen adult male Mollusks began moving forward. The boys shrank back against the log wall, huddling behind Alf.

"What do you mean?" pleaded Alf. "What law? What're you going to do to us?"

Fighting Prawn didn't answer. The men kept coming forward. Behind them, a column of smoke from the fire pit drifted diagonally into the bright-blue sky. James, Prentiss, and Thomas were clinging to Peter, who found he could not breathe.

"NO!" screamed Tubby Ted. "DON'T EAT ME! PLEASE!"

That brought a grim smile to Fighting Prawn's face. "*Eat* you?" he said. "We're not going to eat you."

Peter exhaled, then froze as Fighting Prawn spoke again.

"We're going to feed you to Mister Grin."

CHAPTER 47

A MAGIC ISLAND

Slank and Little Richard, having hidden their dory and the pirates' longboat, set off along the beach. Slank was in the lead; Little Richard walked a few paces back, armed with a flintlock pistol, which he hoped would be effective against spiders.

"Sir," he asked, "where're we going?"

"Around that point there," said Slank, gesturing ahead toward a rocky spit of land.

"So we ain't going into the jungle?" asked Little Richard, hopefully.

"Not right here," said Slank. "This is where Mr. Stache went in, and I don't want us to run into him quite yet, not 'til we find what we're looking for. We'll go around that point, then we'll move inland."

"Oh," said Little Richard unhappily.

Walking on the hard-packed sand at the water's edge,

they quickly reached the rocky point, a jumble of lava boulders. They worked their way through these until Slank, in the lead, peered over the top of a massive weathered rock and beheld a spectacular lagoon, its deep blue water shimmering and sparkling like diamonds in the late-afternoon sun.

In the center of the lagoon's curve a waterfall burst from one of two hillside caves and splashed down onto a cluster of gigantic boulders. Some yards offshore from these was a smaller grouping of smooth black rocks, like a miniature island. The nearest of the rocks rose to a flat spot, like the seat of a chair.

Somebody, or *something*, was sitting in the chair.

Slank blinked and strained to see it more clearly.

"It *can't* be," he muttered.

"What *is* it, Mr. Slank?" said Little Richard.

"It's a . . . *woman*," said Slank. "But it's got . . ."

"A *woman?*" Little Richard, who liked women as much as he hated spiders, scrambled forward, inadvertently knocking Slank aside as hauled himself up on the rock to see.

"Sir?" he said. "I don't see no woman."

Slank stuck his head back up: The rock was empty.

"She was *there*," he said, pointing. "She was *right there*."

Little Richard eyed Slank doubtfully.

"I tell you I saw her!" said Slank. "She had golden hair. And . . . And a . . ."

"A what, Mr. Slank?"

"A tail," Slank said. "Instead of legs, she had a long green tail."

"A tail?" said Little Richard. "This woman that isn't there now had a *tail?*"

"Yes," said Slank.

"So what you're saying, sir," said Little Richard, "is you saw a mermaid."

"I didn't say that!" said Slank. "I said I saw a woman with . . . with a . . . "

". . . a tail," said Little Richard.

"Yes, a tail," said Slank, although now he was starting to wonder himself.

"All right, then," said Little Richard gently. "Maybe what you need, sir, is a little rest."

"I *saw* her," said Slank.

"'Course you did, sir!" said Little Richard. "'Course you did. Now what you need is a nice sit-down in the shade there, and then . . ."

"Look!" exclaimed Slank, gripping the big man's forearm.

Little Richard looked, and there, on the rock, dripping seawater, were *two* mermaids. One with golden hair, one with black hair, both breathtakingly beautiful.

Little Richard tried to speak, but his throat clogged and his face turned red. Finally he spat it out: "TWO!"

"I told you," said Slank.

"What kind of island *is* this?" said Little Richard, gazing wide-eyed at the mermaids. "It's magical, it is."

"Yes, " said Slank, more to himself than to Little Richard. "There's magic here, all right." His hand went under his shirt and, for a moment, curled around the gold locket he wore there. Then he ducked behind the rock, grabbing Little Richard's massive shoulder and pulling down on it.

"Get *down*," he hissed.

Reluctantly, Little Richard tore his eyes from the fish-women and crouched next to Slank.

"But they're so *beautiful*, sir," he said.

"You'll have a better view soon," said Slank. "We're going over there."

"We *are*?" said Little Richard, overjoyed.

"We are," said Slank. "But quietly. We're not going to let them see *us* until we get nice and close, so they can't swim off. Them creatures has what we're after, and I aim to get it from them."

"But we ain't gonna *hurt* them, sir?"

"Only if we have to," said Slank. "Only if they try to keep it."

CHAPTER 48

The Law

For a moment, neither Alf nor the boys could speak; they stared at Fighting Prawn, faces frozen in dread.

Peter broke the silence. "Please, sir," he said. "Who is Mister Grin?" As he spoke, he again sensed something move inside the log structure. The earth beneath him seemed to shake—something in there, something *very* big.

"Mister Grin," said Fighting Prawn, "is a native of Mollusk Island. For many years he was a peaceful neighbor to the Mollusk people: he went his way; we went ours. But then, some years ago, visitors came to our island—sailors—Englishmen, they were. Like you. They thought it would be good sport to hunt Mister Grin."

Something thrashed inside the enclosure; the walls shook. The boys cowered, scurrying back on their bottoms. Even Alf retreated a few feet.

"We urged these men not to harm our old neighbor, but

of course they did not listen to us. We are *savages*, don't forget. The English are *civilized*."

Fighting Prawn smiled, not pleasantly.

"They were good hunters, these Englishmen," he said. "They captured Mister Grin—managed to snare him with grappling hooks, then drag him up the beach and tie him to a tree with ropes. Then they had their sport. They drank their rum and teased him, prodded and poked to see what he would do, used him for their *amusement*. We asked them to stop. But Englishmen do not care what savages think.

"Finally, a young Mollusk boy could no longer bear to hear Mister Grin's roars of pain. That night, when the drunken Englishmen had fallen asleep, the boy crept among them and tried to cut Mister Grin free. An Englishmen awoke and saw the boy. He shot him, in the leg. The boy fell, screaming. Some of our people saw what happened. The boy lay on the ground, bleeding, screaming. And the Englishmen did nothing. Mister Grin was only a few feet away. Mister Grin was so angry by then . . ."

Fighting Prawn looked at the ground, then at the enclosure, and then back to Peter.

"That boy was my son," he said.

"But, sir," said Peter. "That wasn't . . ."

"We attacked the Englishmen then," said Fighting Prawn, ignoring Peter. "They were surprised that we would do that, and even more surprised when we defeated them. In the end, they cried like babies, begged us for mercy. We told them they would have to ask Mister Grin for mercy. He showed them none."

Another movement from inside the logs.

"We released Mister Grin then, because it was not his fault, none of it. But they'd ruined him, you see? Given him a taste for humans. Instead of returning to the jungle, he stayed near our village, watching us, smelling us, wanting us. Lurking, waiting. We had no choice but to capture and kill him."

"But he's still alive," Peter said.

"Yes," said Fighting Prawn. "As fate would have it, another ship arrived on the day we were to do it. So instead of destroying Mister Grin, we put him to work. Now it is our law, to keep the island ours. For Mollusks, not for outsiders."

"But, sir," said Peter, "those were pirates! We're on this island because pirates attacked us also. We feel the same way about them as you do."

"The lad is right." Alf was speaking now. "We mean you no harm."

"Yes, you would say that," said Fighting Prawn. "You visitors *always* say that, and sometimes you may even mean it. But we have learned that you visitors are *always* trouble, pirates or no. You have abused our hospitality, brought disease, taken us as slaves, killed us like animals. . . ."

"But that wasn't us!" exclaimed Peter. "We didn't do those things!"

"You haven't *yet*," said Fighting Prawn. "And Mister Grin will see to it that you never will. That is our law."

He turned and grunted something. Instantly, two men appeared with a ladder of lashed bamboo. They leaned it against the log wall. From within, there came a low growl. Tubby Ted whimpered. Prentiss and Thomas clutched each other, sobbing. James gripped Peter's arm.

"But, sir!" It was Alf speaking now. "You can't mean to . . . I mean, these are just *boys*!"

"No exceptions," said Fighting Prawn. "It's the law."

He grunted something. Four men with spears approached Alf.

"Wait! There's a trunk!" said Peter, exchanging a quick glance with Alf. "It has powers . . . It's . . . It's *magic*, and we think it's on this island! We could help you find it, sir, show you how to use the power!"

Fighting Prawn shook his head in disgust.

"Lying, now," he said. "They all try that, too. Lying to the savages, as though we're children, easily tricked. Here's your *magic*." He spat on the ground.

"But the magic is real!" Alf said. "I seen it with me own eyes. What the boy says is true."

Fighting Prawn looked back and forth between Alf and Peter, and for a moment, Peter thought Alf might have convinced him. But then the old man grunted again to the four men, who prodded Alf roughly toward the ladder, forcing him to climb.

"No!" said Alf, pointing to the logs. "I ain't goin' in there!"

"Then these men will spear you and throw your body over the wall," said Fighting Prawn. "Either way, you *will* go in there."

As he spoke, one of the men pressed a spear point against Alf's chest. Alf winced as he felt the razor-sharp shell penetrate his shirt and prick his chest.

"All right," Alf said, "I'll go without fight. But only if it's just me. *Please.* Not the boys. They's just *boys.*"

"Boys, yes," said Fighting Prawn. "Just like my son."

Prodded from below, his legs now pricked and bleeding, Alf climbed to the top of the wall. He looked over the side, then back at Peter, his face white as a sail.

"Alf?" said Peter.

Alf started to speak, but before he could, he was shoved over the wall, and was gone.

The boys were next. One by one, first Tubby Ted, then James, Prentiss, and Thomas, all sobbing, were driven at spear point up the ladder and over the wall.

Peter was last. He climbed without prodding. At the top, he looked back down at Fighting Prawn and said, "This is wrong. We've done nothing."

"Yes, you have," said Fighting Prawn. "You came to this island." He paused, then added: "You're a brave boy." He looked once to sky and then back to Peter. "Perhaps Mister Grin will have mercy upon you."

Then he motioned to his men. But before they could act, Peter jumped over the wall to join his mates. And Mister Grin.

CHAPTER 49

INTO THE CAVE

"QUIET!" SLANK HISSED.

Slank and Little Richard struggled, sweating, through the darkening but still-hot jungle, staying out of sight as they followed the sweeping curve of the lagoon toward the dark mouth of the cave.

From time to time they peered carefully through the vegetation at the two green-tailed she-fish. Each time, Little Richard stared, almost hypnotized by the creatures; the closer he got, the more beautiful they looked to him.

In twenty minutes they had crept behind the trees to a spot directly up the beach from the rocks where the she-fish sprawled, unmoving, facing out to sea, apparently oblivious to the approach of the two men.

"All right," whispered Slank. "We want to get as close as we can, but not scare 'em. Understand?"

"Yes," said Little Richard, excited at the prospect of getting close, especially to the blond one.

"All right, then," said Slank. "Here goes." He stepped out from the trees, followed by Little Richard. The two men walked down the beach until the gentle lagoon surf lapped at their boots. They were now perhaps twenty-five feet from the rock where the she-fish lay.

"Hello there, ladies!" said Slank, cordially.

The she-fish spun, their bodies now rigid. They stared at the two men with expressionless faces dominated by round, huge, sea-blue eyes.

Beautiful eyes, thought Little Richard. *But not human eyes.*

"My name is Slank," said Slank. "I think you may have run into something I'm looking for."

The she-fish did not speak or move. For twenty seconds there was no sound but the low hiss of the surf.

"We mean you no harm," said Slank.

As reassurance, Little Richard parted his lips in a broad smile. He had nine and a half teeth in all, the color of tree bark.

The instant he opened his mouth, the already wide eyes of the she-fish became even wider. Before Slank could say another word, the creatures had flipped their tails, slithered off the rock, and slid into the lagoon.

"Wait!" shouted Slank, but they were gone. The men's

eyes followed the long, graceful shapes, gliding underwater with astonishing speed to a dark opening in the jumble of ship-sized rocks nearby. The she-fish surfaced there, looked back for a moment at the men, then dove again, their bodies shooting into a dark opening between two massive boulders, and disappearing.

"You IDJIT!" said Slank, turning and throwing a punch that landed on Little Richard's massive trunk, having no effect other than to hurt Slank's fist. "WHAT DID YOU DO?"

"Nothin', I swear!" said Little Richard. "I just smiled at 'em, is all!"

"Well, don't do it again," said Slank. "You scared 'em, and now we got to go in there after 'em." He gestured at the dark opening in the rocks.

"We do?" said Little Richard, who, in addition to spiders, did not care for the dark.

"We do," said Slank, wading into the lagoon toward the big rocks, with Little Richard reluctantly following. As the water reached his waist, Slank pulled the two pistols from his belt, holding them up to keep them dry.

When they reached the cave opening, the water was up to Slank's chest and Little Richard's waist. The two men paused and looked into the cave. In the late dusk they could see only a short distance: on either side, water sloshed against smaller rocks; overhead was a high, sloping, cathedral-like ceiling, formed by massive rocks leaning together; ahead lay a yawning darkness.

"I don't like this," said Little Richard.

"I've seen you whip six men at once in a fight," said Slank. "How can you be afraid of *women?*"

"Those ain't normal women," said Little Richard. "And it's dark."

"Just the same," said Slank, holding his pistols high as he waded into the gloom, "we're goin' in."

They moved forward, the sound of their sloshing echoing back to them in the dark, cavernous space. Soon they were in deep gloom, barely able to make out the cave walls, no longer able to see beneath the surface of the water.

"Hey!" shouted Little Richard, his voice booming off the walls.

Slank spun, pistols leveled. "WHAT?" he shouted.

"I felt something," said Little Richard. "It touched me leg."

"It's your mind playin' tricks," said Slank. "Stop bein' such a baby." But it was bothering him now, the darkness of the water.

They pressed on, the cave entrance now almost out of sight, their eyes straining to pick up what little of the wan dusk filtered in through openings in the boulders high overhead.

What was that?

Now it was Slank's turn to think something had touched him. He kicked out his right leg, but struck nothing. But now he saw it: something was roiling the water around them.

Little Richard saw it too.

"They're here," said the big man, moving close.

"Stand back to back," said Slank. "Get your sword ready."

They moved together, each facing out. The roiling around them was getting more pronounced now. There was a splash, and the tip of a tail. And then several more, from different directions.

There's more than two, thought Slank.

And then a woman's head appeared, streaming hair, circling, a few yards away; then another head, and another, and another.

A LOT more than two.

"What're they doing?" said Little Richard, behind Slank. "What do they want?"

"I don't know," said Slank, trying to shake the thought: *They led us in here. It's a trap.*

Now, in the gloom, they could make out six, perhaps seven heads circling them, moving very fast, still a few yards away, but Slank saw now that the circle they spun was shrinking. Inch by inch, the she-fish were drawing closer, closer. . . .

Then they stopped.

One of them—the men could see now it was the blond

one that they had seen before—was directly in front of Little Richard, just out of his reach—not that he wanted to touch her.

She looked into his face, her face without expression, blue eyes seeming to glow.

Then she smiled.

Little Richard gasped. The she-thing's mouth was a horror: the top overcrowded with a jumped of jagged teeth, more shark than human; the bottom row was a hard, smooth, bony plate, still more fish than human.

Little Richard raised his right arm, and with it, his sword; he meant the gesture purely defensively, but the instant he moved, another she-fish—Slank's glimpse told him it was the black-haired one that had been outside—hissed and darted forward, snakelike, opening her own hideous mouth and clamping her needle-sharp teeth down on his right forearm.

Slank whirled to shoot it, but Little Richard, bellowing in pain, moved faster; he brought his massive left fist down on the she-fish's head. She emitted a blood-chilling screech and fell away into the dark water.

The cave filled with hisses now as the other she-fish erupted in a frenzy of furious motion. Little Richard screamed in pain as another set of teeth sunk into the back of his left thigh; he reached down frantically, trying to knock the thing away. The water around the two men foamed and boiled; Slank swept his pistols back and forth, but could find nothing to aim at; the she-fish were moving too fast, and mostly underwater.

And then they were gone.

For a moment there was no sound in the cave but Slank's breathing and Little Richard's moans as he felt the pain of his wounds, especially the jagged hole in his leg.

Then they surfaced, perhaps twenty feet away. Five—no, six—of them. One of them, the one Little Richard had struck, was clearly hurt, possibly unconscious; the other five were supporting it, making odd, low noises. They were moving away slowly, toward a bend in the cave wall; as they rounded it, Slank could see them looking back toward the men, could see the fury in their glowing blue eyes, could see . . .

Wait a minute.

There was something odd. . . .

Why can I see them so clearly?

Slank squinted for a moment, and then he realized what it was: there was light coming from somewhere around that bend, from deeper in the cave.

Something in there was giving off light.

"Come on," he told Little Richard, moving toward where the she-fish had disappeared around the curve.

"*What?*" said Little Richard, grimacing in pain. "You want to *follow* those devil things?"

"Yes," said Slank, pushing forward, excited now. Little Richard, not wanting to go, but afraid of being alone in the dark water, followed. They reached the bend in the cave wall, and Slank, holding his pistols in front of him, inched forward until he could see around it.

"Well, well," he said softly.

Little Richard leaned around to see, and gasped.

In front of them was a little cove, at the back of which was a rock ledge, perhaps thirty feet across. Lying on the ledge, to the right, was the injured she-fish, still being attended to by the five who had carried it there. Arrayed along the ledge, and in the water in front of it, were many more—Slank estimated two dozen—she-fish. Behind them, on a pile of rocks at the center of the ledge, was the source of the glow that filled the cavern.

The trunk. It was battered and lopsided, light streaming from its many cracks.

"It's mine," said Slank, mostly to himself.

The creatures, keeping their glowing blue eyes fixed on the men, moved slowly toward the center of the cove, gathering in front of the trunk.

"I don't think they mean to give it up," said Little Richard. "They're protecting it."

"Yes, they'd want to keep it," said Slank. "But I don't mean to let them." He turned to Little Richard. "Go get it," he said.

"Me?" said Little Richard. "But . . ."

"GO GET IT," barked Slank, evoking a flurry of hisses from the she-fish. "If they come at you," Slank continued in a calmer voice, "I'll shoot them."

Still, Little Richard hesitated.

"If you don't go in there," said Slank, "I'll shoot *you*."

Little Richard stared at him for a moment, and saw he meant it. Turning back, he took a breath, and began wading toward the she-fish.

The creatures began darting nervously side to side; the hissing increased. Little Richard glanced back over his shoulder, pleadingly, toward Slank, but found himself looking down the barrel of a pistol. He turned away and took another step toward the creatures, who were very agitated now, opening their mouths as they hissed, revealing those terrifying teeth.

It happened in less than a second. One of the she-fish shot from the pack, mouth agape, straight for Little Richard. As he threw his hands up, the cave rang with sudden sound of a pistol shot, magnified by the stone walls. Incredibly—for the creature was moving very fast—Slank's aim was true: the pistol ball struck it in the neck, and it fell back with a gurgling sound, blood spurting from the wound.

The cave now filled with unearthly shrieks and screeches. Another creature, and now a third, lunged at Little Richard, and Slank fired again. This time he missed, but the sound of another shot, and its ricochet on the stone, was apparently too terrifying for the she-fish. As suddenly as they had attacked, they whirled and retreated. Grabbing their two wounded, the creatures flashed their powerful tails and dove, giving the men—and their terrible weapon—a wide berth, swarming from the cove and toward the cave entrance.

Slank, still holding his pistols leveled, watched them go. Little Richard, barely believing he'd been spared, slowly lowered his hands from in front of his face, took a deep breath, and exhaled.

"That was worse than spiders," he said.

"It's a good thing," said Slank, "they don't know there's but one shot per pistol."

Then he turned, slowly, savoring the moment, toward the glowing, now-unguarded trunk.

"And now," he said, "you're mine."

CHAPTER 50

£YES in the DARK

PETER STUMBLED DOWN A STEEP SLOPE of hard-packed dirt that formed the interior wall of the Mollusks' log structure. He couldn't see where he was going, as the dense tree branches overhead blocked out most of the fading dusk-light.

After a few feet the wall became even steeper, almost vertical, and Peter lost his footing, falling . . .

"*UNH.*" Peter had slammed into a body sprawled on the earthen floor.

"Sorry," he said.

"Get *off* me," hissed Tubby Ted.

"Where are the others?" said Peter, scrambling to his feet.

"Here, lad," said Alf, his deep voice reassuring to Peter. "Over here."

As his eyes adjusted to the darkness, he saw Alf's big bulk, with the three smaller forms of James, Thomas, and Prentiss huddled next to him. They were in a corner of the space, but he couldn't see how large it was; only two walls, disappearing off into the gloom.

He took a step toward Alf, and his foot hit something hard and hollow-sounding. It skittered forward a few feet. James bent and picked it up, then dropped it, screaming.

It was a skull.

"It's all right, lad," said Alf, hugging the sobbing boy. "It's all right."

"No it's *not*," said Prentiss. He was pointing at something, a pile of things. Peter peered at it. *Bones*. He looked around, and realized that the floor was covered with them. Bones and skulls. Dozens of skulls.

Then they heard it, from somewhere off in the darkness. Another growl.

"We have to get out of here," whispered Peter. He turned back and tried to scale the wall, but it was too steep to climb, and he couldn't gain either a handhold or a foothold on its smooth, hardpacked surface.

"Here, lad," said Alf, heaving Peter up onto his shoulders. But as high as Peter could reach, the wall was hard, and smooth, and steep.

"It's no use," he said, and Alf set him back on the floor.

Another growl, this one closer.

The boys backed away from the sound, into the corner, Alf and Peter in front of them, all of them peering into the darkness, watching, listening.

Another growl, still louder. And a scraping sound, like claws. And the rumble of a massive weight, shifting and dragging on the hard earth floor. Coming ever closer.

James screamed again, and as he did they all saw what he saw in the distance, in the darkness, coming toward them:

Two ovals, red, glowing, like coals, each with a cruel black vertical slit.

Those are eyes, thought Peter. *But they're impossibly far apart.*

Another growl. The glowing eyes *moved*.

CHAPTER 51

"*B*IRD!"

*F*IGHTING *P*RAWN AND THE REST OF THE *M*OLLUSKS stood outside the cage, silent, waiting. Waiting for the screaming to start, dreading it, knowing that once the screaming started, it would be much longer—hours, sometimes—before it finally stopped.

The Mollusks took no pleasure in enforcing the law. But Fighting Prawn was their leader, the only one who had lived with the outsiders, and he had told them that this, difficult was it was—especially with children—was the only way they could protect themselves, and their island.

And so they waited, as the evening sky darkened into night.

Fighting Prawn, as always, stood closest to the cage, staring at it, absolutely still. The others gathered around him in a loose semicircle, all of them facing the logs, imagining what was happening inside, waiting, waiting. . . .

It was because they were facing the logs that they did not immediately notice the movement high in the trees just outside of the clearing. It was a small child, a girl of three, who saw it first; she cried out to her mother, her tiny voice making the grunt-click sounds for "bird."

"Bird! Bird!" she said.

"Hush," her mother said.

"Bird!" the girl repeated. "Big! There!"

And then her mother looked up and saw it, and her shout of surprise and alarm caused the rest of the Mollusks to look up, too, shouting as the thing swooped through the high branches at the edge of the clearing, coming closer now, clearly far larger than any bird they'd ever seen, its shape difficult to discern in the near-darkness.

The entire tribe was shouting and pointing now. Suddenly, the thing burst from the trees into the clearing, swooping low toward the Mollusks. Some screamed; others ducked; still others ran. A few men hurled spears toward the thing. But it was moving too fast, and in an instant it was over the wall, into the cage, out of sight.

Fighting Prawn, standing calmly amid the chaos of his people, watched the swooping thing pass overhead; for an instant, as it disappeared, he thought that it looked like . . .

But that's impossible.

And then his mind went to something the boy had said: *"It's magic, and we think it's on this island."*

CHAPTER 52

MISTER GRIN

THE GLOWING EYES WERE COMING.

"Get behind me, lads!" shouted Alf, crouching, preparing to fight—*but what*, he wasn't sure.

Peter, ignoring Alf, dropped to hands and knees, looking in the gloom for a weapon. He grabbed a heavy bone—*Must be a leg*, he thought—then found its mate, which he handed to Alf.

The thing was coming fast, now. The cage echoed with the sound of claws scrabbling on the floor, and massive weight being dragged closer, closer. Now Peter could see the massive, flat head. And now the glowing eyes disappeared from view as the thing opened the biggest mouth Peter had ever seen, lined top and bottom with jagged teeth as big as daggers, a gaping cavern of a mouth that easily could have taken him in whole. The cage echoed with a monstrous, bone-chilling roar. Then the enormous mouth snapped shut with a sound like a gunshot and the thing sprang forward at its prey.

"NO!" bellowed Alf, leaping forward to meet it, swinging the leg bone down hard with both hands onto the massive charging snout, and right in time. The bone broke in two; the creature stopped for a moment, as if surprised. Then it snapped again, and lunged at Alf, who sidestepped, trying to draw it away from the boys. His ploy worked; the thing turned toward him, pivoting its huge body, sending its massive tail—a tail, Peter now saw, that was the size of a longboat—sweeping across the wall, sending Peter and the other boys flying.

"COME ON, YOU DEVIL!" Alf was shouting. "COME ON AND FIGHT LIKE A MAN!" He was walking backward, trying to keep his eye on the monster as he looked around desperately for another weapon. Peter lunged to his feet and followed, careful to keep out of the way of that terrible tail, his plan being to toss the other leg bone to Alf. As the tail swept back and forth, Peter jumped over it as though it was a jumprope.

"ALF!" he yelled.

"STAY BACK, BOY!" shouted Alf. "ST—UNH."

Alf was down. He'd tripped on a skull, and he'd hit his head hard. He moaned and rolled sideways, but did not get up. The monster opened its mouth again; it would be eating Alf in another step.

"NO!" screamed Peter, leaping forward, again dodging the sweeping tail, and bringing his bone-club smashing down on the thing's hard, scaly back. "NO! NO! NO!" he shouted, each time striking it again. The monster whirled and snapped, moving far faster than Peter expected. Peter jerked his hands back just far enough, but the bone was caught, instantly crunched to splinters in the monster's massive jaws.

Now it was Peter's turn to scramble backward, with the thing turning in his direction, coming after him . . . coming, coming . . . its glowing eyes strangely dispassionate, a hungry beast about to do its work. As Peter backed away, he simultaneously crouched and felt around his feet for another bone . . . for anything . . . He touched nothing but hard ground. He backed up some more. Hit something hard.

The wall.

He was trapped in the corner.

The monster paused, as if knowing Peter had no way out. It halted and then slowly opened its massive mouth, close enough now that Peter could smell its musty, fetid breath. He could have reached out and touched the dagger teeth that were about to tear into his flesh.

Peter closed his eyes and held out his hands in a futile gesture of self-protection, and as he did . . .

"Peter!" shouted a voice.

Molly!

He opened his eyes and saw her hovering above him, waving something.

"Here!" she shouted, dropping it.

He caught it. *The locket.* He fumbled frantically at it, but could not find a catch.

"It won't open!" he shouted.

The beast moved closer, its jaws wide open.

"There's a button on the side," shouted Molly.

Closer.

Hands shaking, Peter found the button, and the locket sprang open. Instantly his hands disappeared inside a glowing sphere.

"Touch the inside part!" shouted Molly

Peter put his finger into the heart of the sphere, and immediately he felt his body start to rise, felt his feet leave the floor. . . .

Too late.

He saw it in an instant; the jaws were closing, and they would catch him.

Too late.

Instinctively, Peter struck out at the closing jaws; his right hand, with the locket still in it, landed directly on the tip of the monster's snout, which was suffused by the sphere.

The jaws stopped, half open, half closed.

The monster made a noise—not a roar, this time; more of a groan, or even a sigh.

And then, slowly, slowly, the monster began to rise from the floor of the cage, its body perfectly still, and in the light from the locket, Peter—who was also rising, slowly—could finally see its true size. *It has to be twenty-five feet long,* he thought. *Maybe thirty feet. It must weigh a ton.*

But it rose like a feather, the monster did; rose as easy as a bit of ash carried by a wisp of smoke, up, up, and then over the thick log wall. And then, with a flick of its tail, it drifted, still sighing, off into the jungle night.

CHAPTER 53

THE POWER

BLACK STACHE, WITH SMEE and the rest of his raiding party crouched behind him, peered through the dense jungle into the camp of the savages.

It looked to Stache as if the whole lot of them were praying to a giant wall made of wood and mud. They stood silently facing it, man, woman and child.

Stache was intensely interested in what was on the other side of that wall. For only moments earlier, he'd seen the boy—*that* boy, the cause of so much of Stache's troubles— climb a bamboo ladder, say something to the white-haired old savage below, and then disappear over the wall.

Where that boy is, the trunk is nearby. Stache was sure of it. He was eager to lead his men over that wall, but unsure of the disposition of the savages. And so he waited, and watched, and listened.

"NO!"

The shout—from a grown man—came from the other side of the wall. The man sounded terrified. His shout was followed by a loud, unnatural snapping sound, like . . . could that be a *bone*? Stache wondered what could snap a bone like that.

Just then a little girl savage turned his way, pointed, and started shouting. Stache ducked, thinking at first that she'd spotted him. But then he heard a rustle in the branches above. He looked up, and gasped.

A flying girl. Directly over them. Swooping like a bird.

The same girl that had been on the ship. He was sure of it.

"Sir," whispered Smee, pointing, "there's a *mmmpph.*"

"I *see* her, idjit," hissed Stache, clapping his hand over Smee's mouth.

The girl swooped swiftly across the clearing and, as the natives shouted and pointed in alarm, disappeared over the wall.

Stache was worried now. All this flying, he was now certain, had something to do with the treasure he was after. The flying boy had gone over the wall, and now this flying girl. He decided that, savages or no, it was time to find out what was on the other side of that wall.

He signaled to his men. They rose, drawing swords and pistols. Facing the clearing, Stache held his hand up, about to give the signal to attack.

Then his arm dropped, limp, staring in astonishment. His men followed his gaze. Several shouted in alarm, but there was no danger of their being heard by the savages, who were now in loud disarray themselves, many shouting and running frantically to get away from the gigantic creature now emerging from behind the wall.

A crocodile, Stache thought as the thing floated fully into view. *A flying crocodile*.

Stache had seen crocodiles before; he'd seen dozens. But never one this large. Never one *half* the size of this monster. He stood, motionless, as the croc drifted his way, thirty feet in the air, its tail swishing back and forth lazily, its legs moving as though it were swimming. It passed almost directly overhead, then continued off over the jungle treetops.

Stache watched it disappear, then looked at his men, who were looking back at him with expressions ranging from concern to outright terror.

"All right, men," he said. "It's a crocodile. You seen crocodiles before."

"Not flyin', we haven't," said one of the men. "Nor a flyin' girl, neither."

It was an unheard-of display of impudence, but Stache saw that the man spoke for the others. Fearing a mutiny, he forced his voice to stay calm, asking the man, "What's your name, son?"

"Simons," said the man.

"Simons," Stache said gently, making a mental note to kill Simons when he was no longer needed, "I admit it ain't usual to see a flyin' croc. Nor a flyin' girl. But I know what's doin' it. It has to do with this treasure we're after, see? It has a great power, it does, the power to make people fly, and more. Power is better than gold, men. *Much* better than gold. With the power this treasure gives you, you can have all the gold you want for the takin'. That's what we're after, men, and once we gets that trunk, you'll all be sharin' in it."

And if you believe that, you're as stupid as you look, he added to himself.

He saw he had the men's interest now, having brought their minds back to the treasure, having shown the connection between it and the things they'd seen. He pressed his advantage.

"Now, look," he said. "That old croc is gone now. And them savages is run off into the jungle, most of 'em, except that old man out there. There ain't nothin' between us and that wall, and there ain't nothin' behind that wall now except children. And I got a feeling the treasure's right near by them somewhere. It's *right here*, men. Right in our hands."

The men were nodding. He had them now.

"All right then," said Stache. "Grab your swords and . . ."

He stopped, seeing the expressions on the men's face suddenly change as their gazes shifted to something behind him.

He whirled, looked, and cursed.

Now the children, holding hands, were rising slowly into the jungle sky.

CHAPTER 54

SLANK'S PLAN

"PORT," SLANK SAID. "No, port is *left*, idjit! *That* way!"

Little Richard—who, despite years at sea, could never get the port-starboard thing straight in his mind—corrected course.

The huge man was rowing the dory, with Slank in the stern. They were towing Black Stache's longboat, in which sat the battered wooden trunk.

Little Richard, at Slank's order, had carried the trunk from the cave. He'd been reluctant at first—fearful of following the she-fish, and in severe pain from the two gaping bite-wounds they had inflicted. But when he touched the trunk, his mood changed almost instantly: a feeling of warmth, of well-being, of *joy* flooded his battered body. And there was more. . . .

"D'you hear that?" he'd said to Slank, as he slung the trunk—it felt almost weightless—onto his shoulder.

"Hear what?" asked Slank.

"Bells," said Little Richard. "Y'don't hear 'em?"

"No," said Slank, eyeing Little Richard sharply.

But as they had trudged out of the cave, Little Richard still heard the bells, and when they reached the mouth, he noticed something else: the pain from his wounds was gone. He looked down at his forearm, and grunted in surprise.

"What?" said Slank.

"Look," said Little Richard, pointing to his arm.

Slank looked. The wound was gone. Where minutes ago there had been mangled flesh and oozing blood, there was only unbroken skin.

"My leg, too!" said Little Richard, feeling the back of his thigh.

"Put down the trunk," said Slank, sharply.

"But . . ."

"Put it down *now*," said Slank.

Little Richard had trudged to the beach and set the trunk on the sand. As he released it, the sound of bells faded, died. He reached his hand back toward it. . . .

"Leave it *alone*!" said Slank. Reluctantly, Little Richard withdrew his hand.

"I'll stay here with the trunk," said Slank. "You go get the boats. Row the dory back here, and tow that pirate's long-boat with you."

"Why don't we just carry the trunk to the boats?" said Little Richard. "I don't mind carrying it."

Because I don't want you touching it, thought Slank, but all he said was: "Get them boats NOW!"

When Little Richard returned with the boats, Slank loaded the trunk into the trailing longboat, then climbed into the dory and ordered Little Richard to row them back to the pirate ship.

Slank was feeling very, very good about the way things had worked out. First, and most important, he had the trunk. *He had the trunk.*

He also had the longboat, which meant Black Stache was now marooned on the island. Slank smiled.

The fool pirate. He never really knew what he was after. Nor who he was up against.

Slank's plan now was to return to the pirate ship and have Little Richard toss most of the tied-up crew overboard, keeping just enough men—he'd need only two or three—to sail the ship at pistol-point. And when he got where he was going, he'd get rid of those as well. And of course the idjit Little Richard, who knew too much, now.

Yes, things were looking very, very good, Slank thought. Even the night was pleasant. The sun was down now, and a full moon had risen; it hung low over the lagoon, looking impossibly large in the cloudless sky, as though it had drawn closer to Earth to get a better look at this strange island. The light shining from it was bright enough to cast shadows, bright enough that Slank could easily see the deserted beach, and the palm trees beyond, and the dark mass of the mountains.

It was bright enough that, if Slank had been looking at the water behind the longboat, he would have seen something else.

A trail of bubbles, following them.

Getting closer, and closer . . .

$\mathcal{A}$ Close Call

"$\mathcal{H}$ANG ON!" SHOUTED PETER.

"I'm scared!" whimpered Prentiss, looking down as they soared over the wall. "I don't want to fall!"

"You won't fall," said Peter. "You're flying!"

And they were, all of them. Molly was first, followed by Peter, who was holding the hand of Prentiss, who was holding the hand of James, who was holding the hand of Thomas, who was holding the hand of Tubby Ted, who was holding the huge hand of Alf, who hated heights and had his eyes tight shut.

Moments earlier, just after Mister Grin had floated out of the cage, Peter, urged on by the hovering Molly, had each of the others touch the glowing sphere in his hands. Then he'd snapped the locket shut and ordered them all to hold hands as they began to rise.

Peter, the only boy with flying experience, followed Molly, gently towing the others over the wall. As they cleared it, he looked down nervously, concerned that the Mollusks would use their spears to bring them down. But the surprise appearance of the flying Mister Grin had plunged the tribe into disarray. The only one remaining by the wall was the old man, Fighting Prawn. He stood still, watching, expressionless, as Molly, then Peter and the others, floated into view in the now-moonlit sky.

Peter's eyes met the old man's.

"I told you," Peter called down. "There's magic."

Fighting Prawn said nothing, only stared back at Peter. Their eyes remained locked for a moment more, then Peter's attention was drawn away by Molly's shout.

"Peter!" she said. "We must get back to the beach before it wears off! This way!" She turned and swooped low over the dark jungle.

"All right," Peter said to Alf and the boys. "We're going to follow Molly. You need to lean forward, like this." He leaned, and his pull on the others increased.

"Not me," said Tubby Ted, looking down nervously. "I ain't leanin'."

Alf, likewise, remained rigidly vertical, petrified with fear. Prentiss and Thomas were still too stunned to respond. But James—*good old James*—was leaning. With his help, Peter was able to get the little hand-holding clot moving— slowly at first, and then picking up speed—across the clearing, and then over the treetops.

Peter's eyes probed ahead over the moonlit treetops, trying to make out Molly's distant, swooping form. Thus absorbed, Peter didn't notice that, as they left the clearing, they passed directly over Black Stache and his pirate crew. He didn't see Stache raise a pistol and aim it straight at Peter's heart.

It would have been an easy shot, and Stache came *this* close to pulling the trigger. But much as he wanted to kill the boy, he wanted even more—having seen its power—to find the trunk, and he was sure the boy would lead him to it.

Only a few yards away, Fighting Prawn was thinking precisely the same thing.

CHAPTER 56

CAPSIZED

THE FIRST TIME THE DORY LURCHED, Slank assumed it was a wave, although if he'd looked around, he'd have seen that the lagoon was dead calm now, its smooth surface turned silver by the brilliant moon rising in the east.

But Slank wasn't paying attention to the water; his eyes were locked on the trunk resting in the longboat being towed by the dory.

The next time the dory lurched, Slank blamed Little Richard's rowing.

"Stop that!" Slank complained.

"If you'd stop shifting your weight, sir," Little Richard said, "we'd make smart time to the ship."

"I ain't shifting nothing," Slank said. "It's your . . ."

But before he could finish, the longboat rocked violently, nearly taking on water as the trunk slid to the side. Alarmed, Slank lurched to his feet, nearly swamping the dory. He would have gone overboard if Little Richard hadn't turned and grabbed him. Slank lunged for the line and tried to pull the longboat—and the trunk—toward him, but it didn't move.

"Give me a hand, here!" he shouted to Little Richard.

The big man slid next to Slank and leaned over the transom of the dory, which, because of the weight of the two men, was now nearly submerged. The men jerked back suddenly as a hideous gaping mouth of razor-sharp teeth shot, hissing, from the water.

"It's them mermaids!" shouted Little Richard, as he and Slank tumbled backward in the bouncing dory.

The creature came down hard, her teeth sinking into the transom; she twisted her head viciously and tore off a half-moon shaped piece of wood, leaving a jagged half-moon-shaped space, through which water began to spill. As she disappeared, another she-fish attacked to starboard, and then another to port, the two rocking the boat in a deadly game of seesaw. Slank rose, trying to scramble away from the she-fish closest to him, only to be smacked hard from behind by the powerful tail of the other, propelling him over the side, his yell for help cut off when he plunged beneath the surface of the lagoon.

Slank's sudden departure left the dory unbalanced, and before Little Richard could correct it, the she-fish capsized the boat, dumping the big man into the lagoon as well.

The two men thrashed to the surface, struggling to stay afloat in their heavy clothes, weighed down by swords and pistols that they quickly jettisoned and let sink to the bottom.

The water boiled ominously around them. Little Richard screamed as he was bitten on his right leg, then his left.

Slank, paddling furiously, managed to get to the longboat. As he grabbed the gunwale, he felt the searing pain of teeth sinking into his thigh. He let go of the boat to strike at his attacker, and as he did, the longboat went over, and the trunk tumbled into the lagoon, where it . . .

. . . floated.

Slank lunged for it, but missed. *It was moving.* Sitting atop the water surface, barely an inch of it submerged, the trunk turned left, paused, then right, and finally moved off briskly back toward the island, leaving a V of ripples, like a long, fading, arrow in the silver lagoon. In the middle of the V rose parallel lines of bubbles.

Little Richard sputtered to the surface, bleeding, cursing.

"Here," called Slank, and Little Richard paddled over. They clung to the longboat, which was lying hull-up in the water.

Slank lifted his head and squinted across the lagoon. The watery arrow, led by the slowing shrinking trunk, was heading back in the direction they'd come from, back toward the she-fish cave.

"You think you've won, do you?" muttered Slank. "We'll see about that, ladies."

"What are we going to do?" said Little Richard.

In answer, Slank, pulled out his locket, then said: "How are you with heights?"

CHAPTER 57

AN OLD FRIEND

PETER AND THE OTHERS just made it to the beach. The starstuff began wearing off while they were still over the jungle; for a few moments, Peter thought they would be plunged into the thick, dark vegetation underlying the moonlit tree canopy. He didn't relish the thought of being lost in there at night.

But with James's help, Peter was able to drag the little hand-holding group of reluctant fliers into one last swoop-and-soar, and this time, as they reached the apex of their upward curve, he heard Molly just ahead, shouting and pointing, and then saw, to his great relief, the white of the beach, looking like snow under the startlingly bright moon.

"Hang on!" he shouted. "We're coming down over there."

They just cleared the last set of palms—in fact, Alf's feet brushed the highest one, sending a coconut thudding to the sand—and then they crash-landed onto the beach, tumbling and rolling a few yards from where Molly was waiting. They were at the edge of a sandy cove, bounded on either side by steep, rocky hillsides.

For a moment, Alf, James, Prentiss, Thomas, and Tubby Ted stood speechless, brushing off sand and absorbing their disbelief at their flight, and relief at being on the ground again. Then the questions started.

"How did we *do* that?" asked Prentiss. "How could we, I mean . . ."

"And the crocodile!" interrupted Thomas. "How did . . ."

"I'm hungry," said Tubby Ted. "Is there any . . ."

"And that thing!" said James. "That thing we touched! What *was* that? It felt so . . ."

"It was the magic from the trunk, wasn't it, lad," said Alf. "You must've . . ."

"Can we fly *again?*" said James.

"Yes!" said Prentiss and Thomas, simultaneously. "We want to . . ."

"All right, all right," said Peter. "I'll try to explain, though it's a bit, um, strange. But first I have to . . . uh . . . Listen, just wait here a minute."

Peter walked to where Molly was standing, watching him, her expression blank as he approached.

"You came back," he said. "To rescue me." He blushed. "I mean, *us*."

"Yes," she said.

"Thank you," he said.

Molly didn't answer.

"But you said you couldn't," Peter said. "You said you had to get the trunk. You said that was the most important thing."

"It is," she said. "And I should have left you. Now I don't know how much starstuff I have left in that locket, and it's night, and the pirates are on the island, and I fear they already have the trunk. It's been *moving* Peter; I've felt it. Somebody has found it, and whoever it is won't want us to have it. And now those natives will be after us, and that crocodile is loose somewhere, and . . . and I'm just afraid it's *hopeless*."

Peter saw she was crying. He wanted to hug her, but he couldn't, not with Alf and the others watching. He settled for patting her shoulder.

"It'll be all right," he said. "We'll find the trunk."

Molly forced a wan smile. "I appreciate that, Peter. I know you want to help. But at this point I honestly don't know what to do."

"You say you can feel the trunk," said Peter.

"Yes."

"D'you know what direction it's in?"

"No, only that it's moving."

"Well if it is, then somebody's moving it, and perhaps

we'll be able to see it. In the morning, we'll climb that mountain again and have a look."

Molly nodded. "I suppose that's as good a plan as any."

"In the meanwhile," said Peter, "we need to get some sleep, if we can. We can set up a watch, in case somebody comes along. Or that *thing*." He shuddered, thinking about Mister Grin.

"All right," said Molly, her spirits picking up a bit, now that they had a plan.

"And I should give you this back," said Peter, reaching for the locket around his neck. "You might . . ."

"Did you hear that?" Molly said, her hand on Peter's arm.

"What?" said Peter. "I didn't . . ."

"*Shhh*," hissed Molly. She cocked her head, listening, then smiled.

"It's him!" she said, tossing the words back over her shoulder, as she was already running toward the water.

"Who?" said Peter, running to catch her. But her attention was focused ahead, and the sounds she was making were not intended for him.

And then Peter saw a familiar shape—a blunt and grinning snout, sticking up from the moonlit wavelets perhaps ten yards offshore, clicking and chittering in return.

"Ammm!" Peter shouted.

CHAPTER 58

CROSSROADS

BENEATH A THICK TREE CANOPY ringing with monkey howls and other jungle sounds, Black Stache led his band of pirates, following a path that meandered in the general direction that the flying children—and Mister Grin—had gone.

Smee, jumping at every sound, said, "Cap'n, what if that humongous flying lizard landed somewheres ahead, here?"

"Weren't no lizard," said Stache, over his shoulder. "That was a croc."

"Whatever it was, Cap'n," said Smee, "it might be up ahead here. Maybe we should . . ."

He stopped, because Stache had turned, scowling.

"Maybe we should *what*, Smee?"

"W . . . well, Cap'n," stammered Smee, "with that . . . that *thing* flying around here, and those children, *them* flying, too, it's just all so strange on this island, Cap'n, and it bein' night and all, I thought, that is, *we* thought, that is, me and the men here, we thought maybe if we waited 'til daylight, we could . . ."

"You thought?" interrupted Stache. *"You thought?"* He glared at Smee, then at the men standing nervously behind him.

"Y . . . yes," began Smee. "I, that is, we . . ."

"YOU DON'T THINK!" thundered Stache, causing Smee and the others to jump like a gaggle of puppets all attached to the same string. "*I* do the thinking, you understand?"

"Aye, Cap'n," came the chorus of replies.

"Good," said Stache, and resumed walking.

The fact was, Stache—although he would never let his men know—was also quite uneasy about going the same direction as the croc. He was not fond of crocs, having fed people to the beasts on a number of occasions, and seen firsthand the terrible things their jaws could do. And a croc of this monstrous size, *flying* . . .

No, Stache did not relish encountering the thing. But he *had* to find those children. *Flying* children. He had no doubts about it now: *They can fly.* And Stache meant to have the source of that power.

Overhead, the thick tangle opened a bit, and then more, the full tropical moon shining down, nearly as bright as the English sun, illuminating a clearing where two paths intersected. A jungle crossroads.

Stache considered the paths.

"Crenshaw! Bates!" he said. Two men stepped reluctantly forward.

"You two are volunteering for the scouting party," said Stache. "Crenshaw, take this path to the south. Bates, you'll head west. You *listen* and you *look*, but you will not *be heard* and you will not *be seen*. Am I clear on that?"

"Aye . . ."

"Aye, Cap'n."

"We're looking for them kids, or the treasure, or both. You report back to me the moment you see anything of interest. You have 'til the moon's straight overhead. Then we'll be taking the south path . . . that's toward you, Crenshaw. Am I clear on that?" He didn't wait for their answers. "Go!"

As the two scouts trotted off, unhappily, in different directions into the dark jungle, Stache and his men made themselves comfortable in the moonlit clearing. Nobody spoke, but each man, Stache included, was thinking the same thing.

Glad it's not me, going out there alone.

CHAPTER 59

AMMM'S MESSAGE

PETER TROTTED DOWN THE BEACH toward Molly, who was now waist-deep in the moonlit cove, squeaking and chittering as she waded toward the upthrust, grinning snout of Ammm.

James, trotting alongside Peter, said, "What is it? What's she doing?"

"She's talking to the porpoise," said Peter. "His name is Ammm."

"Fish can *talk?*" said James.

"This one can," said Peter.

"What's it saying?" said James, as they reached the water's edge.

"I dunno," said Peter. "I don't speak Porpoise. But Molly does. She'll tell us."

They were now standing next to Molly, with Ammm several feet in front of them, listening politely. Molly, desperate for news from her father, forced herself to remember the mandatory opening formalities of porpoise talk.

"Greetings," she said.

"Greetings," said Ammm.

"Molly teeth green," said Molly.

"Yes," agreed Ammm. "Molly teeth green."

"Molly happy see Ammm," she said. The Porpoise language has 237 words that mean "happy," and Molly had actually chosen the one denoting the happiness derived from having one's belly tickled by seaweed. Ammm doubted that Molly was feeling this particular happiness, but out of politeness used the same word in responding.

"Ammm happy see Molly," he said.

With the formalities concluded, Molly took a breath and frowned in concentration, not wanting to make any mistakes as she got to the critical question:

"Molly father come?"

Ammm paused for several moments, during which Molly did not breathe. Then Ammm said, "Yes. Molly father come."

Molly exhaled, and, in English, said, "Thank heaven."

"What?" said Peter.

"He says my father is coming," said Molly.

"When?" said Peter.

"I don't know," said Molly. Switching back to Porpoise, she said, "When Molly father come?"

"Day," said Ammm.

Molly frowned. "What day?"

Ammm hesitated, as if confused by the question, then repeated: "Day."

"Day," said Molly.

"Day," said Ammm.

"What's he saying?" said Peter.

"I'm not actually sure," said Molly. "I think he's saying 'day,' but my Porpoise is not very good, and the Porpoise language is vague about time. If he *is* saying day, he could mean my father is coming tomorrow, but I think he also could be saying it will be more days."

"I hope he means tomorrow," said Peter.

"Yes," said Molly, "but even that might be too late, if the pirates have the trunk. We must . . ."

She was interrupted by more chittering from Ammm. Molly listened, struggling to follow the sounds. The only part she caught was "bad man."

"Again, please." she said.

Ammm spoke again, more deliberately. This time Molly caught "bad man" again, and "light."

Molly pondered that. *Light. What could he mean by* . . .

"Oh, no," she said.

"What?" said Peter.

"I think he's saying the pirates have the trunk," said Molly.

"Does he know where they are?" said Peter.

"Where bad man?" Molly asked Ammm. "Where light?"

"Molly come," said Ammm. He darted a few yards to the left, toward the rocky, wave-lashed point at the left end of the cove, then repeated: "Molly come."

"He wants us to follow," said Molly. To Ammm, she said, "Molly come."

Ammm whirled and plunged into the water, surfacing just moments later twenty-five yards farther along the beach toward the point of land, chittering "Come!" Peter and James followed trotted diagonally back to the beach, then on a parallel course with the porpoise, who kept popping up to make sure they were with him. Alf and the other boys, thoroughly mystified, trotted along behind.

"What're we doin', lad?" panted Alf.

"Following the porpoise," said Peter.

"But *why?*" shouted Tubby Ted, bringing up the rear.

"It's a talking porpoise!" shouted James. "It's taking us to the treasure!"

"It's *what?*" said Alf and Tubby Ted, at the same time.

"He's right," said Peter, over his shoulder.

"But *who* has the treasure? It's them pirates, is that it, lad?" Alf questioned.

"Yes, we think so," Peter admitted. "And we . . . I mean, Molly, has to get the trunk back from them."

"Well, then! Why didn't ya says so? I wouldn't miss it!" said Alf.

"Same!" said James.

Thomas and Prentiss said nothing, but—not wanting to be left alone on this increasingly strange island—trotted along with the group, as did the panting, incessantly complaining Tubby Ted.

They trotted for a hundred yards, at which point the beach curved sharply to the right, along a steeply rising lava slope. At the end lay the point, where huge ocean rollers—having traveled, unhampered, across thousands of miles of open ocean—slammed, thunderingly, into massive lava formations, sending spray high into the air. Ammm continued to follow the coast, heading out toward the end of the point.

On shore, the little band of humans followed, but as the hard-packed beach sand gave way to sharp, treacherously hole-ridden lava, the footing instantly became near-impossible, and the going very slow. Peter stopped for a moment, and studied the slope.

"Look," he said to Molly. "Ammm has to swim 'round that point. He can't use the land. But we can. It would be a lot quicker for us to just climb this hill and meet him at the water on the other side."

Molly considered the hill, then shook her head.

"We don't know what's on the other side of this hill. It might be another cove, but it might also be more island. We could be back in the jungle, and lost. Besides, Ammm may be leading us to the end of this point."

343

"But we can't keep up with him, not on these rocks," said Peter. He gestured toward the others, who were picking their way over the dark lava rock by rock, with agonizingly slowness. Ammm was far ahead now, an intermittent speck of light gray in the dark roiling water.

"I've got to try to stay with him," said Molly. "I don't dare lose him."

"All right, then," said Peter. "I'll climb this hill, and see what I see. Water or land, either way I'll come back and tell you."

Molly looked doubtful.

"You'll come right back?" she said.

"I'll find you," he said.

Their eyes met for a moment.

"All right," she said.

And with that, Peter was gone, clambering up the steep, rocky hillside, leaving the others to struggle along in pursuit of Ammm, wherever he was leading them.

CHAPTER 60

ᴄ𝖳oo Qᴜɪᴄᴋ ꜰᴏʀ ᴀ ᴄ𝖢ʟᴏᴜᴅ; ᴄ𝖳oo 𝖡ɪɢ ꜰᴏʀ ᴀ 𝖡ɪʀᴅ

Bᴀʀᴇʟʏ ʀɪᴘᴘʟɪɴɢ ᴛʜᴇ ꜱᴜʀꜰᴀᴄᴇ, the trunk glided toward the waterfall at the mouth of the lagoon. The brackish water grew clear, so that from above, long, powerful green tails could be seen propelling the trunk as the mermaids triumphantly bore their prize back to their lair.

Feeling safe now, they raised their heads from the water. The one in the lead—the others called her, in their strange, throaty language, *Teacher*—turned and smiled at her school. Her long, thick hair was blond. Her teeth, white and even, were human now, exposure to the trunk having completed her transformation from fish to mermaid. The other mermaids smiled back at her. Human teeth, all.

So elated were they by their triumph, so absorbed with their prize—their *creator*—that only one of them, a young mermaid in the back of the school, happened to see the thing that flew across the face of the moon, too quick for a cloud, too big for a bird. She grunted an alarm and slapped her tail twice on the water surface.

The other mermaids responded instantly, diving in fright. All but Teacher, who would not leave the *creator*. She wrapped her arms around the trunk defiantly, and looked up at the blackened silhouette swooping toward her.

She recognized it at once, and snarled.

———•◦•———

"Lean forward!" shouted Slank from the bow of the flying longboat. He was still getting the feel of it, his ability to steer shaky and imprecise. In the bright moonlight he could clearly see his target below, as well as the blond-haired she-fish hissing up at him. At the stern, Little Richard, gripping both sides in terror, shifted his weight slightly forward as the longboat dove. Slank leaned to port, lining up the bow with his target. "Steady . . . Steady . . ." The boat hurtled downward. The mermaid did not move.

She's brave, I'll give her that. . . .

As the boat was about to hit the water, Slank leaned back. The bow lifted slightly, avoiding a direct collision with the trunk, but striking the defiant mermaid. Slank felt the thud in his feet.

That's one less to worry about.

The longboat splashed down into the lagoon, its sharp

bow sending up waves on each side. Slank and Little Richard tumbled to the bottom of the boat, which rocked violently for a moment, but did not capsize.

"The trunk!" Slank shouted, struggling to his feet.

"There!" said Little Richard, pointing.

The trunk bobbed in the water astern. Slank thought about diving in after it, but quickly changed his mind.

She-fish.

There were a dozen or more of them, between the boat and the trunk, diving and surfacing frantically, apparently searching for something. It took Slank a moment, but then he understood: *They're looking for the one I hit.*

Whirling, Slank lunged to the bow and looked into the water.

There she is.

Her body was wedged under the prow, floating motionless. Slank grabbed her by the arm and dragged her into the boat. Her face was covered with blood. She was breathing, but barely.

Suddenly there was a wail from the water, and then more. The mermaids had caught sight of their wounded sister, and were surrounding the boat, snarling.

"Throw her back!" shouted Little Richard. "They'll capsize us again!"

"No!" shouted Slank, drawing his knife. "She's our barter!" He grabbed the unconscious mermaid and hauled her upright, holding the knife at her neck. The mermaids wailed and keened in horror.

"LISTEN!" shouted Slank. "I give her to you"—he made a gesture of throwing her over the side—"and you give me that"—he pointed at the trunk. "You understand?"

The mermaids showed no sign of comprehending. Instead, responding to some signal neither man heard or saw, the mermaids flashed their tails and disappeared, leaving only ripples.

Five seconds passed. Ten.

"I don't like this," said Little Richard.

"Get your whip," said Slank, dropping the unconscious mermaid at the bow.

Little Richard uncoiled the bullwhip he kept wrapped around his waist.

"Here they come," he said.

The two men crouched, watching the water. Suddenly, the dark shifting shapes shot up at them through the moon-lit water.

"Here they come!" Slank said.

In a flash of tails, the mermaids slammed the boat, rocking it violently. Slank stabbed blindly down into the water. Little Richard's whip cracked once, twice, but he, too, was having trouble drawing a bead on the swiftly moving creatures. The boat rocked again; again Slank stabbed at the water, this time driving several of the creatures back.

But only for a moment. The mermaids came at them again, then again. Slank and Little Richard lunged frantically back and forth in the boat, grunting, shouting, trying to keep them at bay, trying to keep the wildly gyrating boat from going over. From time to time the knife cut, or the whip connected, each time drawing a scream. The water around the longboat grew cloudy with blood. But the mermaids kept coming, coming, frothing the water around the unsteady longboat.

"THERE!" Slank shouted, pointing, as the mermaids, working together, massed for an attack at the stern, their goal being to pull the transom underwater with their weight. A lash from Little Richard's whip drove them off, sent the bow splashing down, and caused Slank to fall. Rising, he looked behind him to see that the wounded mermaid was . . .

Gone.

She had either slipped or fallen back into the water. The other mermaids, still battling Little Richard at the stern, apparently had not noticed. Slank searched the blood-clouded water around the bow but saw no sign of her.

Meanwhile, as Slank peered into the water at the bow, and Little Richard battled the mermaids at the stern, the trunk, momentarily forgotten by all of them, drifted farther and farther from the longboat, into the night.

CHAPTER 61

CRENSHAW RETURNS

BLACK STACHE HELD UP A HAND, silently stopping Smee and the others, and signaled them off the jungle path. Stache, too, stepped aside, concealing himself amid the enormous leaves of a plant.

The sounds of someone running drew closer. A *native?* Stache crouched and laid his sword across the path. When the runner was upon him, Stache lifted the sword a few inches, and the runner, with a cry of pain, sprawled face-first onto the ground.

"Crenshaw," said Stache, stepping out.

"Cap'n!" said Crenshaw, out of breath. He hurried painfully to his feet.

"Well, man," said Stache. "What is it?"

Crenshaw attempted to answer. "I seen—"

"—that lizard?" said Smee, interrupting.

"Shut up, Smee," said Stache. "Crenshaw?"

"The longboat, Cap'n," said Crenshaw, still gasping for breath.

"The *longboat?*" said Stache, bewildered. "*Our* longboat?" By his recollection, it should have been well down the island.

"Yes, sir. I seen it just now."

"Where?"

"It was . . . *flying,* Cap'n."

"It was *what?*"

"Flying, Cap'n. Up in the air. Like a bird. But it weren't no bird. It was the longboat, sure as I'm standing here."

The other pirates gathered around now, muttering about this strange and unlucky island, where things kept flying that were not supposed to fly.

"Belay that talk!" said Stache. "Crenshaw, where did you see this flying longboat?"

"Up this path, where you sent me. It leads to a beach . . . a lagoon, sir. I'd just gotten there when I sees the longboat pass right in front of the moon, plain as anything. And there was *men* in it."

More muttering from the crew.

"I SAID BELAY IT!" said Stache. To Crenshaw, he said: "How many men? What men?"

"Two, I reckon. One of 'em big as fright, he was. Right across the moon, they flied. Fast as a bird, they was. But it weren't no bird. It was a flying . . ."

"Yes, yes, a longboat," said Stache, eyeing Crenshaw curiously. "And where exactly did this longboat *go?*"

"Can't says for certain, Cap'n. There was trees and such in me way. It went from this ways to that," he said, indicating right to left. "Went past the moon and headed down."

"Down?"

"Yes, Cap'n. Down. I reckon toward the water."

"What about the trunk? The treasure?"

"Didn't see nothing of the sort. Just the flying longboat. She went past and I turned high tail to run back to tell you, and then you tripped me up, and then you asked me what I seen, and then I . . ."

"I KNOW THIS PART, YOU IDJIT!"

"Yes, sir."

Stache reviewed the situation. The trunk could not be far off, that was for certain. When things started flying that should not be flying, the trunk had to be near. But who were these two men, and what were they doing in his longboat?

"All right, men," said Stache. "We double-time down to this lagoon. Crenshaw, you lead the way, and show us where you seen this flying longboat. MOVE!"

Trotting with a pronounced limp, Crenshaw headed back down the path, followed by Stache, and, somewhat more reluctantly, Smee and the others. In a few minutes the path widened. Patches of low fog shone in the moonlight, like tiny puffs of gray cotton. Crenshaw had left out mention of the swirling fog.

Stache smelled the lagoon before he saw it: like a fresh rainfall. From far to his left came the trickling sound of water—a stream, and waterfall that fed the lagoon. Then, above the sounds of the water, he heard distinctly human sounds—grunting, shouting, splashing, the crack of a whip— familiar sounds to a pirate: *fighting*.

The path led to a small sand dune. Stache stopped his men short. By the sound of it, the fight was raging in the water just on the other side. *No reason to join a fight until you know what side you're on.*

Another crack of the whip. Then, a scream: a *woman's* scream.

His men stopped, all eyes on Stache.

"Here's what we do," he whispered. "Whoever's out there, we let them kill each other off. When they're done and the fighting stops, we'll take care of whoever's left. Get your weapons ready." He was thinking: *flying boats and fighting . . . the treasure's at the heart of this.*

Then, drawing his sword, Stache began to creep up the side of the dune.

$\mathcal{P}$ETER'S $\mathcal{D}$ECISION

$\mathcal{P}$ETER'S HANDS WERE BLEEDING, sliced time and again by the jagged lava as he fought his way up the hillside. As he neared the top, the slope became very steep, almost vertical, causing Peter to question the wisdom of his plan. He periodically glanced back down along the hillside, but could no longer see Molly or the others; he wondered if he'd be able to find them again.

Finally he reached the top, and saw immediately that his suspicion had been correct: the hill was in fact a narrow neck, separating the cove from a wide, curved lagoon. The slope on the other side of the hill was as steep as the one he had ascended, leading down to another beach. His swept his gaze along it, starting on the far right, seeing nothing of interest until some huge rock formations in the center of the lagoon curve, near the beach. He focused on these, his eyes straining to pick up details in the moonlight.

After a moment, he saw it: a slim, dark shape on the silver water.

A boat.

Peter squinted. There were people in the boat; there was commotion around it. Pirates, he was sure of it. Who else could it be?

And they've got the trunk, I wager.

Peter considered the situation. He was certain that Ammm, forced to take the water route, was leading Molly around the point to this boat. He decided it made no sense for him to go back down the way he had come, over the rough lava, and try to catch up with Molly. Obviously, he should proceed down to this new beach and wait for the others there.

So he descended, finding the going-down much quicker than the climbing-up had been. He stood on the beach for five long minutes, then five more, then five more, peering down the beach to his right, waiting impatiently for Molly and the others to come into view, remembering how slow their progress had been when he'd left them.

Finally his impatience got the better of him.

I'll just go down and have a look, he thought.

And so he set off, keeping out of the moonlight, staying under the tall palms that edged the beach, trotting toward the big rocks, and the longboat.

CHAPTER 63

GONE AGAIN

FOUR DISTINCT VS APPEARED in the moonlit water, all aimed at the port side of the longboat.

"Broadsides!" Slank called out. Too late.

The mermaids timed their strike perfectly, lifting the port side high just as Little Richard was leaning the wrong way. He fell, flailing, and his massive weight flipped the boat, catapulting Slank into the air, and then into the lagoon.

Slank bobbed to the surface, frantically stabbing into the water and thrashing with his legs, expecting at any second to feel mermaid teeth sink into his flesh. Instead, he felt . . .

He felt the bottom. During the fight, the boat had drifted within ten yards of shore; Slank could stand easily.

Little Richard was also standing, peering nervously at the water, whip at the ready. "Where'd they go?" he asked.

Slank looked around, seeing no sign of tails or splashes,

only the now-gentle lagoon surface, mirroring the moon. Then it hit him.

"Where's the trunk?" he said.

The two men spun in circles. *Gone. Again.*

Slank spat a curse at the sky, then took a deep breath.

"All right," he said. "Let's get the boat ashore."

They grabbed the swamped longboat, walked it to the beach, dumped the water out and hauled the boat onto the sand.

"I don't get it," panted Little Richard, when they were done. "They was after us like banshees, then they was gone!"

Slank had been thinking about that.

"They was trying to rescue the one I had in the boat," he said. "That's why they capsized us. But then they saw she wasn't there, and went looking for her. It's the only explanation."

"But where'd she go?" Little Richard asked.

"I don't care where she went," Slank said. "What I care about is the trunk, and I'm thinking if we didn't see it drift off, them she-devils didn't see it neither."

Slank was studying the lagoon intently now, hands on hips. To the left, fresh water poured in over the waterfall and swirled in a deep pool by the island of rocks. Watching the movement of the foam, Slank detected a slight current, moving to the right, down the curve of the beach.

"Come on!" he said, setting off at a trot.

"Where are we going now?" said Little Richard, none too happy, lumbering behind.

"If the trunk comes ashore," said Slank, "it'll be this way."

CHAPTER 64

"He Surely Will"

KEEPING TO THE MOON-CAST SHADOWS beneath the
palms, Peter trotted along the beach toward the longboat. As
he drew closer, he heard angry shouts, and a cracking sound,
as well as other—stranger—noises; and saw figures in and
around the boat in frenzied activity, apparently fighting.

Who would the pirates be fighting?

He stopped and look back toward the rocky point. There
was still no sign of Ammm, or Molly.

It's taking them forever.

Peter hesitated. On the one hand, he was reluctant to get
too close to the battle ahead, and risk capture; on the other
hand, he was very curious to know who was fighting the
pirates, and where the trunk was. He decided he could risk
getting a little closer.

He had walked no more than twenty feet when he heard
it: a moan, coming from his right, at the water's edge. He

stopped, and heard it again, louder this time. He glanced ahead at the shouting figures, then, keeping his head low, darted down the beach to the water.

He saw her immediately: a girl lying facedown in the shallow water, her long blond hair splayed forward, touching the sand. She appeared to be struggling to crawl onto the beach. Her arms moved feebly, her hands clawing at the wet sand.

Peter ran to the girl, dropping to his knees into the water. He took her by the shoulders and turned her over, and immediately noticed several things. The first was that she was startlingly beautiful, with astonishingly large, luminescent green eyes. The second was that she did not appear to be wearing any clothes, her only covering coming from her lush cascade of hair.

Ordinarily this second thing would have gotten Peter's full attention, but he was much distracted by the third thing, which was blood seeping from a deep gash in her forehead.

Supporting the girl's head in his hands, Peter looked frantically around for something to put over the wound.

My shirt, he thought.

He decided to pull the girl farther up on the sand, so he could rest her head on the beach while he removed his shirt. Getting his hand under her arms, he heaved backward. That was when Peter noticed a fourth, even more startling thing.

She had a tail.

"Aaah!" said Peter, jumping up, dropping her head. The girl, or fish, or whatever she was, moaned piteously, and writhed in pain. Peter stood over her, water dripping from his body.

"Wh . . . who *are* you?" he said.

The mermaid did not answer, but blinked and looked at Peter, as if seeing him for the first time.

Those eyes!

She drew a sharp breath, her expression suddenly fearful.

"It's okay," said Peter, softly, kneeling again. "I won't hurt you."

The mermaid's expression remained wary, but her large eyes closed again. Peter saw she was weakening rapidly as her blood, dark in the moonlight, continued to ooze onto the sand.

"I'm going to put a bandage on you," Peter said, untucking his shirt. "You'll be fine."

But she didn't seem to hear him; her head had slumped sideways now, and the life seemed to be slowly draining from her face. Peter felt certain it was too late for a bandage to do much good, but, not knowing what else to do, he began to pull his shirt over his head, only to get it tangled in . . .

The locket.

Peter slipped it off his neck and looked at it. He'd meant to give it back to Molly, but then Ammm had appeared, and in the excitement he'd forgotten. He had no idea how much, if any, starstuff was left in it. If there was any, it likely wasn't much.

Should I save it? I might need it, against the pirates. Molly might need it. . . .

The mermaid moaned again, a weak sound. A dying sound. Peter looked at her face, then at the locket, then down the still-empty beach toward the rocky point.

"I'm sorry, Molly." He whispered the apology and then snapped open the locket.

Immediately a sphere of golden light blinded him; first his hands, then the rest of his body, experienced the now-familiar warmth and feeling of well-being. Peter wanted to luxuriate in that feeling, but forced himself to invert the locket and pour its contents onto the mermaid's wounded forehead. The warmth quickly drained out of him. The glow spread over the girl's body, then disappeared, like water absorbed by a sponge.

It's working. . . .

In a moment, the glow was gone.

Peter picked up the locket; it still hung open, but was now just lifeless metal. He snapped it shut, and put it back around his neck. He found himself aware of the silence; the splashing and shouting from down the beach had stopped. He started to rise to have a look, when he felt a hand grip his forearm.

Startled, he whirled and saw that the mermaid was

sitting up, her eyes open and focused on Peter. Her wound was gone.

"Are you . . . all right?" Peter asked.

The girl said nothing, but reached her hand out and gently traced her fingers along the side of Peter's face. He blushed. She smiled, a stunningly beautiful smile.

As they stared at each other, Peter heard a splash a few yards offshore and, looking up, saw not one . . . but two . . . no *three* more mermaids. Waist high in the shallow water, they hissed at him and dragged themselves forward. Peter tried to scramble away, but the blond mermaid made an odd, deep-throated sound, and they stopped their advance. An exchange of strange sounds followed. The three other mermaids smiled at Peter, who blushed even more.

This pleasant scene was interrupted by the sudden surfacing of yet another mermaid, who, with barely a glance at Peter, emitted a rapid series of throaty sounds that clearly excited and alarmed the three others. They whirled and, with a flash of their green tails, were gone, underwater. The mermaid whom Peter had rescued hesitated only a moment longer, giving Peter's arm one final squeeze. She offered another radiant smile, slid gracefully forward into the water, and then she, too, was gone.

Seconds later, the whole group of mermaids surfaced twenty yards to Peter's left, making sounds, gesticulating excitedly to one another. Peter stood on his tiptoes but couldn't see. He ran up the beach, and looked back. The mermaids were trying to work their way through the shallows to a dark form lying, wave-lapped, at the water's edge.

Peter blinked, not believing his luck.

The trunk. Unguarded.

Racing through the shallow water, he reached it in seconds. There was no question; even in the brilliant moonlight, he could see the glow through the cracks; the moment his hand touched the rough wood, he felt the familiar warmth.

His attention was drawn away by urgent sounds out in the lagoon. The mermaids, struggling frantically to make their way to him, were waving their arms, and flopping their now-useless tails through the shallow water. The blond mermaid he'd saved was in front. Her eyes met his as she made a series of urgent, but incomprehensible sounds, clearly trying to tell him something.

"What is it?" called Peter. "WhUNNNH."

The clublike wooden handle of Little Richard's whip, two feet of two-inch-diameter oak, slammed into Peter's skull from behind. Peter instantly crumpled to the shallow water, unable to break his fall, and lay facedown, motionless. The mermaids, hissing, lunged forward with teeth bared, but were at a hopeless disadvantage in the shallow water, and scurried back as the whip cracked out at them.

"Forget them," said Slank. "They can't reach us here. Get the trunk. We're going back to the longboat."

"But if we're in the boat, those things'll swamp us again," said Little Richard, gesturing at mermaids.

"Not this time," said Slank. "With what's in the trunk, we can leave the way we come in, flying over them she-devils."

He laughed at the mermaids, who were highly agitated; he noticed that one of them, the blond one, was, despite the risk of the whip, crawling toward Peter, who had not moved.

"Oh, you fancy this lad, do you?" he asked. "You're welcome to him." With his right foot, he gave Peter's motionless form, still facedown, a shove toward the deeper water.

"Get the trunk," said Slank to Little Richard, "and let's get off this miserable island."

Little Richard hoisted the trunk to his shoulder, then glanced down at Peter. "Shouldn't we turn the boy over?" he called to Slank. "If we leave him like that, he'll surely drown."

"Oh, yes," said Slank, not looking back. "He surely will."

CHAPTER 65

HE'S GONE AHEAD

"COME ON," CALLED MOLLY TO THE OTHERS, for what felt to her like the hundredth time. "Can't you go *any* faster?"

They were picking their way with agonizing slowness along the rocky, wave-lashed point, trying to keep from falling on the slippery, irregular, razor-sharp coral, their legs now covered with scrapes and bleeding cuts.

Right behind Molly, as he had been from the start, walked James, steady James. But the others lagged at a considerable distance—Prentiss and Thomas, both miserable but gamely struggling forward, and Alf, far to the rear, now essentially carrying Tubby Ted. Molly had been tempted more than once to leave them behind, but could not bring herself to abandon them. Even with the big sailor to look after them, this strange and scary island required everyone to stick together.

Peter should never have gone off on his own. . . .

She looked ahead and to the right, her eyes searching just beyond the breakers until she caught sight of Ammm, his snout appearing almost white in the moonlight, chittering at her to come, come, come. Peter had been right: Ammm had led them around the point only because he could not lead them by land. The destination was clearly the broad lagoon that now came into view. Molly assumed this meant that Peter was ahead of them, somewhere on the beach by now. She hoped that for once he would show some patience, and wait for her as planned.

At last, the terrain improved, the unforgiving lava giving way to rock and sand. Molly scanned the broad, sweeping curve of beach, but saw no sign of Peter.

Where are you? she wondered.

She glanced back at the others.

"Come *on*," she called out, for what felt like the hundred and first time. Then, urged on by the chittering Ammm, she began trotting along the hard-packed sand, still searching through the night for Peter.

I hope you haven't gotten yourself into trouble.

CHAPTER 66

THE DREAM

PETER HAD NEVER KISSED A GIRL. He had never kissed anybody, at least not technically. Not that he remembered. He did have a memory, dim and dreamlike, of *being* kissed, but that was by a grown-up, a lady. When he recalled this memory, which he sometimes did as he was falling off to sleep, he thought that perhaps the lady might have been his mother. He tried to see her face, but the memory wouldn't allow it. It felt more like a shadow, old and faded by the light.

But he had never kissed a girl. He'd read of it, this girl-kissing; he had heard the older boys at St. Norbert's snicker about it. For most of his life Peter had not understood why anyone, girl or boy, would want to do such an unappetizing thing as put their mouth together with someone else's. Lately, though, since he'd met Molly, the idea seemed less and less repulsive, and more and more intriguing. But still, he had never done it; had never come close.

So he was sure that he was dreaming now, in this strange and unreal moment, in this weightless watery tumble, in this swirl of light, in this burble of strange noises. He must be dreaming, because he was in the arms of a girl, a very beautiful girl, with blond hair and green eyes—*Molly has green eyes*—and this beautiful girl was holding him, and her mouth was touching his mouth, and—the strangest thing—*her breath was becoming Peter's breath.*

The strangest thing. A dream, certainly. But it was a pleasant dream, and Peter decided the best thing to do was simply let go and enjoy it.

CHAPTER 67

As If He Knows Something

Slank looked back at Little Richard, expecting to see him complaining under the weight of the trunk. Instead, the big man had a wide grin on his face, and his strides were enormous—six or eight feet at a step—as if . . .

"Are you all right?" Slank said.

"Never better!" said Little Richard, taking a step that easily carried him fifteen feet before he drifted to a gentle landing.

That did it. Slank, trotting alongside, grabbed Little Richard's shirt to prevent him from flying away. With the contact, Slank's arm immediately felt warm, a little ticklish.

"I'm *fine*, really!" Little Richard said. "Perfect!"

"I can see that."

"I could start singing!"

"No you don't!" Slank hissed.

Little Richard hummed instead, the smile never leaving his face. Slank thought about carrying the trunk himself, but feared that he, too, would fall under its spell, and be unable to think clearly. So instead he acted as Little Richard's ballast, holding the big man down as though he were a human balloon. The two of them bounced and drifted along the beach until, to Slank's relief, they reached the longboat.

"Put it down," said Slank.

Little Richard—his feet were a foot off the ground now—gave Slank a hurt-puppy look.

"But why?" he asked. "Why would I want to do that?"

"Put it down NOW!" Slank ordered.

Little Richard reluctantly obeyed, gently setting the trunk onto the sand. He looked at it wistfully.

"Now, what?" he said.

"Now," said Slank, sloshing around in the shallow water, "we find a rock. Here, this one will do." Grunting, he hefted the rock and waded ashore.

"What're you goin' to do?" said Little Richard.

"Open the trunk," said Slank.

"Good!" said Little Richard.

"I'm not opening it so you can amuse yourself," snapped Slank. "I'm opening it so we can get this boat flying again, and get back to the ship without being swamped by them she-devils. You're not to touch the contents, you understand?"

"Yes," said Little Richard, a hurt puppy again.

Ignoring the trunk's formidably padlocked clasp, Slank focused his efforts on the two old iron hinges. He smashed the rock down on the first; it cracked easily, and on the second blow, fell off completely. He turned to the second hinge, and on the first blow it nearly came free, a puff of golden powder shooting from the widening lid crack and landing on the sand at Slank's feet.

One more blow should do it. . . .

Slank had raised the rock when he heard the bellow of surprise from Little Richard. He whirled just in time to see a wooden club coming straight for his head. He dodged it, diving to the sand, rolling, and jumping up.

Pirates.

Two of them had jumped Little Richard from behind, but two men were no match for him; he rocked forward and easily tossed them head-over-heels onto the sand.

Slank had his dagger out now, its blade flashing in the moonlight. But before he could use it, he felt sharp point of a sword pressing into the back of his neck, felt a trickle of his blood.

"Drop it or die," said Black Stache.

Slank let the dagger fall.

"Now, tell your friend to stop fighting," said Stache, nodding toward Little Richard, who was currently getting the best of three pirates.

"Little Richard!" Slank called out. "That's enough!"

The huge man, as always, obeyed.

"Tie them up," said Stache. "Use the line from the long-boat."

In a minute Stache's men had Slank and Little Richard lying on the beach, arms and legs firmly bound behind their backs.

"You ain't goin' to kill 'em, Cap'n?" said Smee.

"No need for us to do it, with the tide coming in," said Stache, nodding toward a finger of hissing surf, just now touching Slank's ankles. "I like the idea of them having to think about it awhile. And if the sea don't get 'em, there's that big old croc somewheres about, and them savages." He smiled unpleasantly down at Slank, savoring his triumph for another moment, then turned to his men and barked, "Put the trunk in the longboat."

The men hesitated.

"Well?" said Stache.

"Beggin' your pardon, Cap'n," said Smee, "but some of us are thinkin' this here boat is bewitched, bein' as how it was flyin' and all. One of the men seen the dory just down the beach there—it's swamped, and there's a piece tore from the transom, but the oars are still in the oarlocks, and it'll float."

"The dory's too small," said Stache. "True, this boat was flying, but that just shows you the power of the treasure we're taking home. We'll live as kings, men. Kings! Now let's get our treasure back to the ship and get off this cursed island."

The pirates, persuaded, hoisted the trunk into the long-boat, and hauled the boat into to the water. As they shoved off, Stache cast a glance back at Little Richard and Slank, lying bound in the sand. Slank again met his eyes, but this time, instead of looking angry, he almost looked amused.

Why would that be? Stache wondered

"Tide'll be in soon," Stache shouted. "Remember to hold your breath."

The pirates laughed, and Little Richard whimpered, but Slank remained annoyingly calm.

"I'll be fine, Mister Stache," he called back. "But I hope *you* can swim."

"It'll be you doing the swimming, sir, not I," Black Stache answered. The pirates laughed again, dutifully, but Stache was strangely troubled as the longboat, with his men at the oars, surged away from the beach where Slank lay, still regarding him with that infuriating smirk.

As if he knows something, thought Stache. *But what could he know?*

After pondering this a moment more, Stache dismissed the thought of the two men on the beach, and turned his attention forward, in the direction of the *Jolly Roger*, and escape from this island.

He did not see the four fast-moving Vs on the surface of the silver water, heading straight for the longboat.

Little Richard, straining mightily against his bonds, grunted, swore, grunted again; but despite his massive strength, he could not break the stout rope, nor unravel the knots, tied with sailor's skill. Feeling the water lapping at his feet, he whimpered and tried to roll up the beach.

Slank was rolling, too, but sideways. His eyes were on a spot in the sand next to the indentation left by the trunk. A glowing spot, where the puff of golden powder had fallen when he'd been banging off the hinges with the rock.

He rolled over, and then again, until he was on his stomach, the glowing spot to his right and a little below him on the beach. He carefully positioned his body, then rolled toward the spot, onto his back, and . . . *there.*

He immediately felt the pleasing warmth surge through him, felt his body starting to become light. But he didn't want to fly. Focusing, concentrating—he had some practice with this—he directed the brief flash of power into his arms. With all his strength, he pulled. He felt the rope give, then, suddenly, part. He was free. He sat up and quickly untied the ropes on his feet.

"Sir!" said Little Richard, not believing his eyes. "How did you *do* that?"

"Never mind that now," said Slank, scanning the sand

until he found his dagger. "Turn over so I can cut you loose. We need to stay in sight of that longboat."

⸺⸰⸺

The mermaids, having had some experience, now knew exactly how to attack the longboat. They struck the side in perfect unison, very nearly capsizing it and throwing two of Stache's men straight overboard.

Stache could not imagine what massive thing had hit them. *A whale? In the lagoon?*

Smee was on his feet, shouting, "Cap'n! Men overboard!"

"I KNOW, YOU IDJIT" shouted Stache. "SIT DOWN!"

Too late. Smee had further destabilized the boat, which rocked violently and sent the little round man staggering to the side. He lost his balance, and grabbing desperately for something to hold on to, he latched on to the trunk's end handle, pulling the trunk with him as he spilled into the water.

"NO!" bellowed Stache, lunging to grab the trunk. But as he touched it, it was swatted away from him, toward shore, by . . . a tail! A long, green tail. *What kind of whale is that?*

At that instant, the boat was struck again. This time it went over easily, completely upside down. Stache and the rest of the men flew into the water, gasping, sputtering and thrashing their way desperately back to the capsized boat.

Stache grabbed it, then lifted his head as far as he could, looking around frantically for the trunk.

"NOOOO!" he bellowed, as he finally saw it . . . drifting back toward shore.

<hr/>

Slank and Little Richard ran along the beach in the direction of the commotion out on the water. The bellowing and shouting of the pirates meant that the mermaids, as Slank had hoped, were attacking the pirates, for once doing Slank a favor. He smiled as he heard Stache's anguished yell; that told him that the trunk was in the water again.

"There it is!" shouted Little Richard, pointing.

Slank saw the trunk, bobbing in shallow water, not far from another shape, dark and rounded—the dory! If the pirates were right, it would still float. Slank smiled. There might be a way off the island, even without the longboat.

Fifty yards out on the moonlit lagoon, he could just make out the low, dark shape of the longboat, with the pirates clinging to it. Stache and his men had the misfortune of getting caught in the current, and were now drifting toward the mouth of the lagoon, their efforts to swim the longboat to shore going poorly.

"Fare thee well, Captain Stache!" Slank called out.

"That's MINE!" cried Stache.

"Not anymore, it ain't!" laughed Slank. He turned his

attention to the trunk, just offshore now. Still wary of mermaids, Slank was reluctant to venture into the water. To Little Richard, he said, "Pull it up onto dry land. I'll find me another rock."

<hr/>

Molly saw it all, from under the palms: saw the pirates in trouble; saw Slank gloating in triumph; saw the trunk.

Molly knew this was the moment: either she was a Starcatcher, or she wasn't, and if she was, this was when she proved it, with or without Peter.

"I have to go out there," she said.

"I ain't goin' out there," muttered Tubby Ted.

"I can't let that man have the trunk," said Molly. "I have to stop him."

"How?" said James.

"I don't know," said Molly, looking around. "But I have to." She found a coconut on the sand, picked up, hefted it.

"You're going after pirates with a *coconut*?" said Tubby Ted. "You're daft, you are."

"Nevertheless," said Molly, "I'm going."

"So am I," said James, picking up a coconut of his own.

"So am I, miss," said Alf. "I'll take that big one, there."

"If he gets deep enough in the water, you may get some help from Ammm," said Molly. "James and I will take Mr. Slank."

The three of them started down the beach.

"Daft," said Tubby Ted.

———◦———

"Hurry!" Slank yelled to Little Richard, who, still worried about mermaids, was wading cautiously toward the bobbing trunk.

Just as he reached it, Ammm hit him.

No man had ever knocked Little Richard down. But of course Ammm was not a man: Ammm was a sleek hurtling missile, 567 and one-half pounds of ocean-hardened muscle, hurtling through the air and nailing the giant square in the chest with a force that would have killed some men. In Little Richard's case it was enough to knock the breath from his body and send him flailing backward into the shallow water. He got back to his feet, only to feel another massive weight on him. This time it was Alf, who locked his thick arms around the giant's throat, hanging on for dear life as Little Richard, weakened and breath-starved, staggered forward and went down again.

Slank heard the struggle and strode toward the water. He was expecting mermaids, and thus didn't see the two small shapes racing up from behind and leaping onto his back. He felt the impact, then something pulling at his ears—nearly tearing them off—and scratching at his eyes, while at the same time something else was sinking its teeth into his legs. *How many are there?*

Slank screamed and jabbed back with his elbows, sending his assailants flying. He whirled and saw . . .

Children. Two of them: the girl from the ship, and a small boy.

Slank almost laughed: *children.* But then he stumbled, as the girl—*she's very quick*—hooked her leg around his. He fell facedown, and instantly something hard struck his head, again and again. He went dizzy, but managed to writhe sideways to see.

Coconuts. Children are beating me senseless with coconuts.

Blood streaming down his face, Slank lunged to his feet, flailing his arms as he staggered toward the lagoon, the children still clinging to his back and bashing him with coconuts. As blackness closed in, Slank groped desperately for the knife in his belt.

Alf was a very strong man. But Little Richard was inhuman. Despite his initial advantage, Alf realized that Little Richard was slowly gaining the upper hand, peeling Alf's hands away from his neck, and dragging them both back to the beach, where the giant would be able to breathe freely, and Alf would be no match for his monstrous strength.

"Hold on!" Molly shouted to James. "We've got him!"

She bashed the coconut hard, again, onto Slank's skull. Slank shuddered but did not go down. Suddenly the man's right hand swept down toward James.

"Knife!" James screamed, letting go of Slank to dodge the blade.

Now only Molly was holding on. Slank reared back, and against the twinkling black of the night sky, Molly saw a silver swipe of metal as Slank brought the knife toward her, like a man trying to scratch his back. The blade was aimed straight for Molly's face.

She lifted the coconut and blocked the blow. The knife lodged in the coconut, and Slank yanked it free, at the same time pulling the coconut from Molly's grasp. Molly grabbed Slank's right arm and tugged hard. He screamed in pain and fury. She pulled again, harder.

Again the knife flashed toward Molly's face. She let go, falling back into the water. Slank towered over her, the knife held high, his eyes wild with pain and anger. He raised his knife hand to stab her.

"ARRRRGGGGGH!" he bellowed, as Ammm delivered a spine-wracking blow to his back. Slank turned and slashed at the porpoise, only to receive a faceful of water blasted from Ammm's blowhole. As Slank gasped and sputtered, Ammm rose to his tail, reared back, and snapped forward, striking the sailor hard. Slank spun a half circle and splashed down into the water.

Molly got her legs under her. From behind, she heard Ammm chittering and chirping urgently; she didn't get all of it, but the essential message was clear: GO.

Molly grabbed James by the arm, dragging him toward the beach, where she figured she and James could outrun the men. Two steps from the beach, Slank tackled them both. Molly went down, Slank grabbing her by the leg. Behind them the frantic chittering grow louder, but the water here was too shallow for Ammm to help.

Molly, her face covered with sticky sand, felt Slank drag her and James roughly onto the beach. Her heart sank as she saw Tubby, Prentiss, Thomas, and Alf all lying facedown in the sand, Little Richard standing over them.

"Where's the trunk?" shouted Slank.

"Right there," said Little Richard, pointing a few yards down the beach to where the trunk lay at the water's edge, its rough sides lapped by gentle wavelets. Satisfied that it was out of reach of porpoises or mermaids, he left it for a moment, turned, and threw Molly and James roughly to the sand next to Alf and the other children.

"You all right, Mr. Slank?" said Little Richard.

"No," said Slank, touching his bleeding scalp. "I'm not all right."

"What do we do with 'em?" said Little Richard, gesturing to the figures on the sand.

"We kill them," said Slank, quietly. "I've learned my lesson about leaving people alive. We'll start with the brave young lady."

Knife in his right hand, Slank grabbed Molly's hair with his left and yanked her to a sitting position. She grunted in pain, but refused to cry out.

Slank knelt in front of her, his face close to hers, staring into her eyes.

"You wanted that trunk very badly, didn't you, Molly Aster?" he said.

Molly only glared in response.

"Wanted to save it for your daddy, didn't you?" continued Slank. "The great Leonard Aster. The great Starcatcher. Only he wasn't so great, was he? Got on the wrong ship, he did. We fooled him good, the great *Leonard Aster*."

With that, Slank, still holding the knife, reached inside his shirt and slowly pulled out the golden locket. Molly's eyes fell on it, and widened.

"You," she said. "You're . . . you're . . ."

"Yes," Slank said. "I'm one of them. That's why we put the trunk on the *Never Land*, so I could keep an eye on it, while your fool father chased a trunk full of sand onto the *Wasp*. I grant you, we didn't count on you being aboard the *Never Land*. And we surely didn't expect that idiot pirate to come blundering into this business. But it's all cleared up nicely now, isn't it, Molly? And soon the trunk will be in the hands of King Zarboff."

Molly flinched at the name.

"That's right, Molly," said Slank, delighted at the reaction. "At long last, *we* will have the power. You have no idea how *much* power, Molly. It will change *everything*. If only you would live to see it . . .

Slank shifted forward, and brought his knife blade to Molly's neck. She refused to pull back, refused to whimper, staring stonily into Slank's eyes as he began to press the sharp blade against her throat. . . .

"AHOY!"

Slank jerked back, his knife leaving a thin line of blood on Molly's neck. Both of them turned toward the source of the shout—a flat rock, twenty-five yards offshore, its occupant clearly visible in the bright moonlight.

"PETER!" shouted Molly.

Slank spat out a curse. It was impossible! He'd killed this boy himself!

But there he stood, water dripping from his hair, his arms crossed in defiance, surrounded by mermaids, as if they were *guarding* him.

He had one foot on the rock.

The other rested firmly on the trunk.

CHAPTER 68

THE BARGAIN

FOR A MOMENT THEY JUST STARED AT EACH OTHER, across
the silver stretch of lagoon—Slank and Peter—the man and
the boy.

It was Slank who broke the silence.

"Do you see this, boy?" he said, holding up his knife,
twisting it so the blade glinted in the moonlight.

"I see it," answered Peter with a shout.

"Good," said Slank. "Now, understand this. If you don't
do exactly as I say, this knife will be covered with the blood
of your friends here, starting with the young lady." Grabbing
a handful of Molly's hair, Slank jerked her to her feet. She
cried out in pain.

"Molly!" shouted Peter. "Are you all right?"

"Don't listen to him Peter!" she shouted. "Don't let him
. . . OWW!" Slank had silenced her with another yank on
her hair.

"You understand the situation, boy?" Slank shouted.

"I do!" answered Peter.

"Good," said Slank. "Then we can do business."

"Peter, NO!" shouted Molly.

Slank jerked her head again, and again she cried in pain.

"You keep quiet," Slank hissed at her, "or I'll cut your throat just for the satisfaction." He called out to Peter, "I'm curious, boy. How did you get the trunk?"

"I took it when you were talking about killing them," said Peter.

"Clever boy," said Slank. "But how did you get it out there on the rock so quick?"

"My friends helped me," Peter answered, gesturing at the mermaids.

"I see," said Slank. "So the devil-fish are on your side now?"

"They are," said Peter.

And, strangely enough, it was true. Peter still didn't quite understand it. All he knew was that, head throbbing in pain, he'd awakened in the water, in the embrace of the mermaid he'd saved. And, somehow the mermaid was *talking* to him, except that her mouth wasn't moving, and her words were only sort of words, because they were also pictures, and feelings. Peter found that somehow he understood the mermaid—she called herself *Teacher*—effortlessly, and somehow she understood him, and the importance of protecting the trunk—she called it *Creator*—from the bad men. When they heard the struggle on the beach, and saw the trunk unguarded, a plan of action formed instantly in both of their minds at once, as if they were thinking with one brain.

Slank shouted, "If them devil-fish will do as you say, I think we can work ourselves a mutual bargain, boy. I'll trade the life of this girl—the lives of all your friends, here—for that trunk."

Molly started to shout something, but Slank clapped his hand over her mouth. The lagoon was silent, except for the low hiss of the gentle surf and the rumble of the distant waterfall.

"All right," said Peter.

"NO!" shouted Molly, yanking her mouth free.

"Shut up!" said Slank, covering her mouth again. To Peter, he said, "I knew you was a bright boy. A reasonable boy. So you'll understand that I have to add a condition to the bargain."

"What condition?" asked Peter.

"I need safe passage in that dory, back out to the ship," said Slank. "You need to tell them devil-fish to leave me alone."

Peter looked down and exchanged a look with Teacher, who was in the water just in front of the rock where he stood. Then he looked back at Slank.

"They'll leave you alone," said Peter.

"I appreciate you assurance on that," said Slank. "I'm sure you're an honest boy. But just the same, I need me a little *protection*."

"What do you mean?" said Peter.

"I mean the girl goes with me," said Slank. "Your other friends can stay, but she goes with me in the dory, with the trunk. Once I get to the ship, I'll leave her in the dory, and your fish friends can swim her back."

"Peter, don't do it!" It was Alf yelling now. "Once he's got the trunk on the ship, he won't have no reason to let her go!"

"That's right, Peter!" shouted James, sitting up. "Don't do it!"

"Shut them two up!" barked Slank. Little Richard shoved the two protesters back to the sand with his huge right boot. Slank shouted to Peter: "What do you say, boy? Do we have ourselves a bargain?"

"How do I know you'll let her go?" said Peter.

"Because I'm giving you my word," said Slank. "And if you don't agree to my bargain, I give you my word I'll start cutting throats here, and you'll see that my word is good. So what do you say?"

Now the silence was total; even the sounds of surf and water went momentarily quiet, as if the lagoon itself awaited Peter's answer.

"All right, then," said Peter. "I accept your bargain."

Molly tried to shout something, but Slank, anticipating her reaction, kept his hand clamped hard on her mouth.

"There's a good boy," he said. "You just saved your friends' lives. Now, here's what you do. You have two of those devil-fish swim that trunk to shore and shove it ashore right by that dory there. Just two, no more. Then I want them to swim back with their heads high, where I can see them. I want to see *all* of them creature's heads when we row out of here, and I want you to stay on that rock 'til we're gone. You understand all that, boy?"

"Yes," said Peter.

"That's good," said Slank, "because I'll have my knife to this young lady's neck, and there's no human nor fish can move fast enough to keep me from cutting her. You understand, boy?"

"I understand."

"Good," said Slank. "Now, send them devil-fish over with the trunk."

Peter crouched on the rock, exchanging a look with Teacher, who turned to the other mermaids and emitted a long and complex series of guttural sounds. Two of the mermaids, both auburn-haired, swam to the rock. Peter slid the trunk into the water, where it bobbed, corklike, on the surface. The auburn-haired mermaids got behind it, and began propelling it swiftly toward the beached dory.

"That's a fine lad," said Slank, watching the trunk's

389

approach. "A fine lad, indeed."

Peter didn't answer. He stood statue-still on the rock, his eyes trained on Molly. She, too, seemed to be looking at him, but, even given the bright moonlight, was too far away for him to see her face clearly. It was probably just as well, because the look in her eyes, as the trunk came closer and closer to shore, was one of cold fury.

But Slank saw the girl's look, and understood it. It gave him great pleasure.

"The boy likes you very much," he whispered harshly to Molly, keeping his hand firmly clamped over her mouth. "But he's not very savvy, is he?"

Then he laughed as Molly struggled, uselessly, to reply.

CHAPTER 69

ℛEPRIEVE

"𝒫ADDLE, YOU DOGS!" SHOUTED STACHE. "Paddle and kick! We're making headway!"

The exhausted pirates groaned, but complied, for they could see that Stache was right: the capsized longboat, with agonizing slowness, was curving toward the far leftmost of the two points of land that framed the lagoon. As veteran seamen, they all understood the urgency of the situation: if they could not push the longboat over to the point in time, the current would sweep them past it, and out to sea.

So paddle and kick they did, at Stache's urging. So desperate was the situation that even Stache, tucking his sword into his belt, paddled and kicked—it was unheard of: the great pirate himself, reduced to this.

They were nearly even with the end of the point now; it loomed in the moonlight fifty yards away. Too far. None of them could swim that distance; most of them—typically, for pirates—could not swim at all.

"Cap'n," cried Smee. "We ain't gonna make it."

"PADDLE AND KICK!" roared Stache in response, but he, too, saw that it was hopeless; they were clearly past the point now. He considered his options: if he could right the capsized longboat, and bail it, he might have a chance to survive. But there were ten men clinging to the overturned hull. Too many to get the boat floating again. He'd have to get rid of some.

"You men on this side!" he shouted. "Let go!"

The pirates closest to Stache—there were five of them—stared back at him, too stunned to answer.

"I said *let go!*" shouted Stache, awkwardly drawing his sword.

"But, Cap'n," protested the man next to him. "If we . . ."

"*LET GO!*" roared Stache, making his point by clubbing the man's hand with the hilt of his sword; the pirate screamed in pain and released the boat, sliding back into the water.

"Now, you!" shouted Stache, starting to bring the sword down on the next man—this time, blade-first. The second pirate leaped backward, followed quickly by the other three.

Ignoring the men he'd just sentenced to drown, Stache turned to the remaining pirates, who watched him fearfully.

"Now," he said. "We're going to turn this boat over and bail. You men move to . . ."

"Cap'n!" interrupted Smee.

"WHAT IS IT?" bellowed Stache, very close to running Smee through with his sword just to shut him up.

"The men you knocked off?" said Smee.

"What about them?" said Stache.

"They ain't sinking, Cap'n," said Smee.

Stache whirled around and saw it was true: behind him, five heads, and five sets of shoulders, poked up from the surface of the lagoon, steady as rocks.

The discarded crewmen were standing, chest deep. A sandbar extended off the point of land.

The pirates could walk to shore.

CHAPTER 70

ALMOST THERE

SLANK CAREFULLY WATCHED the two auburn-haired mermaids swim back toward the rock where Peter stood. When they were nearly there, he addressed Little Richard.

"Turn the dory over and put the trunk in it," he said.

"What about *them?*" asked Little Richard, gesturing toward Alf and the boys who were facedown on the sand.

"They won't be no trouble," said Slank. "Unless they want the little lady here to get her neck shortened."

He kept a firm grip on Molly as Little Richard waded out to the dory. The big man turned it over easily, and Slank was gratified to see that, other than the half-moon-shaped piece bitten from the transom by the mermaid, the little boat appeared undamaged. It would certainly get them to the ship. If necessary, he could try using the starstuff, but that could prove dicey: trying to fly the boat, and the trunk, and Little Richard, and the girl. Especially the girl: she concerned him most of all. A Starcatcher by blood, she might be real trouble once near the starstuff.

Secretly, Slank had no intention—none at all—of letting Molly go. The boy was a fool to believe otherwise. Instead, Slank could see himself returning to Rundoon as a hero: he would be bringing with him not only the largest harvest of starstuff in human memory, but also a member of a legendary Starcatcher family, the daughter of the great Leonard Aster. King Zarboff would be *very* pleased. The King *loved* pretty girls—he was sure to reward Slank heavily.

Little Richard loaded the trunk into the stern of the upright dory.

"All set, sir," he said.

Slank dragged Molly through the water and lifted her into the bow of the dory. He crouched next to her, knife still poised. Little Richard pushed off, then climbed into the middle seat and took up the oars.

Slank kept his attention fixed on the rock where Peter stood surrounded by the mermaids. None of them appeared to have moved.

"Remember our bargain, boy!" he shouted.

"I remember," replied Peter.

Fool, thought Slank.

The oars dipped, pulled, rose; dipped, pulled, rose. Little Richard's powerful strokes, aided by the seaward current, pulled them rapidly away from the beach, toward the wide mouth of the lagoon. Slank kept his eyes on the rock, but still saw no sign of movement. As it finally slipped from sight in the distance, Peter and the mermaids were still positioned exactly as they had been.

Slank switched his attention to the water, watching for the dreaded Vs. He saw nothing, heard nothing, except for the swirling eddies caused by Little Richard's steady strokes.

In ten minutes' time they reached the mouth of the lagoon, and began to round the rocky point. Slank now fixed his attention on the masts of the *Jolly Roger* and considered what he would do with the ship's crew. They'd likely be unhappy, having been tied up all these hours. Some he would have to throw overboard. Some he would keep to sail the ship, using Little Richard—and the power the starstuff would give him—to control them.

Out of the lagoon, and into open sea, Slank checked the water's surface again: Still no signs of mermaids. He began, for the first time in many hours, to relax. He released his grip on Molly's mouth. She spat, as if disgusted by the taste of his hand.

"There now, young lady," he said. "I'm not so bad, once you get used to me. Which you will, on our voyage to Rundoon."

Molly glared at him, but said nothing.

"He's a fool, your trusting little friend back there," taunted Slank.

"He's a good person," said Molly. "He did what he thought was right. You wouldn't understand that."

As they approached the *Jolly Roger*, which sparkled in the moonlight, Slank could see the inert forms of the hog-tied pirates slumped over the booms, just as he and Little Richard had left them.

"Almost there," he said to Molly. "Welcome to your new home."

CHAPTER 71

A Good Thing

Black Stache slogged to shore, his sword drawn, his men in front of him, where he could see them—especially the ones he'd thrown off the boat. They'd been muttering and grumbling among themselves, and he sensed mutiny in the air.

As they reached dry land, he decided that, given the unusual circumstances, it was time for a little motivational speech.

"Now, men," he said. "I know some of you might be unhappy with the way things has been going."

The men stared sullenly back at him. Stache continued: "But if I hadn't shoved you off the boat back there, you'd be lost at sea now, wouldn't you? We'd *all* be lost! Think about it, men!"

The men frowned, thinking about it. Stache pressed on.

"So it's thanks to me you're standing here, isn't it?

Without your captain, you'd all be dead. Am I right, men? Well? Am I?"

Some of the men were scratching their heads now. A good sign.

"Of *course* I'm right," said Stache. "That's why I'm the captain. And that's why you men do what I say. And right now, I says we march back around to that beach, and kill them buggers what took our treasure, and gets it and ourselves back to the *Jolly Roger*. Well! Then, let's go, men!"

And with that, he passed through the group of them and strode off in the general direction of the waterfalls. From there they could continue on around to the beach. After a few strides, he glanced back: his men, led by Smee, were following. They didn't look none too happy, but they were coming. Stache looked forward, and smiled.

Pirates, he thought. *It's a good thing they're idjits*.

CHAPTER 72

CHANGE OF PLANS

SLANK COULD NOT STOP TALKING. He was almost giddy now, as the dory drew near the *Jolly Roger*. He felt confident that, with the power in the trunk, the crew would be his. It pleased him to have Molly to boast to, to taunt.

"D'you fancy snakes?" he asked her. "Because King Zarboff has a big one. Don't get too close to it, though. It fancies tender young morsels like you." Slank laughed.

"You'll never get to Rundoon," said Molly, her voice even.

Slank cut his laugh short. "Who's to stop me?" he said. "You? Your little trusting friend, back there on the rock?"

"No," said Molly. "My father. He's coming, and he'll find you."

Slank laughed again.

"And what if he does?" he said. "Even if he manages to find me, do you think he's any match for what's in that trunk?"

Molly tried to remain expressionless, but Slank caught a flicker in her eyes.

"Ah," he said. "I see that *you* see my point."

"Yes," said Molly, although that was not what she had seen, not at all. What she had seen, and almost betrayed, was the dark shape coming across the water from the direction of the lagoon mouth, low and fast. She saw it because she was facing the stern; Slank, facing her, did not see it.

"Yes," she said, "I suppose you might be right. There must be a great deal of power in that trunk."

"Oh, indeed there is," said Slank, enjoying the fact that his prize captive was talking now. "More power than has ever fallen to Earth, at least in human times. That's what they say. Power enough to change the world."

"What will you do with it?" asked Molly, desperate to keep Slank's attention, to keep him from turning his head toward the shape in the sky. She worried, too, about Little Richard, who was facing the stern, but his head was bent forward, his attention focused, for now, on his oarwork.

"What will we do?" said Slank. "Why, we'll change the world, of course! We'll *command* the world, we will. Once we kill off you Starcatchers."

The flying shape was close now.

"Do you really think you can do that?" said Molly. "The Starcatchers have a great deal of knowledge, you know. And power."

"True," said Slank. "But we're about to . . ."

He stopped abruptly, staring at Molly, and in that instant she knew that her eyes, tracking the flying shape, had betrayed her. Slank whirled and shouted as he saw it hurtling toward him. Little Richard saw it, too, and raised an oar to hit it, as Slank raised his knife to stab it.

"PETER!" shouted Molly.

"MOLLY, JUMP!" shouted Peter.

And jump she did, launching herself off the bow of the dory, just as Peter swept overhead, his right hand stretched down and reaching for her. She, too, reached up for him, but his hand only brushed hers for an instant, and he was gone. Molly fell into the water.

Slank roared in fury and reached overboard for Molly, grabbing her by the hair; but then he heard Peter's shout. The boy, having turned, was coming back around, diving toward him. Releasing Molly, Slank spun and raised his knife, timing his lunge as the boy swooped in closer, closer, and . . .

Missed.

Peter swerved at the last instant, leaving Slank stabbing the air, and Little Richard swinging his oar at nothing.

Slank looked back at the water, and saw that Molly was . . .

Gone.

He cursed, then checked the stern.

The trunk was still there.

"Out of my way!" he shouted, struggling in the little dory to get past Little Richard without capsizing. With the girl gone, he would take no more chances: He would use the starstuff *now*.

CHAPTER 73

"Just Watch"

MOLLY SANK, FARTHER AND FARTHER DOWN. The moon, at first bright and yellow on the rippling sea surface above her, grew dimmer, and greener. She churned her arms and legs, but made heavy by her clothes, could not swim. Her lungs burned. She was going to drown.

Her right hand tingled with warmth.

Her hand was tingling where Peter had touched her.

Molly held her hand before her face, and, in the watery dimness, she saw the faint glow, and she understood: Peter hadn't been trying to lift her off the boat; he'd been trying to put starstuff on her hand. But was it enough? They'd touched for only the briefest instant. . . .

Forcing herself to ignore her aching lungs, Molly raised her right hand over her head and closer her eyes, focusing on the tingling feeling, willing it to spread, and to lift her.

Please be enough, please . . .

She opened her eyes, but couldn't tell if she'd sunk deeper or not; she was close to losing consciousness. Once more, she closed her eyes.

Please, please. . . .

And then she felt it, the familiar warmth. She opened her eyes underwater and looked up to see the moon, the lovely moon, brighter and less green, much more golden, coming nearer to her now, and nearer, and then . . .

AAAAAHHHH . . . Molly's head broke through the surface, and she leaned back and sucked in all the salt air she could grab with one breath, and . . .

"THERE SHE IS! GET HER!"

It was Slank's voice, coming from behind her. Molly twisted—the starstuff had lifted her halfway out of the sea, so the water was now at her waist—and she saw the dory not twenty feet away, saw Slank hunkered over the trunk, pointing to her; saw the huge man tugging on the oars, turning the dory toward her.

I need to get higher, thought Molly, straining upward. *Come on, come on . . .*

She felt her body rising, but slowly, slowly—too slowly, she saw, as the dory was almost upon her, the giant swinging the stern around, so that Slank, in the stern, could reach for her, and . . .

"Molly! Here!"

Peter didn't just touch her right hand, this time; he

grabbed it. Joining hands, he pulled her upward, and she burst free of the water just as . . .

"GOT HER!" shouted Slank, taking hold of Molly's ankle. He yanked down hard and Molly screamed in pain as her arm felt as though it was coming out of its socket. Peter hung on desperately to her right hand as the far more powerful Slank slowly dragged her down by her left leg, Molly hanging between them, suspended over the water at the stern of the dory.

"GRAB HER OTHER LEG!" Slank yelled to Little Richard, and the big man let go the oars. Molly knew that once the giant took hold of her, she was doomed. She realized she had one chance—just one—as she drew back her left foot and . . .

"*UNNH!*" Slank grunted in pain as Molly drove her left heel into his nose, blood spurting instantly, the shock weakening his grip just enough for Molly to yank her right foot free of his grasp just as Little Richard reached for her, his huge grasping fingers just brushing her leg and . . .

She was free!

Released from Slank's weight, Peter and Molly shot upward together, still holding hands, tumbling, tumbling in the moonlit night sky.

They let go of each other, spreading their arms, steadying themselves, both of them veteran fliers now. In a strangely calm moment, they hovered, catching their breath, about fifty feet above the water and the dory where Slank cursed, holding his bleeding nose.

"Are you all right?" said Peter.

"I'm fine," answered Molly, although in fact her whole body hurt from being a human tug-o'-war rope. Then, stiffly, she added, "Thank you for saving me."

"I owed you one," said Peter, studying her face, surprised by her tone. "What's wrong?"

"Wrong? *Everything* is wrong," hissed Molly. "Peter, *you let Slank have the trunk.* I appreciate your heroics, but all we've done, all we've gone through, counts for *nothing* if that man"—she pointed down at the dory—"has the starstuff. I thought you understood that."

"Molly," said Peter, "I . . ."

"YOU'RE BOTH GOING TO DIE!"

Peter and Molly looked down; Slank, blood streaming down his face, was in the bow of the dory again, glaring up at them, knife in hand. His voice was choked with rage.

"ENJOY YOUR LAST MOMENTS, LOVEBIRDS!" he screamed. "I'M COMING FOR YOU NOW!"

Slank bent to the trunk lid. He'd already bashed one of the hinges off with a rock; now he slid his knife blade under the other hinge, preparing to pry it off.

"Peter!" said Molly. "We must stop him!" She began to lean forward, into a dive, only to be stopped by Peter's hand grabbing her arm. They floated above the sea and the dory.

"Let GO!" she shouted.

"No!" said Peter. "Just watch."

Slank pulled on the knife handle. The trunk hinge popped off easily, as if it had been barely attached, and clattered to the bottom of the dory. Slank looked back up at Peter and Molly, a look of triumph on his face, then turned back to the trunk and lifted the lid.

The trunk was empty.

For two seconds, three, four, Slank remained absolutely motionless. A drop of blood fell from his nose and spattered on the rough wooden bottom of the trunk. Then with a scream of inhuman rage he stood, looked up, drew back his arm and hurled his knife skyward, straight at Peter. It was a perfectly aimed throw, and Slank knew, as he released it, that it would find its mark.

And it would have, except for the starstuff's power flowing through Peter, enhancing his senses, slowing the world down for him. He saw the blade leave Slank's hand, saw it turning in the moonlight, the turns perfectly timed so that the knife's sharp point would penetrate deep into the center of his chest; and Peter saw that if he shifted his body just slightly, and brought his hand up just . . . *Now* . . .

As Slank gaped in disbelief, Peter plucked his knife right out of the air.

"Thank you!" shouted Peter.

Slank, a strangling sound coming from his throat, looked

around furiously for something, anything, to use as a weapon. But there was nothing in the dory, nothing but the empty trunk, mocking him.

"Mr. Slank," said Little Richard. "We're moving. I mean, something's moving us."

Slank looked at the water; it was true. Although Little Richard wasn't touching the oars, the dory, as if acting on its own, was moving away from the island.

Slank looked at the water astern, and there he saw them: the telltale Vs of the mermaids. The dory was picking up speed; the island was receding.

"Good-bye!" called Peter, waving.

"*Bon voyage*, Mr. Slank!" called Molly.

Slank, too stunned to answer, slumped to the bottom of the dory, his back against the empty trunk. He stared back at the boy and the girl who had somehow defeated him.

A boy and a girl.

They waved at him one last time, then, holdings hands, they turned, leaned forward, and swooped down, then up, in a graceful inverted arc, heading back to the island, as Slank and Little Richard, helpless, continued being pushed out to the open sea, in a little boat with an old trunk that had once held the greatest treasure on earth.

CHAPTER 74

The Golden Box

MOLLY FLEW CLOSE TO PETER, so he could hear her over the sound of the air rushing past as they swooped and soared over the sea, heading back to the island.

"What did you do with the starstuff?" she shouted. "How did you do it? Where is it now? Who . . ."

"Wait!" laughed Peter. "One question at a time!"

"Is the starstuff safe?" she asked.

"Yes," he said. "I'm taking you to it now."

"Oh, Peter, thank heaven," she said. "But what happened? Where *were* you? After you left us to climb over the point, we came 'round the long way to the beach, and you weren't there."

"Right," said Peter. "I waited for a while, but there was some kind of fight going on up the beach. So I went up to have a look."

"You were *supposed* to wait for us," said Molly.

"I know," said Peter. "I didn't intend to get close, but then I saw . . ."

Peter hesitated.

"You saw *what?*" said Molly, impatiently.

"I saw a mermaid," said Peter. He looked sideways at Molly, who was staring at him.

"You don't believe me," he said.

"No," she said, slowly. "I do. Do you remember when I told you about the strange things that starstuff does to animals? The minotaurs and such?"

"Yes," said Peter.

"Well, that's where mermaids come from," said Molly. "The trunk must have leaked starstuff into the water."

"Maybe it did," said Peter. "Well anyway, I found this mermaid on the beach, and she was hurt, bleeding from the head, and I had your locket, and there was a little starstuff left, so I gave it to her. I'm sorry, Molly, but I was afraid she would die, and she was so . . . *beautiful.*"

Molly gave Peter a very sharp look, but he missed it.

"Go on," she said, coolly.

"After that," Peter said, "things happened so fast. The starstuff healed the mermaid, and there were these *other* mermaids, and they were all excited about something, and I followed them along the beach, and there was the trunk! With nobody around it! So I ran up to it, and . . . and . . ."

"And *what?*"

"I'm not sure," said Peter. "I think somebody hit me, because I had a raging head pain when I woke up, in the water, and Teacher was holding me."

"Teacher?" said Molly.

"The mermaid I saved," said Peter. "Molly, she saved *me*."

"How do you know her name is Teacher?" said Molly.

"I dunno," said Peter. "I just *know*. I can feel her thoughts, and she can feel mine. Isn't that incredible, Molly?"

"Yes," said Molly, sounding quite unhappy, although Peter didn't notice.

They were at the mouth of the lagoon now; Peter, with Molly following close, altered course slightly, leaning slightly to the right, toward the jumble of rocks at the base of the waterfall in the center of the curving beach.

"So anyway," continued Peter, "I was in the water, with Teacher and the others keeping me afloat, and Teacher told me—not by speaking, you understand, but by . . ."

"Yes, by thinking, you told me that," said Molly.

"Right, by thinking, she told me that she knew about the trunk! She called it Creator. And we decided to find it, so we went back to the beach, and we saw the fight going on, with you and James jumping on Slank, and Alf fighting that huge man. And we saw the trunk was unguarded. And that's when we came up with our plan."

"You and Teacher," said Molly.

"Yes," said Peter. "She's very clever. You'll like her."

"I'm sure," said Molly.

"While you were fighting," said Peter, "we grabbed the trunk and carried it quickly—you won't *believe* how fast the mermaids can swim—out to the rocks. My biggest fear was that we wouldn't be able to open it, but somebody had already bashed at the hinges, and it was easy. And there it was, inside—Molly, it was *amazing*—and I took it out, and hid it behind the rock."

"You *touched* the starstuff?" said Molly. "Peter, in that quantity, it could have killed you!"

"I didn't touch it directly," said Peter. "It was in a locked metal box, a yellow box, like gold. It's very powerful, Molly; much more so than the locket. I only held it in my hands for a moment when I lifted it, and I nearly fainted from that. Anyway, I think the box must have leaked, because there was loose starstuff in the wooden trunk. That's why the trunk glowed so much. I dumped the loose starstuff onto the rock, next to where I hid the metal box. Then I put the wooden trunk on the rock and yelled to Slank."

"A good thing, too," said Molly. "He was about to stab me."

"I know," said Peter. "I was scared to death he'd figure out the trick, but he believed me, and took the trunk. Of course he took you, too; I hadn't expected that."

"I bet Teacher did," muttered Molly.

"What?" said Peter.

"Nothing," said Molly.

"But I had the loose starstuff," said Peter, "so I waited a bit, figuring Slank would let his guard down, then I came after you, with the mermaids following, to make sure Slank didn't come back."

"Thank you, again," said Molly.

"It's nothing," said Peter. "Ah, there's the rock."

Just ahead was the flat rock from which Peter had stood with the wooden trunk. From this, the seaward side, Molly could see that the rock had a ledge just above the water; on that ledge rested a gleaming gold box, radiant in the moonlight, almost too bright to look at directly. Next to it was a small glowing pile, the remains of the leaked starstuff.

As she swooped close, Molly saw mermaids in the water, and several more sitting on the rock. Peter swooped in and landed lightly among them; he had become quite an accomplished flier. Molly alit next to him. The mermaids studied her with frank curiosity.

"Molly," said Peter, "this is Teacher."

She was, as Peter had said, beautiful, her long blond tresses flowing elegantly down her front. Molly felt hideously dowdy in contrast; her dress was wet, her hair a tangled mess.

"I'm sure you two will be great friends," said Peter.

Molly and Teacher eyed each other in the manner of two young women who will never, ever, be great friends.

"I must take care of the starstuff," said Molly. "We're rid of Slank, I hope, but there are still those pirates about."

She bent down to examine the gold chest, only to draw back quickly when two mermaids lunged toward her, hissing.

"They're guarding it," said Peter.

"Well, tell them to stop," said Molly.

Peter turned to Teacher, and they exchanged a look that nearly drove Molly insane with jealousy, though she hid her feelings well. Then Teacher, looking none too happy, grunted something, and the two hissing mermaids retreated.

"You can touch it now," said Peter.

"Thank you," said Molly coldly.

She bent to examine the chest, putting her hand on it, then quickly pulling it away, overwhelmed by the power she felt emanating from it. Peter was right; it was *much* stronger than her locket had been.

Molly was worried. She finally had the starstuff, but what could she do with it? How could she get it off this rock? And if she could, where should she move it? Would it be any safer on the island, with the pirates, and the savages?

Molly felt tired and cold, and no match for the crushing burden of responsibility for solving a problem far beyond her limited Starcatcher training. She wanted to cry, but she did not want Peter to see her cry, and she *especially* did not want Teacher, with her flowing hair, to see her cry. And so she stood and turned toward the sea, and felt the burn of tears, and, not wanting to be seen wiping her eyes, blinked them, first in irritation, and then again in amazement, as she saw it, coming around the point on the right side of the lagoon: a longboat, four oars per side, moving swiftly, guided by the familiar, graceful, arcing form of Ammm . . .

"AHOY!" called a deep voice from the longboat, and Molly didn't care now who saw her cry, because she knew that voice better than any other in the world: the voice of her father.

CHAPTER 75

FOREVER

THEY WERE ON THE BEACH NOW: Peter, Molly, Leonard Aster, Alf, James, Prentiss, Thomas, and Tubby Ted. After his tearful reunion with Molly, Leonard had insisted that she and Peter get off the rock, and that the mermaids keep their distance, while his crew of Starcatchers dealt with the box of starstuff.

From the beach, the scene on the rock looked unearthly: the Starcatchers, five men and three women, were clad head-to-toe in shiny gold-colored clothing, including gloves, boots, and helmets whose face masks had only the smallest of eye slits. They shone like human chandeliers, their gleaming costumes reflecting both the moon—now low in the sky, but still bright—and the brilliant light radiating from the golden starstuff box.

As Leonard and the others on the beach watched, Leonard explained that the shining clothes were, in fact, made of gold: it had been spun into fibers and woven by a process known only to the Starcatchers, who had learned, over the years, that gold, and only gold, could contain the power of the starstuff.

"That's why the Others put this batch of starstuff into that golden box," said Leonard. "But they didn't do it correctly. The box must be constructed so that air itself cannot pass in or out. If it's done right, the starstuff can't escape, and it can't be detected. That's why I found nothing odd about the fact that I felt nothing from the trunk on the *Wasp*—I assumed the golden box inside was made correctly.

"But of course the real reason was that there *was* no starstuff inside the *Wasp* trunk—it was a ruse that, I'm ashamed to say, fooled me completely. The real starstuff box—the one on the *Never Land*—was not made properly; the Others don't have the experience that we have, or the expertise, or the craftsmanship. They couldn't make the box tight enough. And so the box leaked. In fact, it's been leaking since it was back in Scotland; apparently some of it got on a lizard or snake, which transformed into some sort of strange gigantic creature, which managed to escape into Loch Ness. I certainly hope that's the last we hear of *that*.

"In any event," continued Leonard, "we've got the starstuff back now, thanks to you, young lady. You did well, Molly. *Extraordinarily* well—a young Starcatcher, alone, defeating Slank and that giant of his . . ."

"It wasn't just me," said Molly. "It was Peter, too. In fact it was *mostly* Peter."

"Is that so," Leonard said thoughtfully, studying Peter.

"It is, father!" said Molly. "Peter was *wonderful*. There's so much I need to tell you, but for starters, he rescued me from Slank, and he came up with the idea of taking the starstuff out of the trunk."

"That wasn't just me," said Peter, blushing. "That was Teacher's idea, too."

"I suppose," said Molly, coldly.

"Teacher?" said Leonard.

"That mermaid there," said Peter. "The yellow-haired one."

He pointed to where the mermaids were gathered, a few yards offshore. Teacher was the closest, watching them—watching Molly, actually—and looking quite unhappy.

"So you picked up the golden box?" Leonard asked Peter.

"I did," said Peter.

"And how long did you hold it?"

"I don't know," said Peter. "A few seconds, I think. I can't say for sure. As I told Molly, I almost fainted."

"You almost did far worse than that," said Leonard, but softly, to himself.

"What did you say?" said Molly.

"Nothing," said Leonard. "Molly, did you touch the box?"

"Only for the briefest instant," said Molly. "I had to

pull my hand away. I don't know how Peter managed to pick it up."

"Nor do I," said Leonard, studying Peter now with an intensity that Peter found disconcerting. "Nor do I. Tell me, Peter," he said. "How did you fly out to rescue Molly from Slank?"

"I used the loose starstuff," said Peter. "I poured it out of the trunk, and scooped some into my hand."

"I see," said Leonard. "And you gave some to Molly, so she could fly back with you, is that right?"

"Yes," said Peter.

"Molly," said Leonard. "Can you fly now?"

Molly closed her eyes, concentrating.

"No," she said after a few moments. "It's worn off."

"Peter," said Leonard. "Can *you* fly?"

Peter's body immediately started to rise.

"That's odd," he said, hovering a few feet of the ground. "Usually I have to try, but this time . . . I just *thought* about it, and here I am!" He floated gently back down.

"I see," said Leonard, his expression grave.

"Father," said Molly, "What is it? Is something wrong with Peter?"

"Not *wrong*, no," said Leonard. "Not exactly."

"What do you mean?" said Molly and Peter together.

"I mean," said Aster, "that the starstuff may have changed Peter. Just as it changed the fish in this lagoon"—

420

he gestured toward the mermaids—"it can change people, too, if there's enough of it."

Peter was pale. "How did it change me? I don't feel any different."

"Fly," said Leonard.

Immediately, Peter rose again.

"That's how," said Leonard.

"You mean . . . you mean I can just . . . *fly* now? Without needing more starstuff?"

"Yes," said Leonard.

"And it's permanent?" said Peter. "I'll *always* be able to fly?"

"I believe so," said Leonard.

"But that's wonderful!" said Peter, grinning hugely, still floating just off the ground. "I can fly!"

"But, Father," said Molly. "If that's so, why don't all the Starcatchers do what Peter did? Why don't we expose ourselves to enough starstuff that *we* can always fly, as well?"

"For two reasons," said Leonard. "One is that the concentration of starstuff required for the transformation is ordinarily fatal, even for a Starcatcher, let alone a normal person. Peter is very, very lucky; he must have an extraordinary tolerance for starstuff. Most people who picked up that leaking box would have died; in fact, we understand that several *did* die when that box was filled."

"What's the other reason?" said Peter.

"The other reason," said Leonard, "is that the starstuff, in that concentration, causes other changes in humans, beyond just enabling them to fly."

"What do you mean?" said Peter. "What other changes?"

"I don't know, frankly," said Leonard. "There are few cases like yours, of a person surviving the exposure, and each one is unique. But it's possible that . . . that you . . ."

Leonard hesitated.

"That I what?" pressed Peter.

"That you won't get any older."

"*What?*" said Peter.

"That you'll stay as you are," said Leonard. "A boy. Forever."

Peter thought about that for several moments, then spoke, slowly.

"Is that bad?" he said.

"I don't know," said Leonard. "I suppose in some ways, it could be good—never getting old and tired; never becoming frail."

Peter considered that.

"But it could be lonely, too," he said. "Staying the same age, while your friends grow up." He looked at Molly, then quickly looked away.

"Yes," said Leonard. "There is that."

"How will I know?" said Peter. "How will I know if I've changed?"

"I think," said Leonard, "you'll just have to wait. And perhaps I'm mistaken. We can look into this more, when we're back in England; I'll arrange with your family to . . ."

"I have no family," said Peter. "I'm an orphan." He gestured to James, Prentiss, Thomas, and Tubby Ted. "We're all orphans."

"They were on there way to Rundoon," said Molly, with a shudder. "To serve King Zarboff."

"I see," said Leonard to Peter. "Well, then, when we get back to England, you'll stay with us, and we'll sort this out. But for now, we need to deal with the starstuff: I see my people have just about finished their work."

The gold-clad figures on the rock had carefully lifted the leaking golden box and placed it inside a larger, leakproof one, made by Starcatcher artisans. They then sealed this second box and placed it inside a black wooden trunk, much like the decoy one that the Others had loaded onto the *Wasp* back in London, so long ago. The Starcatchers stowed this trunk in the longboat, and removed their golden protective garb. They were now rowing to shore to pick up the others.

"It's a good-sized longboat," said Leonard. "I think it will hold us all. Our ship is anchored 'round that point there. We're to be escorted back to England by two British navy warships, seventy-four guns apiece; we Starcatchers have our friends in the government. The navy will also be escorting the pirate ship out there. Strangest thing: the pirates were all tied up and hung about like laundry."

"Slank," said Molly, and Peter nodded. Peter's hand went to his belt, where he'd tucked Slank's knife.

"We found Mrs. Bumbrake locked below," continued Aster. "She was a bit cranky, but none the worse for wear." Aster's eyes twinkled. "She's looking forward to resuming her care of you, Molly."

"Wonderful!" said Molly, making no effort at all to sound sincere.

"Here we are," said Aster, as prow of the sleek longboat reached the beach. He called to Alf and the boys, "All aboard for England, then!"

He took a step toward the longboat, then stopped at the sound—a harsh SWISH, then a loud and solid THUNKKKK—as a hurtling spear hissed passed his head, and buried its sharp, pink tip deep into the longboat hull.

"Stop right there, Englishman!" hollered Fighting Prawn, a hundred Mollusks behind him.

CHAPTER 76

$\mathcal{P}$ETER'S $\mathcal{P}$LEA

$\mathcal{T}$HE ENTIRE MOLLUSK TRIBE, a hundred strong, were arrayed in a semicircle on the beach around Leonard, Molly, Peter, and the others. The first light of dawn was showing in the sky; it caught the sharpened pink shells that formed the spear-tips of the Mollusk warriors.

They'd crept silently from the jungle while all attention had been focused on the mermaid rock. Now they stood watching, the warriors in front, spears poised, waiting for orders from Fighting Prawn.

"Who on earth are *they*?" whispered Leonard.

"They live here," whispered Peter. "They captured us before, but we got away. They're called the Mollusks. That old man is their leader. He hates Englishmen."

"You might have mentioned this to me, Molly," said Leonard. "The fact that there are hostile natives on the island."

"I forgot," said Molly.

"You *forgot?*" said Leonard.

"There's been a lot happening," said Molly.

As she spoke, Fighting Prawn came forward with the confidence of one who is well aware of the overwhelming superiority of his forces. Ignoring Leonard and the other Starcatchers, he walked up to Peter.

"So, boy," he said. "You were not lying, about the magic."

"No," said Peter.

Fighting Prawn looked around at the others, then at the trunk.

"And there it is," he said. "In that box. Magic that makes people fly, makes animals fly, turns fish into women, or women into fish." He nodded toward the mermaid rock.

"Yes," said Peter.

"We will take it," said Fighting Prawn, signaling with his hand. A dozen warriors started forward toward the longboat. The Starcatcher crew drew their weapons, swords and pistols. The warriors stopped, looking to Fighting Prawn, who turned calmly to Leonard Aster.

"Tell them to drop their weapons," he said.

"No," said Leonard. "We can't let you have that trunk."

"You are not in a position to decide what we can have," said Fighting Prawn. "Your people might hurt some of mine, but there are too many of us. We will win, and you will die." He gestured toward Molly. "I have watched you from the jungle; I can see that you love this girl. Do you want her to die?"

Leonard looked at Molly, then back at Fighting Prawn, and shook his head.

"No," he said.

"Then tell your people to put down their weapons."

"NO!" said Molly.

"She's right!" said Peter. "He'll kill us anyway. They kill ALL strangers on this island. That's what he told us."

"That's true," said Fighting Prawn. "I told you that. But I won't kill you. I need you to show me how the magic works. I can see it has great power. I can see even *you* fear its power. So to use it, I need you. That is your guarantee of safety."

Leonard was silent for a moment, then spoke softly.

"All right," he said.

"Father, don't!" said Molly.

"Molly," said Leonard. "Look around us. He's right. Even if we do all we can"—here he gave Molly a significant look, and touched the locket chain around his neck—"some of us will die. We'll do as he says, *for now*, and perhaps we can . . . ah . . . work something out." Again, he touched his locket chain. He turned to the Starcatcher crew. "Drop your weapons," he said.

Reluctantly, they obeyed.

"Now, tell them to get out of the boat," said Fighting Prawn. "But they're to leave the magic box where it is."

Leonard gave the order, and the Starcatchers joined him on the beach.

Fighting Prawn turned and made a series of grunting and clicking sounds. Immediately the Starcatchers were surrounded by the warriors, who began to prod them to move down the beach.

"Where are they taking us?" said Leonard.

"Just a short distance there," said Fighting Prawn. "I want to take a look at this magic box, but I don't want you close enough to try any Englishman tricks when I do." He gestured to Peter. "You, boy, you come with me. If you try anything, your friends will pay for it, do you understand?"

"Yes," said Peter.

The Mollusks herded the Starcatchers, along with Alf and the other boys, about twenty-five yards down the beach. Fighting Prawn and Peter walked to the longboat, its prow resting on the sand. They climbed inside. The trunk lay in the bow. Fighting Prawn went forward and touched the lid, resting his hand on the smooth, dark wood.

"How does it work, boy?" he said to Peter.

"I don't know," said Peter.

"Don't lie, boy. I've seen you fly."

"Yes," said Peter, "but I don't understand it. It's very powerful, and it can do many things, wonderful things, strange things. But also bad things, if the wrong people have it. And there are . . . Listen, I can't explain all of what's going on—

it's very complicated—but you *must* believe me. You will be much better off, *much* better, if you let that man"—he pointed at Leonard—"take this trunk, and leave this island."

Fighting Prawn shook his head. "If he leaves," he said, "more will come, and more. No, boy. I will keep him, and I will keep this trunk, and with his help I will learn to use its power, and when I do, I will make sure no outsider dares set foot on this island ever again."

Peter was about to try another plea, when he heard the sound behind him: running footsteps slapping on the hard-packed sand. Fighting Prawn heard them too, and their heads turned, and they saw, coming hard, coming fast, a cutthroat crew led by a scowling figure with his sword held high.

Black Stache.

CHAPTER 77

ATTACK

STACHE'S ATTACK WAS PERFECTLY TIMED, thanks to his veteran-pirate grasp of tactics—and a big piece of luck.

He and his men had been watching from the palms as the strangely dressed figures had transferred the treasure into a new wooden trunk. The men, especially Smee, were some-what unnerved by the gleaming gold costumes, but Slank had convinced them that this was an indication of how rich, how fabulous, the treasure was—those who possessed it wore *golden clothes!*

He'd watched as the figures had loaded the trunk into the longboat.

Such a lovely boat; so nice of them to provide it for me.

His plan was to spring the attack just as the longboat reached the beach, and he was about to give the order when—*NO!*—the savages appeared. For several horrid minutes, Stache was filled with rage and despair, thinking all hope was lost.

But then came the incredible stroke of luck. For some reason not clear to Stache, the old savage, the leader, sent all
the others down the beach, leaving only himself and the
boy—*The cursed boy!*—with the longboat. It was *perfect*.

And with a few whispered instructions—the plan was quite
simple—Stache had whispered "Now!" And the attack was on.

It took only seconds: by the time the boy and the old man
had turned their heads, the pirates were at the longboat; by
the time the old savage had shouted, it was in the water,
moving away from shore, with the waddling Smee bringing
up the rear, just barely making it aboard.

By the time the cursed boy had got to his feet, in the
prow, just in front of the old savage, Black Stache was upon
him, his sword drawn back.

"Good-bye, boy," Stache said.

Smiling, he lunged his sword forward, the tip of his blade
aimed at the boy's heart, and . . .

The boy disappeared.

In fact, he flew straight up, but so quickly did he launch
himself that Stache never really saw it, and thus had no
chance to stop the thrust of his sword, which continued right
through, plunging deep into the chest of Fighting Prawn.

$\mathcal{A}$LL THE $\mathcal{T}$IME IN THE $\mathcal{W}$ORLD

$\mathcal{P}$ETER WAS ASCENDING WHEN HE HEARD THE SCREAM; he looked down and saw Stache, a look of puzzlement on his face, pull his sword from Fighting Prawn's chest. Fighting Prawn, still standing, looked down at the blood gushing from the awful wound, then, with a groan, fell backward onto the starstuff trunk.

Peter looked back to the beach, where chaos had erupted. Mollusk warriors, roaring with rage, were sprinting along the sand and into the water, spears cocked. Behind them, a dozen more highly agitated warriors surrounded Leonard, Molly, and the others, ready to strike at the slightest move, the points of their spears almost touching the captives.

"ROW, YOU DOGS!" screamed Stache to his men. "ROW FOR YOUR LIVES!" The pirates, needing no encouragement, were already at the oars, pulling with all their strength. A spear thunked into the side of the longboat, then another, then one just overhead. Stache, in the prow, yanked Fighting Prawn upright, and dragged him to the side of the boat. The old man's face was gray from blood loss, but he blinked, still alive. Stache raised the wounded man up in front of him for the Mollusks on the beach to see.

"*DO YOU WANT TO KILL HIM, THEN?*" bellowed Stache. Afraid of hitting their chief, warriors stopped throwing spears. Some of them, insane with frustration, plunged into the lagoon and began swimming, but the pirate rowers had found their rhythm, and the longboat was moving far too fast for any swimmer to catch.

Stache was getting away. With the Starcatchers unable to move on the beach, and the Mollusks unable to reach him, *Black Stache was getting away.*

Peter swooped through the sky—bright now; the sun was up—toward the longboat, looking for an opening, trying desperately to think of a plan. There was no way he could overpower the pirates without help, without . . .

Teacher.

As he thought of her, he felt her thoughts; she was down there, underwater, fearful of all the commotion, uncertain about what was happening, what she should do . . .

Stop the boat, thought Peter. *Stop the boat.*

He swooped lower. The longboat appeared to be unhindered; if anything, it seemed to be picking up speed.

Stop the boat, thought Peter. *Stop the boat!*

And then he saw it: the flick of a tail in the surging longboat's wake.

Stop the boat!

The longboat lurched, sending Stache backward, cursing.

"ROW!" he bellowed. Another lurch, another.

"WHAT THE DEVIL IS WRONG WITH YOU MEN?"

"We ain't doin' it," shouted one of the pirates. "There's somethin' doin' it to us."

"ROW!" screamed Stache, and the men heaved on the oars, but the longboat had stopped completely now, dead in the water.

Push it back to shore, Peter willed.

Slowly, despite the screams of Stache and the furious efforts of the pirates, the boat, Peter floating just behind it, began to move back toward shore, toward the waiting Mollusks . . . a hundred yards away, then fifty, then twenty-five . . .

The warriors stood, spears in hand, waiting . . . .

"LISTEN TO ME!" shrieked Stache, desperation filling his voice. He held up his sword, red from hilt to tip with Fighting Prawn's blood, then held it against the old man's throat. "IF YOU COME NEAR THIS BOAT, I WILL CUT OFF HIS HEAD, D'YOU UNDERSTAND, SAVAGES?"

The Mollusks didn't understand his words, but his gestures were clear. They hesitated, watching as the boat, with Peter hovering above it, came closer to shore, closer . . .

And then it stopped, ten yards offshore. The mermaids could propel it no farther, the water too shallow. The Mollusks stood on the shore, watching. The sailors, exhausted and fearful, slumped at the oars. Stache, in the prow, held the body of Fighting Prawn, still gushing blood.

He's going to die soon, thought Peter. *If he dies, the Mollusks will kill us all.*

"Let him go!" he shouted to Stache.

Stache looked up with a hate-filled glare.

"Why don't you *make* me let him go, boy?" he said.

"All right," said Peter, drawing Slank's dagger.

He swooped straight at Stache, praying that the pirate's first instinct would be to defend himself, rather than carry out his threat to kill Fighting Prawn. He was right. Releasing the old man's unconscious body, which slumped to the floor of the longboat, Stache raised his blade, getting it up just in time to parry Peter's thrust—and in the process cutting a gash in Peter's right arm.

Peter grunted in pain as he soared back up. Blood dripped from his arm now, onto his hand, making the knife grip slippery.

"Come on back, boy!" shouted Stache. "Let me finish you off."

Peter turned, rolled and dove again; this time it was Stache who did the thrusting, and Peter the parrying. Twice more, he swooped; twice more he just avoided Stache's sword. Peter saw the problem: he had the shorter weapon, and could not get past Stache's longer one. He could keep attacking, but eventually Stache would likely nick him again, unless . . .

Peter was not a student of swordplay, but he'd noticed that when Stache lunged with his right, sword-holding hand, he threw his left out, as if for balance. He swooped again to test this observation; sure enough, the left hand was out there.

If I can feint him . . . If I can change directions quickly enough.

"COME ON, BOY!" bellowed Stache. "STOP FLITTING ABOUT LIKE A MOSQUITO! COME FIGHT ME LIKE A MAN!"

"I'm coming," said Peter. He took a breath, rolled, and dove again, aiming, as before, directly at Stache's body, watching for the thrust. . . .

Here it comes. . . .

Peter twisted his body and shot to his right, and as he did he switched his knife to his left hand and slashed downward with it, and it happened too fast for him to see, but he could feel it as he flashed past, feel the knife finding a target, and then, as he shot upward, he heard the scream, and turned to look down upon the vision of Black Stache, holding his sword in his right hand, and looking in horror at the bleeding stump where the left had been.

Several things happened then, in quick succession.

The first was that Peter caught a thought from Teacher. More of a feeling, really: a feeling of stark terror. *Something dangerous was in the lagoon.*

The second was that the pirates, seeing their captain grievously wounded, abandoned the stranded longboat, leaping into the water and sprinting toward the beach.

The third was that the Mollusk warriors started after the pirates, only to stop suddenly when they saw, lumbering from the lagoon and onto the sand, the reason for the mermaids' distress: Mister Grin. The giant reptile looked left, at the Mollusks, and then right, at the fleeing pirates, then left again, then right, as if deciding which would be dinner, and which dessert.

The fourth thing was that Smee, who had loyally remained in the longboat with Stache, wrapped his shirt around his captain's bleeding stump, and managed to drag him out of the longboat, and get him stumbling, in shock, toward shore.

The fifth thing was that Peter flew up the beach to where Molly and the others were being held at spear point, swooped down, and before the Mollusk guards could move, grabbed Leonard Aster's locket chain and yanked the locket from Leonard's neck. He flew back to the longboat, now vacant except for the motionless, blood-covered form of Fighting Prawn. He landed next to the old man and gently turned him over, exposing the wound.

He heard shouting from the shore; the Mollusks, keeping an eye on the still-motionless Mister Grin, were coming.

Fighting Prawn looked dead; his eyes were open but had rolled back, leaving only the whites exposed.

Peter fumbled with Leonard Aster's locket.

Please, please . . .

He got the locket open saw the glow, poured it all onto the old man's chest.

Please . . .

The shouting was close now, the warriors splashing to the longboat. . . .

Please . . .

The Mollusks were on him, now, hands grabbing his arms, trying to pull him away from the old man, who . . .

. . . who opened his eyes.

Thank you.

The warriors, still holding Peter, grunt-clicked something. Fighting Prawn answered with similar clicks. Then he smiled. It was a weak smile, but a smile just the same.

More shouts from the warriors, but this time, shouts of joy.

Fighting Prawn looked at Peter.

"You saved me, boy," he said.

Peter shrugged.

"Why?" said Fighting Prawn.

"To save my friends," answered Peter.

"All right then, boy," said Fighting Prawn, touching Peter's arm. "You have saved your friends."

The old man said something to the warriors; they let Peter go. He stood, and looked down the beach to his left; Molly and the others were free now, no longer surrounded by guards, but were not coming his way; instead, they stood nervously, warily. He looked to his right, and saw why: Mister Grin was still on the beach, unmoving.

A bit farther, stumbling toward the sand with the help of by Smee, was Black Stache. The pirate was holding his left arm under his right armpit, wailing in pain. At the edge of the water, he stopped, looking down in horror at something tumbling in the gentle surf.

"IT'S ME HAND, SMEE!" he screamed. "ME HAND!"

"Yes, Cap'n," said Smee. "Now you need to . . ."

"GET ME HAND, SMEE!" wailed Stache.

"But, Cap'n," said Smee, "it's . . ."

"PICK UP ME HAND!"

"All right," said Smee, leaning over reluctantly, then leaping back, shouting, "RUN, CAP'N! RUN!"

Stache looked up and saw it: Mister Grin was coming right at them. Supported by Smee, Stache began to stumble down the beach in the direction his crew had gone.

"Hurry, Smee!" he shouted. "Faster!"

Behind them, Mister Grin lumbered up to where they'd been standing. Smelling something, he swept his enormous snout back and forth, until, having found his quarry, he opened his enormous jaws, engulfing Black Stache's hand. He swallowed it in one easy gulp. Then, after a moment's pause, he set off down the beach, on the trail of the famous, fearsome pirate, moving slowly and easily, as if he knew he had all the time in the world.

CHAPTER 79

The Last Moment

THE SUN WAS HIGH NOW, the sky a brilliant blue. A perfect day on the island.

The Mollusks—generous hosts, when they weren't trying to kill you—had brought a feast to the beach for their guests: smoked fish and luscious tropical fruits, served on glossy green leaves; gourds of cool water; sweet coconut meat right from the shell.

The Mollusks took pleasure in watching their guests eat, especially Peter and the boys, who hadn't had a decent meal in weeks. They ate like hungry dogs, licking the leaves clean, gratefully accepting more, and more, and more, until even Tubby Ted was satisfied. He finally could eat no more, emitting a belch so massive that it propelled him backward onto the sand, where he lay groaning, his belly bulging skyward. The others roared with laughter, except for Peter, who, throughout the meal, had seemed oddly distant, distracted.

With the feast concluded, everyone gathered by the long-boat, which, with its precious cargo, had been guarded by four Starcatchers and four stout Mollusk warriors, in case the pirates returned. But all was quiet; even the lagoon was placid, as if resting after a tense, eventful night. Offshore the mermaids lazed by their rock; Ammm and his brethren porpoises glided in the shallows, waiting to lead the longboat back to the ship.

As the Starcatchers readied the longboat, Leonard Aster thanked Fighting Prawn and the Mollusk tribe for their hospitality.

"You mean," said Fighting Prawn, "for not killing you?"

"Yes," said Leonard. "It was very gracious of you."

"Don't mention it," said Fighting Prawn.

"Do you," said Leonard, "I mean, does your tribe, shake hands?"

"No," said Fighting Prawn. "We kiss on the lips."

"Oh," said Leonard, looking very alarmed.

"I'm joking," said Fighting Prawn, extending his hand, which Leonard took with great relief.

Leonard turned to Peter and the boys, standing on the sand with Alf and Molly.

"Time to shove off," Leonard said. "In a week's time, you'll all be back home safe in England, and this will be nothing but a dream. Ready, then? All aboard!"

They all moved to the boat—all, that is, save one. Peter remained where he was.

"Peter," said Molly. "Are you coming?"

"Yes, Peter," said James. "Come on!"

"Come along, lad!" said Alf. "We're goin' home!"

Peter shook his head.

"I'm not going," he said.

"What?" The question erupted almost simultaneously from Leonard, Molly, Alf, and James. Fighting Prawn stepped closer to Peter, listening.

"I'm staying here," said Peter.

"But . . . *why?*" asked Molly.

"I've been thinking about this," said Peter. "England's not my home. The closest thing I had to a home there was St. Norbert's, and I'm not going back there."

"You don't have to go back there," said Leonard. "I told you—you can live with our family. It's the least we can do—Molly's told me all you've done to help the St— to help us, the risks you took, not to mention saving her life. And I saw for myself, not too hours ago, your bravery and resourcefulness, saving the trunk from that pirate."

"And saving my life," said Fighting Prawn, softly.

"The point is," said Leonard, "you have a home with us. You *and* your mates."

Peter was quiet for a moment, then took a deep breath, and spoke.

"That's very generous, sir," he said. "I'm sure you have a wonderful home, and part of me"—he glanced at Molly, then away—"wants very much to say yes. But I can't."

"But, Peter, *why?*" said Molly, her eyes glistening.

"Because I'm not who I was," said Peter. "I've *changed,*

Molly. I can do things now that I couldn't do before. If I did those things in England, I'd be a *freak*, a circus sideshow. I'd have to hide what I've become. Here, on this island, I have the freedom to be who I am."

"Peter," said Leonard, "I won't deny that what you say is true. Molly and I . . . all of us"—he gestured to the Starcatchers in the longboat—"must hide who we are. Yes, your situation is a bit different. But it's not *that* different. You wouldn't be alone. You would be one of us."

"Yes, for a while," said Peter, with a hint of bitterness. "But then you'd move on, wouldn't you? And if you're right about me, I wouldn't. I'd stay the young flying boy, while you went on through your lives, as normal people do." Peter looked at Molly, and she saw that his eyes were glistening, too.

Leonard's response came in a slow and somber voice.

"Peter," he said, "I feel a great weight of responsibility for this. If not for me—for us—none of this would have happened to you. So I will ask you, one last time—I *plead* with you—to please come to England with us, and allow us to protect you, and care for you."

"I'm sorry," said Peter. "No."

Molly buried her face in her hands, muffling a sob.

"I'm sorry," Peter whispered.

In the ensuing silence, James stepped away from the longboat, and went to stand next to Peter.

"If he stays," said James, "I stay."

"No, James!" said Peter. "You don't understand. I've changed! You can go back to England and . . ."

443

". . . and be an orphan?" said James. "And go to another school? And never have another chance for an adventure like the one I've had here? And leave my best friend in the world behind? No, Peter. I've changed, too. And if you stay, I stay."

"If they stay," said Prentiss, marching up the sand, "so do I."

"And I," said Thomas, marching right behind Prentiss.

"There'll be more food, right?" said Tubby Ted, bringing up the rear.

And now they stood together on the beach, the five boys from St. Norbert's.

Peter looked at Alf, a hint of a question in his eye.

The big man shook his head.

"Sorry, lad," he said. "I'm an old man, and I've had all the adventures I want to have. I've got to go." He stepped forward, opening his arms. Peter ran to him and was swept up in a powerful bear hug. They stood there for a moment, Peter's feet dangling, his face buried in Alf's shoulder. Then the big man set him down, and they turned away from each other, tears streaming down their faces.

"Well, then," said Leonard, finding his own throat surprisingly tight. "I suppose I can't *force* you boys to come back with us. Or, rather, I *could*, but given what Peter has done for us, it wouldn't be right. So *I* will not stand in your way, Peter. But what about our hosts? This is their island, after all. . . ."

All eyes turned to Fighting Prawn.

"The boy saved my life," said the old man. "He is welcome here, and so are his friends. They have the protection of the Mollusk people for as long as they choose to remain."

"Thank you," said Peter.

"Yes," said Leonard. "My thanks as well. But Peter, I hope you understand there are grave dangers on this island. The pirates are loose, and if Black Stache survives the wound you inflicted on him, he will want your blood, and will stop at nothing to spill it."

"I know that," said Peter, touching the knife in his belt. "I'll be ready."

"There's also that enormous crocodile," said Leonard, "and other deadly beasts, I'm sure. And who knows what other dangers."

"I'm not afraid," said Peter.

"No, I can see you're not," said Leonard. "You're a very brave young man. Perhaps a bit *too* brave for your own good. So if we're going to have to leave you—and it appears we are—I'm going to leave something with you, for your protection."

"What do you mean?" said Peter.

"Give me a moment, and I'll show you," said Leonard. To Fighting Prawn, he said, "Would it be difficult for one of your people to bring me a bird?"

"A bird?" said Fighting Prawn.

"Yes," said Leonard. "Can your people catch me one? Alive?"

"Of course," said Fighting Prawn. "The Mollusks are great hunters." He turned to his tribespeople and grunt-clicked a brief message; instantly, a half-dozen young men darted into the jungle.

"They will not be long," said Fighting Prawn.

"Excellent," said Leonard. "Now, Peter, if you'll just give me a few minutes . . ."

Leonard climbed into the longboat and conferred in a low voice with two of the Starcatchers. They quickly donned their gold protective costumes, then went to the wooden trunk and, with great care, opened the lid, then busied themselves doing something with the box inside.

In five minutes they were done; they closed the trunk lid, and handed a small golden sack and another small object to Leonard. Leonard put the sack into his coat pocket, and carried the other in his hand back to the beach.

"All right, Peter," he said. "First, I'm going to give you this." He stretched out his hand; in it was a Starcatcher locket, a gleaming orb on a golden chain.

"But, why?" said Peter. "I mean, since I've changed, I can fly without . . ."

"You can fly, yes," said Leonard. "But you may well need starstuff some day, especially its healing powers." He fastened the locket around Peter's neck. "Keep it with you always, and use it wisely," he said.

"I will," said Peter, his hand touching the chain.

"And now," said Leonard, looking around, "we need the . . . Ah, here they are."

The young Mollusk hunters were returning from the jungle, trotting down the beach, the one in front proudly holding something in his upraised hand. As he drew near, Peter saw that it was a bird, small but extraordinarily beautiful, its body and wings a startling emerald green, its delicate, darting head a brilliant summer-daisy yellow.

"Perfect!" said Leonard. "If I may . . ." he held out his left hand, and the hunter gently placed the bird on his palm. Leonard gently curled his fingers around the delicate creature. With his right hand, he reached into his coat pocket and pulled out the golden sack. He loosened the drawstring, carefully placed the bird inside, then pulled the drawstring tight again, and let the sack rest on his palm.

For a full minute, nothing happened. Everyone— Starcatchers, Mollusks, and boys—stared at the sack, waiting.

And then they heard it.

"Bells!" said Alf. "It's the bells!"

It was coming from the sack, but it felt as though it was in the air all around them: a lovely, delicate tinkling sound, a happy sound, a *mischievous* sound . . .

And Peter understood it.

He stared at the sack, his eyes wide.

"That's right," said Leonard, smiling. "She's talking to you."

"But . . . *who* is?" said Peter.

"She is," said Leonard, as he loosened the drawstring and pulled the golden sack down. And there, standing on Leonard's palm, looking directly at Peter, oblivious to the gasps of the boys, and the shouts of the Mollusks, was . . .

"It's a *fairy*," said Peter.

"Yes," said Leonard. "Or at least that's the name that's been given to these creatures. So we'll call her that, Peter. She's your fairy, and she'll watch over you."

The fairy, in a shimmer of gold, sprang from Leonard's hand and darted to Peter, flitting around his head, filling his ears with her magical bell sounds.

"Those are my friends," Peter said.

"Who're you talking to?" said James.

"The fairy!" said Peter. "Don't you hear her talking?"

"No," said James. "Just the bells."

The fairy darted over to Molly, circled her twice, and darted back to Peter.

"Yes," said Peter, "that's Molly."

More bell sounds.

"No she's not!" said Peter.

"What did she call me?" said Molly.

"Err, nothing," said Peter.

Leonard laughed. "Looks like you've got a jealous fairy," he said. "She'll be a handful, that one. But she'll watch over you, Peter; that's her job."

"Thank you," said Peter, not entirely certain that he wanted a fairy.

"All right, then," said Leonard. "We've got to get back to the ship." Solemn now, he put out his hand to Peter, and Peter shook it.

"Good-bye, Peter," Leonard said. "Thank you for all you've done, and be careful."

"Yes, sir," said Peter. "I will."

Leonard turned and got into the longboat. Alf was already seated with the rest of the Starcatchers. Only Molly remained on the sand. Peter took a step toward her, and she toward him. The other boys stepped away, giving them a place to converse in private.

"Good-bye, Peter," Molly said. "Thank you for all you did for m . . . for us."

"Good-bye, Molly," said Peter.

They looked at each other for a few moments, both trying to think of something to say, both failing. Then Molly began to turn.

"Wait," said Peter.

Molly turned back, her eyes questioning,

"Maybe . . ." said Peter, and he stopped.

"Maybe what?" said Molly.

"Maybe, I was thinking, since I can fly," said Peter, "maybe I could come to see you some time, in England. I could fly there!"

Molly smiled. "That would be nice, Peter. That would be lovely."

Another few moments passed.

"I suppose it will have to be soon," said Peter. "Because

you're going to be getting older, and I guess I'm . . . not."

"Yes," said Molly, fighting to keep her smile. "I suppose that's so."

"Well, then," said Peter.

"Yes," said Molly.

And then, because he didn't want her to see him cry, Peter turned away, and so Molly turned away. She had taken two steps toward the longboat when she felt his hand on her shoulder, and she turned, and he held her, then, and she held him, just for a moment, the last moment they would ever have when they were both the same age.

And then, eyes burning, Molly ran to the longboat and jumped in, and the Mollusks grabbed the boat's sides and slid it into the water, and the Starcatchers pulled on the oars, and the longboat, with Ammm leading the way, glided away from the beach. Molly sat in the stern, next to her father, looking back at Peter, who stood alone at the water's edge. His mates, farther up on the beach, were waving; but Peter was only watching, and Molly knew he was watching only her.

And she was right: Peter watched her until she was only a dot at the mouth of the lagoon, and then she was gone. He turned and trudged up the beach, to where Fighting Prawn stood with James and the others.

"You'll need wood," said Fighting Prawn.

"What?" said Peter.

"To make your dwelling," said Fighting Prawn. "And for your cooking fire. You'll need wood."

"I suppose that's so," said Peter.

"Driftwood is good," said Fighting Prawn. "Look along the beach. Bring the wood back here, and my people will show you what to do."

"Thank you," said Peter.

The boys split up, looking for wood. Peter walked along the waterline. He thought about flying, but decided he felt more like walking; he was feeling numb, and happy to have a task to keep him occupied. He'd walked several hundred yards when he saw it, sliding back and forth on the sand in the gentle surf: a piece of wood, painted, about six feet long.

He walked to it, picked it up. There were letters on the bottom, letters he'd seen before, on the ship that had carried him from London, the ship that had broken up on the reef that guarded this island. The letters said:

NEVER LAND

Peter looked at it. And then looked around him—at the lagoon; at the rock where the mermaids (Mermaids!) lounged; at the palm-fringed beach; at the tinkling fairy flitting over his head; at his new friends the Mollusks; at the jungle-covered, pirate-infested mountains looming over it all.

Then he looked at the board again, and he laughed out loud.

"That's exactly where I am," he said.